Chicken Soup for the Soul.

Inspiration for the Young at Heart

D0062811

Chicken Soup for the Soul: Inspiration for the Young at Heart
101 Stories of Inspiration, Humor, and Wisdom about Life at a Certain Age
Jack Canfield, Mark Victor Hansen, Amy Newmark

Published by Chicken Soup for the Soul Publishing, LLC   www.chickensoup.com
Copyright © 2011 by Chicken Soup for the Soul Publishing, LLC. All Rights Reserved.
No part of this publication may be reproduced, stored in a retrieval system or transmitted in any form or by any means, electronic, mechanical, photocopying, recording or otherwise, without the written permission of the publisher.

CSS, Chicken Soup for the Soul, and its Logo and Marks are trademarks of Chicken Soup for the Soul Publishing LLC.

The publisher gratefully acknowledges the many publishers and individuals who granted Chicken Soup for the Soul permission to reprint the cited material.

Front cover photo courtesy of iStockphoto.com/dmbaker (© darren baker).
Back cover and interior photos courtesy of Photos.com

Cover and Interior Design & Layout by Pneuma Books, LLC
For more info on Pneuma Books, visit www.pneumabooks.com

Distributed to the booktrade by Simon & Schuster. SAN: 200-2442

Publisher's Cataloging-in-Publication Data
(Prepared by The Donohue Group)

Chicken soup for the soul : inspiration for the young at heart : 101 stories of
  inspiration, humor, and wisdom about life at a certain age / [compiled by]
  Jack Canfield, Mark Victor Hansen, [and] Amy Newmark.

     p. ; cm.

Summary: A collection of 101 true stories from people over sixty, with upbeat and
often funny stories about romance, travel, new careers and hobbies, adventures,
volunteer work, sports, families, new homes, new interests, and the joys of retirement.
  ISBN: 978-1-935096-71-9

  1. Older people--Conduct of life--Literary collections. 2. Older people--Conduct of
life--Anecdotes. 3. Older people's writings. I. Canfield, Jack, 1944- II. Hansen, Mark
Victor. III. Newmark, Amy. IV. Title: Inspiration for the young at heart

PN6071.O5 C483 2011
810.8/02/09285   2011924784

PRINTED IN THE UNITED STATES OF AMERICA
on acid∞free paper
20 19 18 17 16 15 14 13 12 11   01 02 03 04 05 06 07 08 09 10

Chicken Soup for the Soul®

Inspiration for the Young at Heart

101 Stories of Inspiration, Humor, and Wisdom about Life at a Certain Age

Jack Canfield
Mark Victor Hansen
Amy Newmark

Chicken Soup for the Soul Publishing, LLC
Cos Cob, CT

Chicken Soup for the Soul
www.chickensoup.com

Contents

❶
~New Adventures~

❷
~Turning Back the Clock~

❸

~Never Too Late for Romance~

❹

~New Careers~

❺

~When a Husband Retires~

❻

~The Privileges of Age~

❼

~New Passions~

❽

~Who're You Calling Old?~

❾

~Go For It~

Sunday	Monday	Tuesday	Wednesday	Thursday	Friday	Saturday
		1 brunch at Smiths	**2** Work 9-1	**3** babysit Jessica	**4** work 9-1	**5** Pack
6 Pier 3 at 4 sharp	**7** CRUISE!!	**8**	**9**	**10**	**11**	**12**
13	**14** work 9-1	**15** Jessica ☺	**16** Work 9-1	**17** Dog Shelter	**18** work 9-1	**19** Golf with Gene
20	**21** Work 9-1	**22** Dr. Miller - 10:30	**23** work 9-1	**24** dog shelter	**25** Work 9-1	**26** Dinner Party 7:00
27 DC trip 27th-29th	**28**	**29**	**30** Work 9-1	**31** Dog Shelter		

Inspiration for the Young at Heart

New Adventures

GO 60

It is only in adventure that some people succeed in knowing themselves — in finding themselves.
~André Gide

"I can't do this," I told my husband as we donned bright blue jumpsuits accessorized with more bells and whistles than I could count. A walkie-talkie hung from my hip. Silver rings decorated shoulders and arms, providing anchor points for attaching cap, sunglasses and wrist hankie. Since I've never been into fashion statements, my appearance wasn't the problem. My emotions were the issue. I was scared.

Earlier that morning we stood beneath the behemoth Sydney Harbour Bridge, the largest long span bridge ever constructed. It is 440 feet from water level to the top of the span. I looked up at the miniscule stick figures on the top of the structure, thinking that in five hours I would become one of those indeterminate silhouettes that drew the attention of passersby. Soon I would become one of those tiny climbers.

I could easily have walked away from this excursion, one I was attempting only at the behest of my husband who had wanted to attempt this folly "forever." What saved us, or at least saved his dream, was my determination to try sixty new things in the year of my sixtieth birthday. This was it. I needed the experience to apply toward what was becoming a challenging goal.

It started with an epiphany. I was bemoaning the approach of my sixtieth birthday in an e-mail to my younger brother. I typed something along the lines of "I will be 60 in a few weeks." When I looked back over the message, my mind read the "60" as "GO." That's when I decided to GO for 60.

Because I travel frequently, many of the entries in my "GO" diary involve experiences in foreign countries. Licking the bum of a green ant in the Daintree Rainforest in Australia is a good example. Eating pierogies in Gdansk is another.

Opportunities abounded on the home front, as well. I had never used a gas grill, preferring to let my husband man, excuse the expression, the barbeque. However, in his absence, with guests waiting to be fed, I read the notes I had prepared under his tutelage and fired it up. If I hadn't had my GO for 60 goal in mind, I most likely would have baked the pork chops in the oven. I did overcook them slightly, something which was, unfortunately, not a new experience for me.

On Election Day in November, I worked the polls, a sixteen-hour marathon that I found alternately stimulating and boring. A highlight of the day was a visit by a rattlesnake. It provided a couple of hours of diversion as we poll workers debated its party affiliation.

I took a Mexican cooking class—the molé was delicious—and cranked out homemade pasta. I water-skied on Lake Powell and I drove on the left side of the road in Australia, both of which served quite nicely to elevate my heart rate. As I neared my sixty-first birthday, my list numbered only fifty-four. It was time to get busy. So, I signed up for docent training at a local museum and sponge-painted a bathroom.

What was my favorite adventure of the year? It's impossible to say. The experiences varied from mundane—setting up a blog—to life changing—signing a book contract. I toured the Hermitage in St. Petersburg and had a formal bra fitting.

The unquestionable success of my GO for 60 year was the shift in my mindset. I might never have agreed to the bridge climb, which, by the way, was not the least bit frightening once we got underway, had I not been looking to add to THE LIST. What a pity it would have been to miss the exhilaration and beauty of that experience. Before the GO Year, I shunned suggestions for activities that I perceived as boring. Because of this "go for it" commitment, I enjoyed an after-noon at a horse race track and trudged up a steep trail in Hawaii to be rewarded by the phenomenal views from the top of Diamond Head Crater.

I continue to seek out new experiences. I don't say "no" as quickly as I once did. I have become far more aware of the world of opportunities that awaits every one of us. Newspapers and local magazines teem with announcements, from musical performances to how-to classes. Make your own beads, anyone? There are lectures on topics from travel to financial security, and ongoing requests for volunteers in every field imaginable.

Stay close to home. Travel afar. Make new friends. Go wild with old ones. Read. Write. Ride a horse. Horse around. I've already got my sights on my seventieth year!

~Susan Tornga

A Star Is Born

Fame is a fickle food upon a shifting plate.
~Emily Dickinson

My wife, Ellie, and I have spent one Wednesday a month for the last five years as volunteer bartenders at our local theater, the Francis Wilson Playhouse in Clearwater, Florida. This past month, we were, as usual, at our stations behind the bar, at 7:15 p.m., ready to serve the patrons for the current play. A large number of walk-ins, together with the season ticket holders assured us that the auditorium would be full for the production of *Kitchen Witches*.

The theater group had become like family to us, but I was surprised to see the director walk up to me fifteen minutes before the play was to start. By this time, he was usually behind the stage curtains waiting for the play to begin.

"My friend Ray, I have something important to ask you."

"What's that?"

"I would like you to be in tonight's play."

Having never been in a live theatrical production, I was taken aback.

"I've never done any acting before. What's the part? And will I have lines to say?"

"Oh, you don't have any lines. As you probably know, the play is about two television cooking show hostesses, Dolly and Izzie, who were always rivals. They are now forced to appear on the same cooking show and they feud constantly."

"Yes, I read the write-up on the play in the newspaper."

"Well, about fifteen minutes into the second act, they are going to have a cook off with strawberry shortcake as the item they are making. I need you to be the judge of the contest."

"Okay. But what do I do?"

"Just sit near the stage and when the emcee of the show announces your name as the judge you join the ladies onstage. Just ad-lib it from there."

"Sounds easy. I can handle that."

The first act of the play passed by quickly, with constant laughter from the audience.

At intermission, I was back serving wine, soda and snacks, doing my bartending job. Then the house lights blinked, signaling that it was time for everyone to return to their seats for the second act. My moment of stardom had almost arrived. I would be making my big debut.

I sat about four rows back from the front and waited for the request to come onto the stage.

"Now, would our judge for the strawberry shortcake contest, Ray Weaver, please come forward?"

I jumped up quickly and made my way to the steps. As I started up them, I decided to make the most of my first stage appearance and deliberately stumbled. The audience roared with laughter. Dolly and Izzie rushed forward to help me to the center stage.

Dolly began to interview me. "Let's tell our audience what you do for a living, Mr. Weaver."

"Oh, I'm retired now. But I do a lot of writing."

"What kind of writing?"

"Suspense stories and magazine articles. And oh, yes, I can read too."

A lady in the front row yelled, "You tell them honey."

"Are you married?"

I raised my left hand, looked down at my ring finger and answered. "Oh, yes. I'm married. And she's still alive. I think."

Now, I was on a roll.

Izzie, looking as though she had enough of the question and answer period, came forward with a long black plastic apron, which she placed on the front part of my body.

As this point, I started to get worried. I was wearing my dress slacks and a nice sports jacket. Why did I need this big plastic apron?

As the two ladies each picked up a large dish of strawberry shortcake, covered with whipped cream, and walked up to me from either side, I started to sweat.

First Dolly shoveled a large spoonful of the treat into my mouth. I tasted, chewed slowly and swallowed. Then Izzie approached me with a large spoonful of her dessert. She thrust it into my mouth, getting whipped cream all over my chin.

I chewed and swallowed even slower.

"Well, Judge Ray, we need you to tell us which of us makes the better strawberry shortcake," Dolly demanded.

I looked from one lady to the other. Now, I was really cautious. I was certain that no matter which one I chose, the other was going to let me have it in the face with her berries and cream.

Finally, I said, "Well, Dolly, I'm sorry. But, I have to choose Izzie's."

Izzie smiled. The audience clapped loudly. Dolly started to push me toward the exit stairs.

Then, Izzie rushed over to me. "Wait, I need the apron back." She whipped the apron off, leaned over and gave me a brief kiss on the cheek.

Now, unable to think of a way to prolong my stage appearance, I made my way back to my seat as the audience briefly applauded.

My wife leaned over and said, "Nice job. Look out, Broadway."

I was somewhat disappointed however that I was not called up onto the stage after the play had ended, when the actors took their final bows and received a standing ovation.

As I prepared to leave the theater after the show, a little old lady walked up to me and grabbed my arm. "Let's see. I know you from somewhere? Where do I know you from?"

I smiled and said. "I'm the bartender."

She looked at me with a puzzled expression on her face. "You know, I never saw that play."

~Raymond P. Weaver

Birthday Pageant

Taking joy in living is a woman's best cosmetic.
~Rosalind Russell

How would I observe my sixtieth birthday? How would I honor the beginning of a new decade? Birthdays have always been important to me. As a matter of fact, I schedule a whole birthday month rather than just one day!

Every July, I fill the calendar with activities that make me happy. My husband is always supportive of the plans since they bring him pleasure also. Walks in the woods with our dogs. A paddleboat ride at the lake. An outdoor concert featuring old-time rock and roll, or perhaps even better, folk songs from the 1960s.

Some years I am exceptionally blessed and my family visits from out of town during July. Food. Laughter. Old stories that bring joy and tears. Life doesn't get any better.

However, for my sixtieth birthday I decided to outdo myself. I had discovered that the Ms. Senior Michigan Pageant was going to be held at the local senior center. In order to be a contestant, you had to be at least sixty years old. Lo and behold, the pageant was to be held on my actual birth date! My husband agreed with me that it was a sign that I needed to sign up.

Watching Miss America was a rite of passage when I was growing up, but it had never occurred to me to take part in a pageant. As a matter of fact, my lifestyle doesn't include fancy dresses.

Nevertheless, I knew this was an opportunity to step out of my comfort zone and have a learning experience. Contestants would have a one-on-one interview with the judges, deliver a statement of life philosophy, show off a talent, and exhibit poise during a walk across stage in an evening gown. It sounded like fun. Scary too!

Although I do sing and dance a little, I didn't feel that was my way to shine. Instead I prepared a humorous monologue about a miscommunication created by my hearing loss. Oh boy, I have now added comedian to my bio!

The interview and statement of philosophy were interesting. A year later, I have still not decided how I felt about the evening gown walk. I did feel like a princess in my sparkly blue dress with the swishy skirt. On the other hand, it felt silly to walk across stage and pose for the audience.

My husband, of course, thought I was the absolute best. The judges, however, had someone else in mind as the winner. I didn't win or place, but I did have a wonderful birthday celebration.

My youngest niece was impressed with my participation. In honor of my birthday, she drew a picture of me in my blue sparkle dress that made me thinner and blonder than I really am. The rendition of my dress was much more accurate. I framed the drawing and hung it up to remind me that it is exciting to step out of my comfort zone.

The Ms. Senior Michigan Pageant was a terrific way to begin my sixties. I cannot wait to see what is next, but I bet it will be something really interesting! The best is yet to come.

~Mary Ellen Warner

Zipping over Fear

Courage is the power to let go of the familiar.
~Raymond Lindquist

My heart thudded as the guide outfitted me in gear that screamed "Danger." A thick leather glove encased my right hand and a helmet hugged my head. Sturdy straps gripped each thigh, meeting in the back to circle my waist, exerting a powerful thong-like effect. I was a middle-aged woman whose only brushes with athleticism included the yoga mat and treadmill. Already, I was regretting my impulsive decision to step off this platform and entrust myself to the wobbly-looking steel cable that disappeared over the ravine and into the far-flung foliage of the Costa Rican rainforest.

As a child, I had avidly watched Tarzan movies and then wildly swung from vine to vine, down at my best friend's farm, gliding across creeks and skidding through the leaves. Despite such glorious flights, when I grew up a fear of heights seized me. I avoided towers, rooftop gardens and mountaintops. I became a ground-floor person.

Yet, when I learned it was possible to fly over the rainforest canopy, something in me wanted to soar again. The concept seemed both ecological and romantic. I would see the tops of trees and glimpse toucans, howler monkeys and other elusive creatures. I would be one with nature, in the purest and simplest of ways.

But the moment I arrived at the zip line site, my stomach clamped into a series of world-class knots. My hands became rainforest moist.

My image of myself flying across the treetops collided with a picture of me crashing into the ground.

"You will love this," one of the guides, Carlos, promised. Six other people had signed up for the ordeal and all of them also looked impossibly fearless, fit and agile.

I listened to a guide instructing us on how to sit, tilted slightly back, our ankles casually crossed, as if we were not hurtling through thin air. He showed us how to stop, pulling down with our gloved right hand.

"This is very safe," Carlos assured me. "Perhaps you can go first. You will like it."

Before I could step back, Carlos clipped me to the steel cable that stretched to somewhere far away in the deep primordial forest. "Sit back, relax. The guide at the other end will hold up two hands to show you when to stop."

As instructed, I clung to my cords with my left hand. My right, gloved hand was slightly behind me, holding the overhead cable so I would not twirl uncontrollably.

"Don't grip the cable, it will slow you. Just hover the hand over the line," Carlos coached. My hand hovered. My stomach quivered. And then I was sailing across the line, the wind in my face, and the treetops all around me. I felt free and alive.

As I approached the platform, the guide signaled me to stop. I pulled down on the cable, but didn't slow. I jerked my hand down again but kept zooming forward. The guide caught me, just before I was one with a tree trunk. Then he taught me the rest of the lesson: "Put one hand over the other and pull yourself up to stop."

Before I had a chance to reconsider, I was hooked up to the next line and soared off into another set of treetops. Each ride was exhilarating, a vibrant whisk through the trees, a submersion in the loamy scent of forest, the air ripe with rain. Each line gave me a short swift flirtation with danger, a rush of fear as the tree platform loomed ahead and then a comforting sense of safety when my feet touched. The last line, the eleventh one, was a long ride over a picturesque river. I savored every moment: the glimpse of blue morpho butterfly, the rich wands of branches, the dark hulk of opossum in a neighboring tree, the sure, sheer abandonment of tethered flight.

Then, the guides were helping me out of my gear. The earth felt comforting as I stepped out of my harness and took off my helmet. I was shaking but happy as I said a grateful goodbye to the guides and the other flyers.

As I rode past the thick forest I had just "flown" over, I felt a deep sense of connection and satisfaction. I probably still couldn't climb a mountain or blithely peer over a building top to enjoy a scenic view, but I could fly through the brimming beauty of a rainforest. For me, it was the height of bravery.

~Deborah Shouse

Blackberry Magic

Nobody can do for little children what grandparents do.
Grandparents sort of sprinkle stardust over the lives of little children.
~Alex Haley

Blackberry pie. Is summer ever complete without at least one day devoted to picking blackberries and making a blackberry pie?

There's a ritual connected with blackberry picking. Rule number one is that it can't be planned. You just have to be out taking a walk and you spot some blackberry bushes. "BLACKBERRIES!" someone shouts, and drawn by some ancient and unexplainable law of nature, you run towards the bushes. Soon, your hands, your arms, your clothes are bathed in that sticky purple nectar.

I succumbed to the lure of the blackberry just this past week. True to the ritual, I did not plan to go berry picking. With my foster grandchildren, seven-year-old Mark and nine-year-old Jennie, as my companions, we had set out to take our new Village dog, Sammy, for a walk down the country road near home. Jennie spotted the blackberry bushes first and let out a scream of delight, "BLACKBERRIES!" You could almost hear the dog thinking, "So much for taking me for a walk."

We plunged into the glorious cache of blackberries, squeezing and squishing, reaching out with bare arms towards the blackest and sweetest of that luscious fruit, dodging those nasty thorns. Drat! Why weren't we smart enough to wear long pants? We were being faithful to ritual, that's why. We were all wearing shorts and, of course, had no container for the berries we were picking.

We improvised. The plastic bag we brought along for Sammy's business (never been used I assure you) served the purpose. Magically, the bag began to fill.

"Is this enough for a pie, Grandpa Hank?"

"No Mark, we need more. I think it takes three or four cups for a pie."

The day was hot. I felt my T-shirt sticking to my body. Mark was wearing a goodly portion of his haul on his shirt. "Ouch," yelled Jennie, as the thorns attacked her bare legs. The three of us (and Sammy, who waited patiently in the shade) stuck to our task, intent on making these black beauties our own.

"Mark, don't pick the ones that are still red," admonished Jennie. "I'm not," replied Mark indignantly. "Geez, I know THAT much."

Still, it was obvious from the kids' enthusiasm that they were having a ball. Forgotten for the moment was the grief they carried as victims of abuse and neglect. All that mattered was that they were enjoying this warm summer day picking blackberries.

Mark yelled across the road to a woman passing by, "You know what? We're gonna make a blackberry pie all by ourselves."

"With vanilla ice cream on top," chimed in Jennie.

The bag was bulging with berries as we returned to my apartment. I had never made any kind of pie in my whole life but there was no way I was NOT going to bake a pie for these kids. With the help of a recipe from the Internet and ready-made pie shells from Safeway, the kids and I put together a blackberry pie fit for the gods.

In the great scheme of things, I suppose the experience of picking wild blackberries and baking a pie with a couple of foster kids is no big deal. But it's a memory this old guy will savor for a long time. I dare to hope that the kids will, too.

~Hank Mattimore

Did You Ride that Thing?

Four wheels move the body. Two wheels move the soul.
~Author Unknown

Just before turning fifty years old, and having flown home after an exhilarating trip from California to the East Coast on a pearl white Honda Helix 250 scooter, I got the itch to ride a real motorcycle. I was ready to shed the scooter image and become a motorcycle mama riding a genuine, throw-your-leg-over, gear-shifting two-wheeler. I just needed to learn how.

A friend loaned me her small Kawasaki motorcycle, and with minimal instructions, I took off. To bolster my courage, I pep-talked and coached myself aloud through the neighborhood. "You can do this! Ease out on the clutch. A little more throttle. That's it." There was a tiny delay at each stoplight when the bike stalled out, but I was able to get it going and move along after a few tries at restarting. Thankfully, the folks in the cars behind me were patient.

Finally, everything was in sync, and I was on my way to practice in another small neighborhood. As I tried to turn around in a cul-de-sac, the engine died. Once, twice, six times I went through the start-up and take-off procedure. No luck. Disgusted, I flung the kickstand down with my left foot, dismounted, and circled that motorcycle, eyeing it like it was a schoolyard enemy ready for a fight. Walking around the bike, I spoke to it, repeating a few choice playground words I'd heard growing up. I felt a lot better. After throwing my leg over the seat, I turned the key, eased out the clutch, and rolled on the throttle. To my surprise, the Kawasaki started moving forward and kept going while I shifted into second and then third gears. I was riding! That bike and I had come to an understanding.

With practice on the back roads and the Motorcycle Safety Foundation course under my belt, my skill and confidence grew. But the reactions of my friends and family leaned more toward skepticism. Shaking her head in disbelief, my mother said, "Oh, I don't want to know about this."

"Oh, my god! You're riding that motorcycle?" one friend wailed as she looked toward the curb where I'd parked. Before too long, she bragged that her place was one of my first destinations.

Eighteen years later, I look back and see that motorcycling opened the world to me. I've ridden in four countries: the United States, Mexico, Canada, and New Zealand. Through all my travels, some with friends and some solo, I've learned about the places I've been and about myself. I have grown as an individual as well as a rider.

My knowledge of geography, using maps, driving distances and the timing for each leg of a ride increased with practice. These skills have made me an astute planner and have taken me to places where the sights are even more wondrous when you experience them from the vantage point of a motorcycle.

One of the most meaningful things I discovered is that I am a strong and capable rider. I can handle my motorcycle and myself in the world, meeting the challenges of heavy traffic, flash floods and sketchy road conditions. The freeways of Los Angeles, Dallas, Atlanta, and Denver are harrowing, but I learned to navigate through each city. Sometimes bad weather has caught me on my bike, such as that time in Taos, New Mexico, when it hailed and plastered a white covering over the road. My riding partner and I pulled over, retrieved our umbrellas from our gear, moved away from our bikes, and waited for the passing cars to clear a path for us. I even conquered the scariest moments of my riding life — negotiating the dark, uneven, unpaved tunnel on the way to Milford Sound and traversing bridges that drivers shared with railroad tracks in New Zealand.

While I love traveling with friends, it thrills me to be on my own, making all the decisions, and pointing my candy apple red Honda Goldwing in the direction I choose. "Do you ever get lonely when you're riding by yourself?" people often ask. Not at all. The motorcycle is a built-in conversation starter. Add being a lone woman rider on a big red bike to the mix, and there is instant conversation at any fuel or rest stop. Most often, men will ask, "Did you ride that thing all the way here by yourself?" Afterward, they tell their own motorcycling history, which bikes they rode or about the bike that's stored in their garage. One fellow helped me with a difficult gas nozzle at a fuel station and then began to tell his story. Before I knew it, he pulled up his shirt to show me the scar that remained from an accident he'd had while riding drunk.

Women will usually come out with an encouraging "'Atta girl!" or mention that they wish they could ride. My standard answer is, "You can." Then I share the phone number of the Motorcycle Safety Foundation, so they can find out where to get riding lessons, and tell them about Women on Wheels, the motorcycling organization to which I belong.

Other riders want to know where you've been and where you're going and to share their tales. It's not uncommon for strangers to sit down together when they happen to meet at a restaurant or to ride together for a few miles. These brief encounters show that the mere act of riding stimulates comradeship.

Most important, some of my dearest and deepest friendships have come through motorcycling. It was our love for the sport and adventure that brought us together, but our friendships have blossomed and developed and endured over time. It's simple. You come to respect, admire, and even love people with whom you have a mutual interdependence. Although each of us is fully capable of handling her bike and riding on her own, when out on the road together, we ride as a unit—a team. What affects one, affects all. So, we adhere to a certain standard of riding and communicate through signals. We learn each others' riding styles and strengths, the way each sits in her saddle, and how far we can ride before someone requires gas. It's the best of all worlds: time on the bike, a ride through glorious country, and good friends with whom to share the experience.

I came to motorcycling in the second half of my life—when I was ready to inject a bit of excitement, but mature enough to handle it with safety and care. Sure, it's risky. But it's calculated risk that makes life interesting and infuses us with energy.

~Annis Cassells

"I told Fred if he wants to feel the wind rushing through his hair he'd better unbutton his shirt."

What a Riot

Old age is an excellent time for outrage.
My goal is to say or do at least one outrageous thing every week.
~Louis Kronenberger

What an experience! Grandma spending a day creating some havoc with our Keepers-of-the-Peace. It was exhausting and exhilarating, mystifying and satisfying. I played my role well, knowing it served a good purpose. The uniformed officers may have been surprised at the level of enthusiasm exhibited by my cohorts. We played our roles with gusto: cops and rioters alike.

It was a beautiful spring morning when black and whites approached a crowd, including yours truly, with sirens wailing, lights flashing, horns blowing, brakes screeching, and a mystical smoke screen materializing. Dozens of cops exploded from the squad cars and crouched behind protective car doors. Next, they formed the notorious shoulder-to-shoulder offense line and I heard commands from a bullhorn along with the sounds of light firearms and heavier weapons. The officers advanced toward the unruly crowd. All this happened while we, the rioters, were throwing bottles, waving placards, and yelling repulsive phrases. As the uniforms approached, I heard a young peace officer bellow, "Hey, Grandma, back off." I turned toward the voice and found the officer looking directly at me. Of course, all the officers were dressed for a real confrontation. They wore full riot gear including bulletproof vests, helmets and face protectors, shields and nightsticks.

The fact that I was a rather plump, gray-haired, seventy-something grandma didn't faze the young man nor did his yelling deter me. I continued throwing the near-empty plastic water bottles—as hard as I could—still carrying a somber black placard with bright red lettering stating, "COPS SUCK." I was shrieking all the nasty clichés about cops that I could bring myself to voice, and he just glared. His "Hey, Grandma" command really ticked me off. Who did this kid think he was facing? Just another grandma? No way. Did I bombard him with bottles? Absolutely. Did I yell? You bet I did, as loud as my aged voice allowed.

My young, mouthy adversary, dressed for battle, pointed his nightstick directly at this grandma—not touching, but it seemed so very close. It was time for me to reverse direction, and I began slowly retreating. My eyes remain focused on the approaching nightstick. It was strangely frightening, yet invigorating.

It was now a couple of hours into the exercise and I was sweating. My brow was damp and my palms were wet. I was at war with the police—granted a controlled war, but nonetheless, a war.

At this point in my story, it seems appropriate to make the reader aware of the purpose behind these activities—the who, what, where, when, and why.

Well, the bellowing young man was one of about 100 peace officers, from various communities, involved in Mobile Field Training in Southern California. This confrontation took place in a huge, fenced, empty area and was designed to give the officers experience in riot control—as realistic as possible—hence the impersonating rioters. These pretenders—at least 100 of us, volunteers all—were told to harass the police and show aggressive behavior but without any physical contact. I feel we gave them a taunting worth remembering.

Appearing next was the coup de grâce—the mounted officers. Until you have had a horse sporting protective gear, with an officer atop also sporting protective gear, pointing a wooden spear directly at your torso, you don't know real intimidation. As these mounted steeds approached, four abreast, I took heed. My water bottles were dropped, the placard hit the ground, and my throat closed so I couldn't yell.

Grandma had met her match. The officers on foot I could handle, but these officers atop such huge and magnificent beasts quelled my thunder. There was no real danger—this I knew—yet it felt like the appropriate time to find a seat in the shade and become a spectator. I was tired and found the visual experience inviting, minus the physical involvement. I sat and was spellbound by the remainder of the exercise.

Once more I say, "What an experience!" Would I do it again? In a heartbeat!

What will the next activity be for this seventy-something grandma? I can't imagine, but I anxiously await the call to serve!

~Jane Goodwin

The Honeymoon

You will do foolish things, but do them with enthusiasm.
~Colette

Keith and I were blessed to find love at age sixty. I had planned a trip to Florida with a friend and when she had a change in plans it became the perfect honeymoon for us. Neither Keith nor I had ever been to Florida, and the thought of palm trees, warmth, and sun after a cold, rainy Oregon winter was a dream come true.

Our first day was amazing. Driving from Orlando toward Cape Canaveral, we were curious about a group of people who had stopped along the roadside and were looking up into the sky. We pulled over to find out why they were there. Suddenly, we were gazing in awe at a shuttle blasting off and disappearing into space with a spiraling vapor trail. Later, a walk on the beach hand-in-hand and a romantic candlelight dinner capped off an incredible day.

"Let's explore the St. Petersburg area tomorrow," Keith suggested, little knowing what that next day held in store.

Driving west to St. Petersburg, we continued wandering southward into Fort DeSoto State Park. We were pleasantly surprised to be greeted with a sign that read, "#1 Beach in America in 2005." Wisps of clouds floated in an azure sky. A postcard had shown the beach covered with bodies, but we shared the warm, caressing waves and beautiful palm-shaded shore with only one other family. To our delight, a group of graceful dolphins swam by as we gazed from the pier. We spotted the angular form of a huge frigate bird soaring high above.

"Frigate birds are usually only seen along shore when a storm is brewing," a passing park ranger told us. No hint of that—what a treat!

After a swim on the idyllic beach, we continued exploring southward, trekking over a magnificent cabled bridge that stretched over the bay with no end in sight. Hunger overtook us as we reached civilization again on the far shore. Unable to find a park nearby, we stopped to munch local vegetables and fruit on a dead end street just off the freeway. A bench seemed to invite visitors, but we chose to sit in the shade of our rented PT Cruiser and observe the neighborhood. I watched a young man stroll across the street with a weed eater, and envisioned him heading to an elderly neighbor's house to help with yard work.

Suddenly a sheriff's car appeared on the right side of our vehicle, and a young officer quickly approached with his hand on his gun. I had a sudden vision of a chubby Barney Fife.

"What are you doing here?" he asked.

"Having lunch and drinking my buttermilk," I replied as I held up the milk carton. "Is there a problem, officer?"

"Well, yes—if you are selling drugs," he said.

Selling drugs? How absurd! I laughed aloud. The young officer flushed, and looked at me sternly, as my husband Keith jabbed me in the ribs.

"What are you doing having lunch in the ghetto, then," the officer said, "unless you want to be carjacked?"

I gazed in disbelief at the neighborhood homes. What did he mean, ghetto? It was not an affluent neighborhood by any means, but certainly not my idea of a ghetto.

. Suddenly another officer appeared by Keith's door, and I saw in the side view mirror that a second sheriff's car had pulled in behind our vehicle. As my husband was asked for his license, he tried to explain that our plight was just an innocent mistake. Gradually, the young officers began to realize we really were just lost tourists from

Oregon, not drug dealers. We were only too glad to follow their directions to leave the area and get back on the freeway.

"What were you doing, laughing at that officer?" Keith sputtered. "Did you want to get us arrested?"

"I can't believe they thought we were drug dealers. I should have pulled out my county ID badge that shows I'm an Alcohol/Drug Prevention Specialist and let him look at that," I said.

"Oh yeah—I'm sure he would think you were just using that as a cover!" Keith retorted.

"Do you think a drug dealer would choose a grandmotherly car like a PT Cruiser? I'd have a Corvette or a Cadillac for sure," I quipped, choking with laughter. Looking down the freeway, I gasped, "Oh, please hurry, and find a rest area soon," as I held my sides and tears ran down my cheeks. Two senior citizens accused of being drug dealers on their honeymoon. This was one day we would surely long remember!

~Yvonne Kays

Personal Magnetism

Humor is just another defense against the universe.
~Mel Brooks

My great-grandma lived to be 102. She was stubborn and never gave up on things. When I tried to wear Great-Grandma's antique pearls, I discovered that I must have inherited her sticking power.

One of my nephews was getting married. Where I live, in the Pacific Northwest, clothing is mostly casual—think flannel shirts and blue jeans. I'm okay with casual, but I relished the chance to dress up.

The ceremony took place in early fall, when Oregon trees put on a spectacular show that rivals East Coast fall splendor. The couple had chosen a garden setting to take advantage of the changing leaves. In October, the garden blazed with striking reds, oranges and yellows, contrasting with a backdrop of dark green firs and Indian summer sky. I settled on wearing a dressy cranberry-colored pantsuit, which would go perfectly with my great-grandmother's pearls.

If Great-Grandma was as far-sighted as I've become, there's no way she could have put on that necklace by herself. The pearls were gorgeous, but the findings were intricate and tiny. I'd had trouble hooking the clasp even before I started wearing bifocals.

Now, even with a magnifying glass, the fastener looked microscopic. I knew I'd never get the necklace hooked on my own, and

I lived alone, not counting my fifteen-year-old cat Oliver. Then I remembered something I'd seen in the drugstore.

Like a lot of drugstores, this one had an entire section devoted to products for older people. Canes, walkers and raised toilet seats vied for my attention, along with pill splitters, pill boxes and pill organizers to help people remember to take their morning and night-time meds. They had long poles for grabbing out-of-reach things so you wouldn't have to bend over. They sold cell phones with over-sized buttons, and a lamp that turned on automatically, so robbers wouldn't know you lived alone.

Then, on a display hook I spotted what I was searching for. Hiding behind the eyeglass repair kits—complete with the world's tiniest screwdriver and a packet of tinier screws—hung the perfect solution for fastening necklaces like my string of pearls. For those of us with arthritic hands or dimming eyesight, the package promised no less than a miracle.

I knocked off all the eyeglass kits getting it, but finally dug out a miracle necklace helper and examined the package's contents, which included a couple of small magnets. All you did was connect a little magnet to each end of the necklace. That was it. I was expecting something more dramatic, but the package promised to fasten any necklace and save my eyes. I bought several sets.

The day of my nephew's wedding, I donned the cranberry pantsuit and the pearls. I looked stunning—if I may say so—and proudly allowed one of the groomsmen to usher me to the family section. The metal folding chair wasn't the most comfortable seat, but I reminded myself that this was a "Northwest Casual" wedding, not a formal affair in a basilica.

The wedding march began—not the traditional one, but a flute and guitar version of the Beatles' "Here Comes the Sun." During the processional, the bridesmaids, in wine-colored satin as colorful as surrounding trees, did that special walk up the aisle. My nephew looked handsome in his suit and pink tie.

The big moment arrived. The bride was beautiful, in a cloud

of white chiffon that complemented her long auburn hair. Everyone rose.

Everyone except me.

I tried to stand but felt intense pressure on my neck. I put a hand to my throat, as the pearls pressed against my neck. The pearl necklace's magnets clung to the back of the metal chair. I was stuck.

I couldn't ask for help, lest I call attention to myself. I sat there smiling, hoping no one would notice my face turning the same shade of red as my outfit.

By the time I'd discretely disconnected myself from the chair, my nephew was kissing his bride. I was too embarrassed to explain why I didn't stand for the bride that day, or why my neck had pearl-like rope burns. Besides, I'm stubborn too. If I make it to age 102, I'll attribute my longevity to my great-grandmother's good genes and my own personal magnetism.

~Linda S. Clare

Crime Fighter

You can't turn back the clock. But you can wind it up again.
~Bonnie Prudden

Okay, I'd retired. So, now what? I traveled a bit and dabbled in a few hobbies. But I was looking for something more stimulating, something I could really sink my teeth into — while I still had teeth.

An article in my local newspaper caught my eye. It described an offering at the police department called the Citizens Police Academy. Various facets of police work would be covered during the fourteen-week course. Topics ranged from patrol functions to investigations, crime prevention, narcotics, SWAT team duties and, in general, the importance of public involvement in the policing process.

I eagerly signed up and never missed a class. Each week various police officers, an assistant district attorney, and even a superior court judge presented our instruction.

One of the highlights was a ride-along with a patrol officer, intended to run no longer than four hours. But it was so interesting that I stayed on with the officer (and his canine) through practically his entire ten-hour shift. By the time we returned to the station, we'd logged in fifty-three miles on the odometer, just cruising around town.

We made a number of traffic stops for driving violations and then looked for someone evading an arrest warrant. Later we searched for a juvenile reported to be drunk in a pool hall. I was even allowed to search the ladies room for her. We responded to a radio call of a robbery in progress at the shopping mall, racing there on the freeway at breakneck speed, but arriving too late to apprehend him. The canine in the caged enclosure in back went nuts the whole way because he knew he was going to work soon. Late that night we arrested a drunk and followed another patrol car to transport him to jail. (We couldn't take on passengers because of the canine.) All this occurred in just one night in my sleepy hometown!

At the conclusion of the Citizens Academy program, I'd made up my mind. I decided to find out how I could get more involved.

On our own, another private citizen and I organized a fundraiser to purchase bulletproof vests for the three police canines. Why not? They're at risk, too. We publicized the event in the newspapers and then secured a booth at an upcoming street fair in town. We designed flyers to distribute before and during the fair, and I took photos of each of the canines and had a local printing company convert them into life-size cardboard cut-outs.

We used these eye-catching freestanding posters to decorate our booth. We collected donations from the public attending the event and then pounded the pavement for a few months afterward, obtaining even more contributions from many local businesses. Ultimately, we raised enough money to purchase assault vests for all three dogs, with roughly $10,000 left over for future vest replacement! The mayor even presented us with commendations during the monthly city council meeting, flanked by the canines sporting their protective vests.

Soon after that, I applied to become an official police volunteer and got accepted into the VIPS (Volunteer in Police Service) program. I work a minimum of sixteen hours a month but usually put in as much time as I'm able to give. Assignments cover a wide range of activities, from various administrative tasks inside the police station to actual street duty in full uniform with another volunteer in a marked police car.

Every two years we renew our driving skills qualification on a police obstacle course. We use the two-way radio and on-board computer during our patrols, communicating our activities to the police dispatchers. We direct traffic at accident scenes, cruise the shopping malls, and patrol neighborhoods for homeowners on vacation or for complaints of vandalism, loitering, and other matters not requiring police officers' immediate involvement. Just the presence of a patrol car in a neighborhood is often enough to make a would-be criminal go elsewhere.

Inside the police station, I track the fifty or so false burglar alarms triggered weekly. I counsel the offenders by telephone regarding excessive false alarms, warning them of possible fines if the false alarms continue. I also assist officers at the culmination ceremonies for the Drug Awareness and Resistance Education (DARE) program for school-age children, as well as at other community events such as parades or high school graduations.

At SWAT team training exercises, volunteers role-play in various simulated rescue and assault situations. Sometimes I play the suspect and other times, the victim. In one scenario, acted out in an abandoned building, I portrayed the bad guy (my favorite role). I squeezed into one of the five-foot high gym lockers in a locker room with only a bottle of water and my radium-dial wristwatch for company. Finally after a half hour, one of the canines sniffed out my hiding place. I was extracted from the locker, made to kneel down and be handcuffed. The more I struggled, the tighter the cuffs got. (Keep that in mind for future reference!) I had to laugh when the handler placed yellow crime scene caution tape around a fresh pile of dog poop left by an excited canine before leaving in search of a bag for cleanup.

During some of these training exercises, we use handguns containing simulated ammunition (marking cartridges). We wear bulletproof vests like the rest of the SWAT team and protective headgear since they'd be shooting back at us as well. After each scenario concludes, the team leader critiques the team's performance. He checks the number of "hits" the volunteers took by counting the half-dozen or so colored markers left on our vests and helmets, including one on my exposed ring finger, breaking the skin, the first time I got hit.

Since that baptism by fire (power), I've learned to wear protective gloves!

One of my favorite duties is assisting the juvenile crimes detective in a program called Juvenile Diversion. It's a one-time opportunity for juveniles arrested for minor nonviolent crimes to take part in a re-education process instead of being placed into the juvenile justice system. After reading the arrest reports to verify eligibility to participate, I schedule the hearings presided over by the detective and a marriage and family therapist, and attend the hearings myself. Afterward, I follow up to ensure that each juvenile successfully completes the program by doing the mandated assignments—working a specified number of community service hours and submitting a written essay on such topics as what they learned from the arrest experience, the dangers of marijuana and other drugs, the cost of shoplifting to the public, etc. I monitor the offenders throughout their six-month probation period, checking for any subsequent arrest activity, which automatically fails them from the Diversion program and sends them into the juvenile justice system after all.

As the "eyes and ears" of the police, we perform a vital role in the community policing process. It's more than just a volunteer job. By increasing public awareness and helping to reduce crime, this partnership instills a sense of wellbeing, improving not only my life but the quality of life within the whole community.

See? It's not just kids anymore who can play cops and robbers!

~Annette Langer

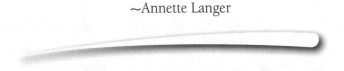

The Kindness of Strangers

Real generosity is doing something nice for someone who will never find out.
~Frank A. Clark

We were in for a whole new way of life when, in July of 1990, we retired and moved from an oceanfront condo on the island of Key Biscayne, Florida, to a horse farm in Winchester, Kentucky, with a pre-Civil War home. One of the best parts of the move was getting to know the people in this small community. Even before we left Florida we had a preview of the friendliness of the residents and their willingness to help even strangers like us. "Your lower field is flooded," was the first long-distance call we received in Florida from the former owner of the farm. The second call came three days later and it held a hint of hysteria. "Now your fences are down. This is the worst flood I have ever seen in Winchester."

So we knew about the damage before we moved, but we didn't figure on how much it would bother us once we arrived. Every time we went to town we passed those pathetic fences lying face down and covered with the silt washed in by the raging waters in June. The trouble was we didn't own a tractor and, frankly, were shocked at the price to buy one. We stewed every day as it began to sink in that we knew very little about farm living and taking care of many acres of land.

One day, our neighbor said, "You know, I need to rotate my cattle. Reckon if I use my tractor and mend your fence, could I use your lower fields?" Talk about gifts from heaven! But it seemed like the best kind of gift—we needed him and he needed us. So, he mended our fences and moved his cattle onto our fields. Not only were our fences fixed, but his cattle kept the field neat and clean and we didn't have to wince every time we passed by. It also gave us time to inspect our other fields. We found more fences down, gates bent under the weight of silt, and more need for a tractor and a Bush Hog.

Our neighbor brought his tractor and tools and mended the fences on our other fields and he re-hung the gates too. And the day came when we opened one gate and then another and herded his cattle onto our next fields. "Isn't it wonderful how we need each other and can each supply the needs of the other?" I said to my husband. We smiled, not believing our good fortune. And we thought, "Gosh, I wonder what he would've done for new fields if we hadn't been here with ours? I mean, we could've bought a tractor and Bush Hog and tried to do all that work ourselves, but he couldn't buy new acres of grazing land so easily." It felt good, this thought.

One night our neighbor asked my husband, "Want to ride with me to check on my farm and my cattle?" So my husband did and when he came home he walked in, scratched his head, smiled and said, "Do you know what? He didn't need our fields at all. He has 150 acres not even being used!" I went to sleep that night thinking about the kindness in our new community and how our new neighbor found a way to help us by claiming he needed us.

~Jean Brody

North Star

If we should be blessed by some great reward, such as fame or fortune, it's the fruit of a seed planted by us in the past.

~Bodhidharma

At sixty-five, I never expected to be a star. So when it happened last summer the experience was all the sweeter. For years, I had expected my plays and screenplays to bring money and fame, but that was not to be. In June of 2009, that all changed. My play *Butterscotch*, which I had written twenty years earlier, and was later published by a major dramatic house and produced in small towns across the country, was chosen to be top billing for the summer season at the Opera House Theatre in Philipsburg, Montana.

Opening night was June 26, and I was there. After flying and driving more than 2,000 exhausting miles, my sweetheart Donald, niece Kim, and I were alerted by our GPS to pull off the two-lane highway onto a dusty road that showed no signs of civilization, let alone a theatre. A big colorful sign, "Welcome to Philipsburg," was surrounded by a herd of snoozing cattle. If we were greeted by comatose livestock, what else could we expect in this Rocky Mountain hamlet? Rodeo riders, mineral prospectors, goat auctions? Not so. A half mile along we came upon an historic, charmingly restored town, once the center of a thriving mining industry.

In Philipsburg (population 930 citizens in winter), we found the opera house located off the main street, which was fortuitously called

Broadway. This was a good omen. Though bedraggled and hungry, we stopped to see the old theatre that had hosted opera companies in the late 1890s. The owner informed us (or should I say warned us) that at the previous night's showing of another play the audience numbered thirty-two. How many people would come tonight — after we trekked two-thirds of the way across the country for the Montana premiere of my play? My heart sank.

Still hoping for the best, we settled into a surprisingly luxurious suite fit for sovereign occupancy, and then went out for sandwiches. At the luncheonette, we overheard two tourists discussing "that show *Butterscotch*." It seemed they had phoned for tickets and failed to receive a call back, and assumed the show was sold out. I knew better. I introduced myself as the playwright, and assured Dora and Liz that plenty of seats were available. At the local newspaper office, we were greeted royally by the editor and her staff of four. And, yes, they would be at the show. "The whole town knows you're here," said the editor.

Apparently, the PR machine in Philipsburg had worked overtime. I was beginning to feel like a celebrity. Someone had spread the word around town, and around the state too, I hoped. On the street, a jewelry vendor said that of course she'd heard about *Butterscotch* and would be there that evening. Now assured of an audience of eight, I rested easy. Maybe even a few more people would appear to help fill those other 192 seats.

That evening, when we arrived at the theatre, I was bewildered by the party atmosphere. A classic 1948 Plymouth sedan sat out front. (Butterscotch of the title is a 1947 candy-colored Ford.) Throngs of people had come — friendly, sophisticated locals, retirees and tourists — not a weathered cowpoke among them. Inside the theatre, we were amazed as an eager crowd poured in until the house was nearly full. Later I learned that 167 seats had been sold.

The first laugh was slow in coming, but excitement began to build, and then the play caught fire. The audience laughed and some even cried, including several men, one of whom later whispered to me: "Don't tell my wife, but I got teary at the end."

We were a hit. I was as overjoyed as if I had heard the play was moving to the other off-Broadway in New York City. Outside, the cast and crew formed a reception line as if we'd been wed or knighted. Photos were snapped and hugs exchanged. I expected a hail of confetti or instant rice. Maybe even a tiara. Vacationers Dora and Liz were there, and so were the newspaper editors and even the mayor of Philipsburg. I wondered who else could have been in attendance: a Hollywood producer or hot agent, Spielberg, maybe Tom Hanks? Amid all this pageantry, I allowed myself fanciful pipe dreams.

At the after-party next door at the Silver Mill Saloon, it seemed the whole audience showed up. I didn't know if it was me and the cast, or the free buffet that accounted for their presence, but I was humbled, asked to sign autographs and pose for photos. I was thankful we had come to Philipsburg. What a night it had been! The next day we packed our bags, loaded them in the rental car and headed home, back to reality. Reign over. Queen for only a day, but what a day it had been.

~Barbara L. Smith

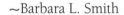

Sunday	Monday	Tuesday	Wednesday	Thursday	Friday	Saturday
		1 brunch at Smiths	2 Work 9-1	3 babysit Jessica	4 work 9-1	5 Pack
6 Pier 3 at 4 sharp	7 CRUISE!!	8	9	10	11	12
13	14 work 9-1	15 Jessica ☺	16 Work 9-1	17 Dog Shelter	18 work 9-1	19 Golf with Gene
20	21 Work 9-1	22 Dr. Miller - 10:30	23 work 9-1	24 dog shelter	25 Work 9-1	26 Dinner Party 7:00
27 DC trip 27th-29th	28	29	30 Work 9-1	31 Dog Shelter		

Inspiration
for the
Young
at
Heart

Turning Back the Clock

Mommy-Come-Lately

The great thing about getting older
is that you don't lose all the other ages you've been.
~Madeleine L'Engle

"Mom, how old are you?" my fifteen-year-old daughter Maddy asked me yesterday while we were fluffing up the pillows on the couch.

"I'm fifty-nine, sweetheart," I said, as though everything about this conversation and where it might lead was perfectly normal.

"Oh, that's what I thought. When I told my friend Sarah that you were fifty-nine, she couldn't believe it. She said her mom is only thirty-eight."

"Well, did you tell her that's how old your big sister is?" I asked.

But Maddy's phone must have vibrated. When I turned around she was off in Text Message Land. End of story for her. A day of memories for me.

While Maddy's used to having an Older Mom, I don't know if I will ever get used to being one.

It's not that I got a late start. My first daughters, Samantha Sunshine and Jasmine Moondance, were born in 1969 and 1975 respectively—like bookends to my intensely counterculture years in Washington, D.C. and San Francisco.

By the time I met and married Tripp in 1983 and he shouldered responsibility for my daughters, I was ready for a normal family—though since we ended up with twelve children, our family would prove to be not very normal after all.

Bearing children over a couple of decades has led to some sitcom moments—like being pregnant at the same time as my oldest daughter and swapping maternity clothes with her. Sober ones too—like breaking the news to her that her newborn brother Jonny had Down syndrome, just as she was expecting her own first child.

Madeleine was Number Nine, born a year after Jonny. She is what we call "normal," if you consider a little girl who could belt out tunes like Patti Lupone and who needed no coaxing to sing—anytime, anywhere—normal. Plus there's her Doris Day demeanor/Pollyanna personality. No matter the setting—public or home—Maddy is the most consistently cheerful, upbeat, and enthusiastic person I've ever met.

From her early years I suspected that people wondered if I was her grandmother. Though these days, in trendier locales, there is no lack of graying new moms who let their biological clocks keep ticking until seconds before the final alarm. They're now sitting at back-to-school night in those teensy-tiny chairs surrounded by parents young enough to be their children too.

The only difference between them and me is that I once sat in those teensy chairs as a normal young mom. And now I've been sitting in them for thirty-eight years. The novelty's worn off. The body begins to protest.

Last fall, when my youngest son started kindergarten—you see, it wasn't crazy enough that my husband and I forgot to stop having kids, we also didn't get the memo that said we were too old to adopt a few more—a mother called me to arrange a Play Date. How to explain that I just can't do Play Dates anymore?

I have twelve grandchildren already. I really should be just a grandma—you know, that wonderful woman who picks up the grandchildren and devotes a day to making them feel special while their mom stays home and does laundry and rids the refrigerator of moldering leftovers. That wonderful grandma who has time to tell stories and bake cookies at her house, then takes the kids home and collapses for a few days before going out with her friends to swap pictures and stories. Or play golf.

Instead I'm still in the trenches, with my own refrigerator to clean, mountains of laundry from six still-at-home kids (eight when the guys are home from college), grocery shopping, and shuttling of the next generation — well, my next next generation — to soccer, play practice, voice and piano.

I'm exhausted — in my worst moments muttering things like, "I know you had a plan, God, but what could you have been thinking?"

But I'm grateful as I pick myself up and — much like the Energizer Bunny — press on with the art and science of mothering.

"But you don't look fifty-nine!" people tell me — at least on my good days. These kids keep me young because I'm not allowed to feel old. Being an older mother in some way is like drinking from a Fountain of Youth.

But then again, I wonder: what if I let my hair go gray?

I remember years ago when Maddy asked me why I was older than the other mommies, and for a moment I wished that I could be like all the others — young and pretty and full of energy.

Then I remembered that once upon a time I had been a young and pretty and energetic mom. And I remembered how back then it was always about me. And that's the difference between being a mother of young children at the appropriate age and being one at mine.

I guess that's the upside of being an older mother. Children have changed me, made the rough edges smooth, the hard places soft. I'm just becoming aware of how the pieces come together and life begins to make sense even though there's still so much to learn. It gives me an inkling what God may have been thinking after all — giving me this second generation of children at the perfect time!

~Barbara Curtis

Dye Hard, Too

You can't hide your true colours as you approach the autumn of your life.
~Author Unknown

I woke up Friday and my hair was purple. I am not talking about grandma-got-a-bad-consult-from-the-cosmetology-student purple. Oh no. This was more like HazMat-clean-up-needed-in-aisle-12-large-woman-plowed-through-the-grape-plutonium purple. Not coincidentally, that was my last day at my job.

I bet you're already thinking those two things are related? Bingo! The whole thing had been five months in the making. It was all my hairdresser's fault.

After ten years of close calls with Dear John letters from my merger-crazed company, my job was being eliminated and I faced early retirement. It was July and I had just run into my hairdresser at the conversational nexus of the universe, the Walmart parking lot. She was young, hip and at that moment, had the most amazing purple hair. I loved it! In the span of sixty seconds I had complimented her, announced my impending joblessness and vowed to dye my own hair purple on my critical departure day.

For thirty years, I had been the local talking head for a very large company and my career duties had included lobbying and media relations as well as reputation management for every company issue. Every conversation—at the mall, at the gas pumps, at the grocery store—ultimately revealed itself as a potential pothole. Conservative, polished and professional defined my demeanor, and because I drove a car that was emblazoned with the company logo on the driver's door, I rarely traveled incognito.

During the five months before my departure, the thought of having purple hair became more and more compelling, like that intense, pure light so many people report seeing during a near-death experience. It was calling to me, daring me to declare myself and take that first giant step into the unknown. It represented everything I had been in my way-former life and nothing from my present. I wanted to look in the mirror that first day of a past career and be reminded that there would be no glory in retreating.

On dyeing day, the minute the purple infusion passed critical mass, my husband began telling people that my chameleon suit was off and the woman he married was back. Funny. I don't remember having purple hair in our wedding pictures but I'm happy he saw it even then.

Twenty-four hours before the end of my employment, I left the salon loving the new me (or the old me). It was early evening. The sky was painted with that late-autumn light and there were holiday sparks in the air. My hair was purple and perfectly coiffed. All was right with the world.

I headed right back to the office and by 10:00 p.m. I had packed up my last news clipping, dumped my last e-mail and faced only my formal exit for my last day. So I woke up Friday and my hair was purple. The difference was, it was daylight.

My daughter once reviewed a particularly evocative Dali piece and described it as similar to seeing an injured dog at the side of the road. You don't want to look but you can't look away. Yes, it was like that. My hair radiated purple in the sunlight. The healthy shine that accompanied the extra care my stylist had provided served as a hall of mirrors to bounce back every glint of illumination one hundred times over. My husband described my first step out of the back porch shadows as "a Kodak moment."

Because I had envisioned my last day so clearly, I had a solid plan for how that evening would unfold as well: dinner at a favorite Italian restaurant followed by shopping in several favorite stores. I did generally forget that my hair was purple, even on the very first day, but I was quickly reminded during each new interaction—at the mall, at the gas pumps, at the grocery store. The logo that made me a target was now off my car door and on my head. What I hadn't factored into my exit day celebration was how I would respond to reactions from strangers about the bold new me.

Our first stop was dinner. The restaurant had lots of ambiance (meaning it was very dark in there) but there was no shielding the clerks and patrons at the upscale women's boutique when we moved on to shopping. Purple hair on a middle-aged mom didn't seem to sit too well with the young sales staff and I had apparently been causing quite a stir.

Without other customers to interfere with their sniping, all three young clerks had convened in a tight clump behind the counter to get an unobstructed view of the fabulous me. My daughter was furious when we left the store; my husband only shook his head as I got the pantomime version of what had been happening behind my back. I wasn't angry. Or hurt. Only amused. For the first time in a very long time, I didn't need to worry about what other people were thinking and I didn't care that they were probably asking: "Who does she think she is?" I know who I am, so despite my daughter's disgust, I went back inside the store.

Faces went white as I approached; I leaned in and half-whispered to get their attention. "Ladies, I know you were talking about my purple hair, but it's okay." The one my daughter had impugned as the ringleader took a step back. All three tried their best to cover that "Uh Oh!" look that confirmed their guilt. I shared my story about my drive to be fearless in the face of this uncertainty and I had them laughing with me, not at me, when I left the second time. Maybe I helped them with a life lesson, too.

"Old age ain't no place for sissies," Bette Davis said. Well, neither is middle-aged unemployment.

A few weeks later I visited Baltimore and learned what happens when a purple-haired woman lands there in the midst of football season. Absolutely nothing. To strangers there, I was just another Raven-haired beauty. "Normal" is such a fickle filter!

The whole experience has been so liberating; it's been like finally trashing the stilettos for a comfy pair of flip-flops. As each day passes, I feel less like a woman who has dyed her hair purple and more like a reinvented woman, who—by the way—has purple hair. It's more than just semantics. Live hard, play hard, dye hard, too.

One of the last things to get packed in the exodus from my office was a handmade poster from my daughter. Five colors of markers flowed across the page to form these words: "If you are lucky enough to be different than everyone else, don't change." Well said.

I'm different and I'm happy and I'm making my own luck these days. My deep purple hair is an indicator that I am no longer defined by anyone's view of me. Each look in the mirror reminds me that life on the far side of employment is still filled with amazing moments—joyous, rich and colorful!

~Mitchell Kyd

Living on the Edge

To remain young while growing old is the highest blessing.
~German Proverb

"**G**et down!" our guide shouted, as a wall of water rushed over the yellow inflatable raft, tossing it like a foam ball in a wind tunnel. I wedged my foot under the bumper seat, slid to the slick bottom, and hung onto the perimeter rope, hoping desperately that my oar would still be in the raft when the frothing frenzy was over. Seconds later, as our rubber boat bounced away from the explosive waves, we heard the next stern command: "Paddle!" So we paddled—hard—until the swift water of the Zambezi River in central Africa relaxed into a steady flow.

Our crew, which consisted of a newlywed couple from Ireland, a twenty-ish couple from London, a young man from Australia, and my husband Larry and me (old enough to be grandparents of everyone else), had just navigated Morning Glory, a Class V rapid. Several diagonal shifts off the right-hand wall of water fed into a big hole at the bottom that submerged the raft before lifting it back to the surface and tossing it towards the next big rapid, Stairway to Heaven, in one of the most thrilling rides I've ever experienced.

It's a good thing I didn't check the Internet before booking this trip. I might not have opted to tackle what the British Canoe Union describes as "the wildest one-day whitewater run in the world with extremely difficult, long and violent rapids, steep gradients, big drops and pressure areas." Had I known how dangerous the Zambezi rapids in Zambia can be (several people drown on similar trips every year), I might have skipped this excursion.

But I relish challenges. On my refrigerator at home is a poster that says, "Every so often, push your luck." It's a reminder of my decision to leave a stifling twenty-nine-year marriage that was as bland and unsatisfying as plain yogurt. The only happiness in my life during that time came from watching my children grow into responsible and successful young adults. Instead of spontaneity and adventure, life had become overwhelmed by complacency, even hostility. The time came to push my luck and set my spirit free.

The first step is always the hardest because we don't know what lies ahead. I worried about my children and the long-term effects of ending the marriage. I worried about finances and my ability to continue providing a similar lifestyle. I worried about time—having enough to work and care for my youngest daughter, who was still living at home.

For the first time ever, I was on my own. I had gone directly from my parents' house to college to marriage. Finding out that I could teach school, buy the groceries, balance the checkbook, mow the lawn, and get my daughter to swim practice on time boosted my confidence. But when those dense waves splashed over my head, threatening to wash away the rest of my life, I hoped I wasn't pushing my luck too far.

Eventually, I found someone who also believed age shouldn't be a deterrent to trying new things. When I remarried, I gave my new husband a T-shirt that proclaimed, "If you're not living on the edge, you're taking up too much space." That became our mantra. Now, in spite of—or more properly, in addition to—normal family obligations, we enjoy tiptoeing on the edge occasionally. I haven't gone bungee jumping or leaped from a soaring airplane—yet. Still, I've found unexpected rewards and confidence from deliberately stepping out of my comfort zone. Besides, unforgettable experiences happen when you're open to uncommon adventures and willing to take a chance on yourself.

Having rafted on whitewater numerous times, we looked

forward to the Zambezi River excursion, with its view of the spectacular Victoria Falls. Huge volumes of roaring water thunder over a tall, craggy wall and crash into a deep, narrow canyon before rushing away in the river, creating a perfect confluence of whitewater.

Vincent, our guide, had the cocky confidence of a person in charge, a good thing for our crew of novices. The first rapid was a level five called the Boiling Pot. Here a wall of water forms to cushion the raft against the rocky gorge (nasty if you crash) and lifts you over the eddy. On the first attempt our crew paddled haphazardly, and we missed the current that would carry us over the rapid. We tried again, synced our paddles, and—to Vincent's relief—successfully maneuvered through the fray. From then on we were invincible.

Our raft stayed upright throughout the trip, and no one became a swimmer (fell into the river). With a touch of sadistic humor, the Australian fellow had threatened to sabotage the raft, so we could all experience the river water firsthand. He backed off after we saw a crocodile sunning itself on the riverbank.

Rapid number seven, a Class V high-volume run, was the longest and most technical rapid on our trip—so difficult that outwardly-fearless Vincent made the cross sign and lifted his eyes to heaven when we successfully avoided two dangerous rocks.

On the eighth rapid, our group voted to take the 50/50 spill route instead of the safer, less daring route. This took us over a challenging series of three runs that totally submerged and spun our raft like a toy boat caught under the bathtub faucet. For what seemed like minutes we were engulfed in a towering rush of water, pushing our luck. But adrenaline kicked in, and everyone paddled furiously until we approached calmer water.

In all we navigated five Class V rapids, the most difficult allowed for raft passage, plus numerous IIIs and IVs. We walked around Commercial Suicide, a Class VI, before tackling the last run, Gnashing Jaws of Death, from which we emerged soaked and exhausted.

But even then it was too soon to celebrate. Exiting the canyon required climbing a steep 700-foot incline on a crude ladder built of gnarled tree branches while carrying oars, helmets, and life jackets.

The adrenaline rush that propelled us through the rapids had vanished, leaving us hot, thirsty, and tired. But quitting wasn't an option. I resorted to "monkey walking" up the ladder on all fours to scale the rocky hillside.

At the top I washed dust from my parched throat with a cool drink. Then exhilaration kicked in. I had accomplished an adventure that people half my age wouldn't even try.

Now, when I'm faced with challenges from family or career—some as daunting as riding the rapids—I remember that day on the Zambezi. I'm not afraid to push my luck because the rewards of trying and succeeding are too great not to take the chance.

~Beverly Burmeier

"Of course we'll be okay. When we were your age, whitewater rafting was how we went to school."

The Other Toy Story

Just about the time a woman thinks her work is done, she becomes a grandmother.

~Edward H. Dreschnack

For those of us raised in a gentler time, visiting a toy store in today's world can be a daunting experience. It's not that we didn't have our own difficulties a generation ago—we stood in line for the latest shipment of Strawberry Shortcake dolls, waited to adopt a Cabbage Patch or kept up with the latest Atari game. Still, those hurdles were nothing compared to what we experience now when we go in search of toys for the grandkids.

Years ago, a barrage of television commercials around the holidays helped us a little. Children wanted whatever flashed across the screen, and for us, an actual image and name we could pronounce was a good start. Today, we're on our own.

Being told, "Get them anything—they like whatever you choose," may be well-intended advice, but useless, nevertheless. Sure, they'll like anything. That's why there are rows of different lunch boxes, a myriad of craft projects and board games, miles of train sets and shelves of different action figures. After I insisted I needed clearer directions, my daughters were more specific: "It has to be a Game Boy Advantage 2, not just Game Boy or Advantage 1, but 2 and not a Game Cube; she wants pink first, then black but definitely not blue; it's the one that turns into a jet plane, not a tank or helicopter, but a jet; if you can't get the duck, then get the monkey, then the kitten, then the frog, but not the dog, she already has the dog." I jotted down the instructions as quickly as possible.

Armed with the shopping list I'd run by my daughters several times, I set out on a Tuesday (the day with the fewest shoppers) and as early in the morning as possible. Hanging on to a shred of pride, I walked past the young man in the red shirt. I was not ready to admit defeat, not within a few feet of the entrance.

Starting with the easy items, I headed for the doll section. All I needed was a simple doll stroller. How hard could that be? Thirty years ago, there was one choice; today, I could opt for the walking/running stroller, an umbrella stroller, a stroller for twins or the super-model with the rod of learning beads and balls to entertain the passenger, and—when that passenger is tired—can be folded back into a bed. Did someone forget the passenger is just a doll?

And, speaking of dolls. Today, they eat, wet their diapers, speak full sentences, change facial expressions—everything but pay for themselves. One realistic newborn started wailing whenever I walked near it. I stood there, pleading with the doll, "Please, stop that, be quiet, shhhhh. Please..." Looking over my shoulder for witnesses, I slipped away, feeling guilty that I had disturbed that sleeping chunk of plastic. Whatever happened to the plain, empty-eyed, curly-haired dolls that did nothing but lie there?

I was elated to find one item sitting right at the front of its section. The joy, however, was short-lived as I realized the item came in a box, unassembled. From the sound of 100 different parts rattling around inside that box, I knew the words "easy to assemble" applied to those with MIT engineering degrees. The devil on my shoulder urged me to buy it anyway and let my son-in-law deal with the hours of frustration. Maybe supplying the "batteries not included" would help me look a little better.

The final stop was in the electronics department. Confident I had this one down, I marched up to the counter and read off my list, which sounded something like "Pokamong Peekachu Venge da Nivia." Tilting his head, the clerk looked me square in the eyes and asked, "Huh?" I tried the name a few more times until he figured out what I was trying to say. When he informed me he thought the store was out of stock, my face began to tighten, then twist; I could feel heat working its way from my neck to my hairline as I growled through clenched teeth, "Look again." He scurried into the supply room and found one.

An hour and a half after starting my search, I was back in the car with the toys safely stored in the trunk. I had weathered this venture, fortunately finding every item on my list. My heart rate had returned to almost normal, and the beads of perspiration had begun to dry. Although I was proud of myself for tackling this feat and felt a sense of achievement in braving the maze of a modern toy store, next time I will grab that kid in the red shirt as soon as I push through the doors.

~Alison Shelton

Never Too Old

Anyone who stops learning is old, whether at twenty or eighty.
~Henry Ford

A young woman sprawled at her desk and thrust a leg into the aisle. It would be hard to miss her painted toenails, floppy sandals, and skintight jeans. She turned her head and two rings above her left eyebrow glistened. Five gold studs decorated her earlobe.

Across the aisle another youthful female dragged in a backpack on wheels. She plopped the bulging luggage in the aisle next to the painted toenails and blocked the passageway.

My desk was two rows from the front, next to the wall. I couldn't view the entire room without craning my neck, but I didn't need binoculars to determine I stood out like Grandma Moses in a kindergarten class. I didn't wear size six jeans. I didn't have a cell phone stuck to my ear, and I didn't carry a backpack or water bottle. The students surrounding me exhibited confidence and ease, while my head throbbed and my stomach released barrels of gastric acid.

Before this new adventure our son often phoned and asked, "What is my retired mother doing today?" My answers bored even me. Except for a few volunteer jobs, retirement days were anything but exciting. I had even sunk to reading junk magazines and racy books. Obviously I needed a drastic change to stimulate my mind and increase my brainpower before my gray matter turned to sludge.

Luckily I stumbled upon a deal too good to pass up—my

reason for being in a college classroom. Senior citizens in our town are allowed to audit classes at the university free of charge. When I scanned the myriad of classes offered in the catalog, my eyes locked on a class in creative writing. This was my chance to try something new, learn writing skills, and regain a sense of purpose.

Once I made up my mind to attend a college class, I attacked the intricacies of registration with the exuberance of King Kong on a rampage. This procedure proved not for the fainthearted.

My saga began the day before classes started. An hour before the appointed time to register, cars circled the parking lot like a sluggish chain gang searching for an escape route. After I found a coveted parking space, I trekked across campus with hoards of senior citizens in search of the registration building. This is precisely why little old ladies wear white tennis shoes.

With gray being the predominant hair color, I joined a long line of senior citizens. By the time I made it to the woman at the computer who held my fate at her fingertips, my varicose veins and patience had been severely tested.

"The creative writing class is already full," mumbled the registrar with all the compassion of a robot.

"Oh, no. It can't be. My heart is set on the writing class." I detest whiners, but that is exactly what I was.

She rolled her eyes and sighed. "We can only accommodate a limited number. We give first preference to paying students." When I didn't budge, she muttered, "I suppose you could go to class tomorrow and ask the professor if he will allow you to stay." She dismissed me with a flick of her fingers toward the door.

A half hour before class time the next day I stationed myself outside the designated classroom. The minutes crawled by while my heart pounded. My nerves became frazzled, my armpits rained sweat, and my legs weakened. But wannabe writers are determined people, particularly if we are retirees on a mission.

Eventually a man with a professorial demeanor approached room 378. I blundered forward, hoping I had the right person, and blurted, "I… er… um… please, I want to audit your writing class."

"Okay," he said. That was it. No drum roll, no brass band. I was a student again.

It feels peculiar to be seventy in the midst of young college students. I hadn't been in a classroom for fifty years. Did I feel self-conscious? You bet! Despite the incongruity of my age, the class proved to be the experience I expected and more. The professor led us through the study of characters, dialogue, point of view, and plot. When the class ended I knew how much I didn't know. With his permission, I audited the class a second time. The next semester I switched to a poetry writing class and audited that class twice.

I learned almost as much from the students as I did from the professors. The students' clothes, mannerisms, and decorative tattoos created fodder for future stories. Their youthful energy lifted my spirits. Their insights, imagination, and intelligence amazed me. When I learned about their full-time jobs, their families, and their financial difficulties, in addition to the stress of college, I was humbled.

The young students and I had much in common after all. We struggled together to improve our writing. We risked making public our fragile thoughts and private feelings. We trusted each other to be charitable when we revealed our written words. We shared failings, celebrated victories, and worried about grades. Putting ideas on paper helped us make sense of our lives and that proved a worthy reward. And no one will forget the first time we read aloud a story or poem and felt proud of our work.

The university frequently entertains guest authors and I avail myself of this opportunity. To expand my reading material, I subscribe to writer's magazines and buy dozens of books. The writing classes inspired me to join a writer's group. This new niche in my life has given me numerous friends. And to keep the brain cells clicking, I continue to take classes in literature, philosophy, sociology, and more. But writing will remain a lifetime hobby.

It is a cliché to say one is never too old to learn, but it is true. Retirement doesn't mean one's brain needs to be put on hold. Returning to college took perseverance, a sense of humor, and guts. Only students can appreciate the inner glow of accomplishment when we have worked hard, completed an assignment, and feel a little bit wiser—no matter what our age.

~Barbara Brady

Slumber Party

Age merely shows what children we remain.
~Johann Wolfgang von Goethe

A group of us like to stay and think young, so we developed "Senior Slumber," a slumber party for us more... mature women. It may sound crazy but it is something we look forward to during our long, dreary Midwest winters. Early in the year we begin planning the annual event, setting a date during a warm summer month.

The event begins early in the morning, when we leave town and make a couple of stops at garden centers, craft stores or antique shops along the way to our party location. Recently, I suggested we stop visiting the antique stores. I found them a bit depressing seeing that my precious childhood memories were now labeled "antiques."

Once we arrive, we drop our luggage and head out for fun. The contents of our slumber luggage have changed from baby doll pajamas, Ouija boards, potato chips and candy bars to nightgowns, pills, bladder leak protection pads, and sugar-free candy.

After our first dinner we enjoy a relaxing sunset wine and cheese cruise. Once we have returned to land we build a bonfire and make s'mores. When the mosquitoes come out, we go in.

After an evening of talking and playing cards it is time to slumber. Okay, so maybe we go to bed before the ten o'clock news has finished and we sleep in beds instead of in sleeping bags on the floor, but our attitudes are youthful. We have yet to Saran Wrap a toilet seat or short sheet a bed, but we have fun.

On the second day of the event we have breakfast and take a trip to an Amish store, craft store or maybe spend a little time on the dock watching the fish swim by, sometimes with our eyes closed. After lunch, whether we eat in or out, we are always up for a rousing game of cards. Before dinner we take another bracing pontoon ride and come back and begin the annual Corn Hole tournament. So what if we move the boards closer together than the rules state? We have fun. Somehow I usually manage to finish the tournament in a prizewinning position. My strategy is to remain relaxed while throwing the little corn-filled bags, although I have realized over the years that maybe that relaxed attitude comes from the Dramamine I take for the high-powered pontooning.

Playing cards is a continual activity throughout the event, as well as eating, and we find that relaxing in the sun can still be exercise as we pass around the sunscreen until dinner time. Maybe we are beyond the half-century mark but it does not mean that we can't have fun. Strenuous kids' activities might have gone by the wayside but we have found tubing behind a pontoon boat can be as much fun as a speedboat.

On the last day we make good use of every minute. Some of us read a book, others go shopping in the little college town, and one of us sits down at the computer and writes about the event.

After two days of eating, talking, playing cards, and pontoon excursions, our jaws may be tired, but our sanity and attitudes are restored, giving us new memories to enjoy throughout the next cold, dark winter.

Probably one of our finest moments came while we were sitting on the dock as the sun was setting. Sharing our thoughts and laughing, we saw a boat full of young men slow down and begin to cruise by us. They were hooting and howling, saying things like, "Hey baby, what are you girls doing tonight?" as they approached us. They did not realize how sound travels across a still lake, and we heard one of the "gentlemen" say, "Hey, they are old." The boat turned and sped away.

Maturing in body, but not in heart, with our young spirits still intact, we are the same girls who slumbered at parties many years ago.

~CR Rae

Foreign Travel with Twenty-Somethings

While one finds company in himself and his pursuits,
he cannot feel old, no matter what his years may be.
~Amos Bronson Alcott

"Y ou're spending six weeks in Costa Rica studying Spanish with college students?" exclaimed my friend. "You're older and retired! Aren't you nervous about traveling to a foreign country with younger people? You could end up rejected and alone!"

My friend was verbalizing my fears about my upcoming trip.

During the university's orientation I was relieved to see older people among the group. Then at the airport I was alarmed as I watched my peers hug the departing students and realized they were relatives staying behind. On the airplane I watched young friends engaged in lively conversations punctuated with laughter. I sat alone and pretended to read a book.

We arrived in San José and moved in with host families who spoke no English. When classes began I observed the students and the differences between my generation and theirs: I didn't have tattoos, wear skimpy tops, display a pierced bellybutton or use the word "like" with every other word. I searched for similarities: we spoke English, we wanted to learn Spanish, and we were sharing an adventure. That was a start.

During a weekend trip I feared no one would want me as a roommate. I was grateful when two girls asked if I would room with them. The next day we hiked 500 meters straight down into a rainforest. The return walk up was grueling. At the top, shapely Pam approached. "You kicked my butt on that climb and I work out four days a week." I sensed I earned her respect.

Back in San José I went shopping with several girls. I watched perfect figures try on revealing tops. I giggled while they checked out cute guys. I was enjoying "hanging out" with girls who were too young to date my son. We discussed parents, religion, racism, values, and dating. They probed for my views on these issues, forcing me to dust off opinions I hadn't examined in years.

I felt comfortable with the group during our next excursion. Suspended from a single cable, I soared from one jungle platform to the next. The trees below looked like stalks of broccoli. While returning in a van, I shared a seat, chocolate, and conversation with animated Katy. She confided that at first the students had doubts about my joining the trip because I was older.

"We, like, don't have those feelings about you anymore," she said with a smile. "We think, like, you're cool! When we, like, get older, we want to be just like you."

I, like, felt tears in my eyes.

When we returned to the States, I expected my new friends and I would go our separate ways. We would no longer have Costa Rica and Spanish to bring us together.

Like, I was wrong!

We continued the relationships that grew while hiking in a rainforest, bouncing along mountain roads, and sharing a sky ride over the jungle.

Traveling to Costa Rica with a group of twenty-somethings was rewarding… because our friendships became stronger than our differences.

My new peer group is, like, awesome!

~Miriam Hill

A New Prescription

When it comes to staying young, a mind-lift beats a face-lift any day.
~Marty Bucella

There are three little words that seem to precede any sort of advice I get these days. "At your age," my son says that I should not jog or I could break bones. "At your age," his girlfriend says I can "get away" with wearing anything but mini-skirts. Frankly, I never really cared to jog or wear mini-skirts at any age, but especially at my age, I don't like to be told what I can or can't do.

So imagine my dismay when my optometrist told me that at my age, I should update my eyeglass prescription to trifocals. "At your age," he told me, "it is fairly common."

I don't know if I want clearer vision. Maybe it's a tool of denial, but at my age a little bit of nearsightedness can be kind when I look in the mirror. I don't see the deepening wrinkles and increasing gray. My backside isn't sagging. I just need some new underwear.

Pointing out personal safety, my optometrist prevailed. The vision technician helped me choose some new frames. I am sorely out of sync with today's fashion because I leaned toward thin, wire-rimmed granny glasses. They were cheaper. The girl frowned and handed me some thick, dark angular frames. I slipped them on and she beamed.

"Those eyeglasses make you look twenty years younger," she said seriously. I peered closely into the mirror. She was right! I barely recognized myself. I straightened my back, feeling confident and, well, youthful. Why is it that I suddenly felt twenty years younger? I was taught that what was inside counts. External effects shouldn't matter. But by golly, these eyeglasses had a strange and positive effect on me.

"What you wear really does affect how you see yourself," she said, grinning at her own optometric pun. On the way home, I decided to shop for a new outfit to go with my new glasses. My usual style did not go with these contemporary frames and I chose summer capris in sunny colors. I found myself trying on open-toed sandals instead of practical flats. Since my toes were going to be displayed to the public, I got a pedicure for the first time in years.

Why had I quietly aged into dreary-looking clothing? I went through my closet and saw that an old woman had slowly moved in. There's nothing wrong with comfortable clothes, sweatpants, elastic banded jeans, thick holiday sweaters and easy slip-on shoes in brown and black. But wearing them made me feel like I was cocooning. Maybe, like a butterfly, it was time to emerge for my second life. I reminded myself that I didn't have to skimp on my own clothing budget now that there were no more school clothes to buy for the kids, no prom dresses or graduation suits. Maybe it was time for me to dress for a successful second half of my life.

Today, alongside the comfy clothes, there are pretty silk dresses, linen suits, colorful skirts and fun shoes. And because I need a good reason to wear these outfits, I go out to new restaurants, concerts and social gatherings. In the past, I'd decline partly because I never had anything to wear. I used to say, "Why buy anything? I never go anywhere."

My favorite new outfits include zippy new exercise clothes. Hiking shorts. Yoga pants. Swimsuits. At my age, Lycra is more like a medical prescription. New clothes in general help you feel youthful inside and out. They are more important than we know. After all, Mark Twain once said, "Clothes make the man. Naked people have little or no influence on society."

"Aren't you glad you updated your prescription?" my son asked.

"You're getting out more." He's right. I love my new vision on life and new clothes.

And at my age, I just might go jogging in a mini-skirt with my new eyeglasses. Okay, maybe I won't. But I can if I want to. I just happen to have a more suitable outfit that matches this fabulous new prescription.

~Lori Phillips

21

Grow Older, Act Younger

That man never grows old who keeps a child in his heart.
~Richard Steele, Sr.

My husband, Bob, and I were recently browsing in a large bookstore. I was looking through books on antiques and he was in the music aisle. He wore headphones that were available so shoppers could hear samples of CDs. Then I saw something else he was doing. He was dancing—not ballerina-style, but be-bopping along to the beat.

And that's when I realized that there was no way he would have done this when he was in his twenties or thirties. But now, in our retirement years, he was comfortable dancing like a teenager in public. I went over to him and touched his shoulder. "People will see you," I whispered. "You're acting like a kid."

"I don't care," he said, still dancing. "It's not only okay to act like a kid again, it's grand!"

He put the headphones on me. I could hear the irresistible beat of The Temptations singing, "My Girl." He mouthed the words "go ahead" to me. He knew I loved to dance with fierce abandon to Motown music, but only in my pajamas in the privacy of our living room. I looked around the store to make sure no one was watching. He moved the headphones away from my ear and said, "It doesn't matter if anybody sees you."

When I was younger, I would have not only been dancing to

the Temptations in this very public place, I would have been singing along as well. But on this day, I couldn't break out of my self-imposed mold. I handed him back the headphones.

I think that the reason my husband allows himself to act like a kid now has to do with perspective. What's important to him at this stage are the vital issues in life — family, health and happiness. He's told me many times, "At my age, lots of things fall into the 'it doesn't matter' category. Why don't you start thinking about it too? It only makes you happier."

He was lovingly teaching me to learn what really matters and what doesn't.

I began to wonder if part of this self-consciousness has to do with getting too caught up in setting a "proper" example for our children. I've noticed that when my friends' kids have left the nest, my friends begin to act differently. They wear more colorful clothing, purples and bright reds, and don't care about giggling uncontrollably in public. But we don't have to wait until our children leave to do these kinds of things. And maybe, that would be an even more "proper" example to set for our kids.

My pal Kate recently sent me an e-mail. I've heard from her many times about wanting to set a good example for her children. But her children have left the nest. Her message read, "I don't care anymore about how I act." The last part of her e-mail read, "If I can't sleep and decide to drive three hours to Maine, then that's exactly what I'll do. I feel the best I've ever felt. For all my gray hairs and wrinkles, I really like being my age." Kate has freed herself from stereotypic age pangs.

The night before my wedding, when I was twenty-six years old, I went out to dinner with my parents. I was wearing a skimpy dress that showed a little cleavage. I heard my dad whisper his concerns about this to my mom. And she said, "This is the only time she can get away with it. She won't be able to when she's older." So what did that mean? We older folks have to button up to the neck and wear only modest clothes?

Our "it doesn't matter" category gets bigger as we age. I used to obsess for hours about something I said or did that seemed foolish. Now I frequently ask myself the question, "Ten years from now, is this silly thing you just did going to make any difference?" Usually the answer is, "No, of course not."

Conversely, I often ask myself, "If you don't do this now, are you going to regret it later?" I asked myself that question when we were in the bookstore that day.

As I walked away, I turned and looked back at my husband in the CD aisle. He was having a blast, unselfconsciously moving to the rhythm of the music. Were people staring at him? Some were. Did it matter to him? Not in the least. At that moment, I decided that I wasn't going to miss any more time acting like an adult when I'd much rather act like a kid. I slowly made my way back to him, forcing out thoughts such as, "I don't dance well and everyone will see that." It wasn't that I was afraid of dancing. I was afraid of looking foolish.

I stood next to him and put on another set of headphones. Then I pressed "play" on a Four Tops CD. Intentionally, I closed my eyes so I wouldn't look around. And with no finesse whatsoever, I tapped my feet in time to the music. Then I let loose and boogalooed just like I used to years ago. When I opened my eyes and looked over at my husband, he was laughing—not at me but at the childlike joy in my face and in my heart.

So I think we should never lose sight of the delight of being a kid. It's liberating. It's therapeutic. And frankly, it becomes easier the more we try.

Although I wish I had learned all this years ago, there's no point in that kind of regret. From now on, I'm going to applaud the child in me. If I'm not wearing what most people my age wear, so what. If I act goofy, it doesn't matter. And if I'm at a concert, I'm going to stand up and dance with the rest of the kids.

The older I get, the younger I intend to act. And I'll have a grand old time doing it.

~Saralee Perel

22

Some Occasions Call for Purple

Growing old is mandatory; growing up is optional.
~Chili Davis

Standing in the accessory aisle, all decked out in crazy hats and wild colored scarves, my best friend Diana and I looked at each other and at that very moment read each other's minds. We burst into laughter and all I could whisper between gasps of air was, "Oh no, we're actually wearing purple!"

We were remembering a poem I had sent her about getting old, wearing purple and living life as a wonderfully, outrageous adventure. It described zany behaviors such as giggling a lot and making promises to never wear plastic rain bonnets. Back then, Diana's comment was, "That will probably be us someday." And, here we were, she in her big, purple hat and me in my mismatched blue hat and purple scarf. To top it off, we were actually taking pictures of each other — right in the aisle of the department store. Needless to say, the sales clerk thought we were crazy, but we gave her a look that said, "We've earned the right to every bit of this silliness."

You see, we've discovered that being "young at heart" is only limited by the boundaries we set for ourselves. Challenges arise, and even though our health may set some restrictions and finances may control our options, dreams don't come to an end. Spontaneity needs to continue, and most of all, laughter should be as routine as breathing.

Many years ago, Diana and I worked for the same company and quickly became friends. We shared a similar background, and had children and grandchildren who were close in age. Our daughters even shared the same first name and red hair. What is the chance of that?

Over time, I changed jobs and we both relocated several times. Each move took us farther away from each other, but distance did not hinder our relationship. Even though we lived far apart, our phone calls always picked up right where we left off. Through the years, our conversations have run the gamut—from trying to solve the problems of the world, needing a missing ingredient in a recipe, trying to top one another with our grandchild's latest achievement, or dreaming about retirement. But, it is the times when we reminisce about our childhood that we laugh the hardest.

"I was a tomboy when I was growing up. My brothers and I did the craziest things...." As Diana shared her story, our nostalgic conversation got me to wondering. When is it that we cross the line from daredevil and fun-loving, to serious and worried human beings? Do we really have to lose our "joy," or is it just buried under the responsibilities and life-issues that become part of our daily routine? Reminiscing reminds us of who we were and tempts us to find that "child" in us again.

Last year, I decided to go to college, forty years after my high school graduation. Many funny stories have come out of the experience and yes, at times it has also been quite a challenge. Sharing these moments with my best friend has reminded us both that we are not too old to enjoy life, and that, as we get older, sometimes we have to create our own adventures.

So, lately our conversations have taken on an entirely different nature. We have started planning some escapades... a shared "bucket list" of sorts, but we are calling it our "life list." You see, it is not a list of things we want to do before we die, but rather, a compilation of adventures we want to embark on as we live life to the fullest. It may be as simple as snapping pictures of each other in outrageous sunglasses while vacationing at the beach, or as fabulous as stomping grapes at a vineyard in Italy (or most likely California).

Wherever our adventures take us, we have promised to encourage each other to look at life through the eyes of our youth and giggle a lot along the way! And we have definitely agreed that the color purple needs to remain in our wardrobes, if for no other reason than to make a statement that we will always be "young at heart."

~Donna Weaver

23

Jump of Youth

The aging process has you firmly in its grasp
if you never get the urge to throw a snowball.
~Doug Larson

When friends and family sent me "over the hill" birthday cards, I wondered what life as a senior citizen would offer. As weariness ached in my joints and thoughts of unfulfilled dreams wrinkled my brow, I hoped that my existence had mattered to someone. Then, a winter activity with my grandson opened a door for me to rediscover youthful memories.

The winter weather had come just weeks after one of those October "over the hill" birthdays. Snow was plentiful and the hill at Old Main was usually packed with serious sledders. As my grandson and I approached the hill, we were delighted to see only two small groups that had escaped the confines of home on a school night. There were a few college students obviously taking a break from their studies, and several teenage boys who could not resist the day's new snowfall to build a jump over a bale of hay.

My grandson and I tested a variety of runs, laughing as we raced past each other like Olympic competitors. The powdery snow was gradually becoming packed. Each pass over a run made it icier, and we picked up speed as we raced to the hay below.

The teenage boys were intent on developing the ideal jump. They had strategically placed a bale of hay two-thirds of the way down the sloping hill. After packing each new addition of snow, one after another, they would speed over the jump. The college students were willing to test the younger boys' creation and were eagerly cheered on. More snow was packed, more runs were made, more cheers for successful runs and groans for painful landings filled the night air.

As I trudged up the hill with my bright pink plastic toboggan, I enviously watched the boys brave their Olympic jump. I was in awe of the airborne moment just before they crashed to the ground. One daredevil on a tube was free-falling as his tube slid on without him. Another boy leaped towards the sky only to crash down on his side. I wished I didn't have to fear broken bones.

The hill was filled with laughter and cheers for each boy's unique style as he flew over the jump. Olympic scoring became obvious by the volume of the cheers or groans. A few more college students had shown up, and each had his turn at the jump with no hesitation. My grandson and I were the only ones on the hill who had not taken the risk of embarrassing ourselves. The boys had a way of making a wipeout look like a grand feat, but I was sure that a grandma would only look like an old fool.

I longed to join them, as their enthusiasm was contagious. A run near the trees had become icy and the speed that created made the dips and bumps more thrilling. Once I got too close to the trees and almost wiped out. The close call only made the chilled evening more exciting. I was taking risks. The adrenaline rush overruled my cold limbs and tired muscles. Without realizing it, each run I took brought me closer to the boys' jump.

I had no intention of taking the jump, but on one run my grandson was trying to beat me down the slope. I pushed off, gaining incredible speed. Earlier, I had realized that a plastic toboggan has little maneuverability. Now, as I was accidentally heading for the jump, I saw only two choices: tip off my toboggan and painfully slide into a tree, or hang on and become an airborne fool. I hung on and prayed for a miraculously soft landing.

I hit the jump straight on and was airborne. The flight was short but invigorating. Then, gravity took over, and I met the earth with a crashing blow. Pain surged through my body as I heard the male chorus cheering and applauding. "Did you see her take that jump?" My Olympic score would definitely have been a nine.

The next morning, as I soaked my aching body, a smile crossed my face. I must have looked ridiculous on that cold, icy hill. I imagined a news broadcaster reporting, "Late last night, a local granny reclaimed her childhood on Old Main's jump of youth."

~Penelope Burbank

24

A Glorious Ride

*If wrinkles must be written on our brows,
let them not be written upon the heart. The spirit should never grow old.*
~James A. Garfield

Bold, wild, adventurous—not words I would use to describe my mother-in-law. I'd heard the stories about Gran as a young girl, daring to ride a calf back from the stream on her parents' farm and getting bucked off. But she grew up and calmed down. Marrying late in life, she lost her husband after only three years. Then she did the only thing she knew to do. She went back to work as a hairdresser and quietly raised her only child, my husband. After working more than forty years, she retired in her mid-seventies to settle into a semi-reclusive life. Sedate, solitary, dignified—now that was the Gran I knew.

So it surprised us all when she told my younger son, Jeremy, she wanted him to take her for a ride in his Jeep Wrangler—with the top down. Cautious Gran? The meticulous hair stylist?

For three years, Jeremy intended to grant his grandmother's wish, but something always got in the way. Finally, he picked up the phone one day just after her eighty-fifth birthday and called her. "We're coming up tomorrow. I'm going to take you for that ride in my Jeep."

Gran could barely contain her excitement. "I can't wait!"

The next morning, Jeremy and his dad hopped in the Jeep and drove the three-hour trip into the rolling foothills of middle

Tennessee. Making a brief stop at Gran's, they unsnapped the windows and pulled off the Jeep's top. Then they buckled Gran into the front passenger seat and headed for her seven-acre parcel of land near Sycamore Lake.

I saw the pictures of her later, perched on the leather seat with the sun shining on her face and the wind blowing through her hair. Well, sort of. Actually, she covered her head with a scarf and put Jeremy's golf cap on top for good measure. Gran is particular about her hair after all. But the wind didn't detract from her exhilaration. The ride down the bumpy dirt road to her property did nothing to spoil her excitement. Even the mud spewing past her windowless door when they got stuck on the trail couldn't diminish her joy.

Later that day Gran called me, tired but eager to talk about her adventure. "That was a long time coming but well worth the wait. It was a glorious ride!"

As I move into my senior years, I want to remember Gran's example. Raising my family, I often became so busy with work and church, home and activities that I forgot to take delight in the moment. Sometimes I let life rush past, like wind past a Jeep, or allowed the bumpy ride and the spewing mud to steal my joy. But Jeremy and Gran didn't. They took the chance at an adventure and made memories that weekend, sweet memories that will last across the years.

Thanks to Gran, I am learning how to make life a glorious ride.

~Tracy Crump

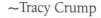

Sunday	Monday	Tuesday	Wednesday	Thursday	Friday	Saturday
		1 brunch at Smiths	2 Work 9-1	3 babysit Jessica	4 work 9-1	5 Pack
6 Pier 3 at 4 sharp	7 CRUISE!!	8	9	10	11	12
13	14 work 9-1	15 Jessica ☺	16 Work 9-1	17 Dog Shelter	18 work 9-1	19 Golf with Gene
20	21 Work 9-1	22 Dr. Miller - 10:30	23 work 9-1	24 dog shelter	25 Work 9-1	26 Dinner Party 7:00
27 DC trip 27th-29th	28	29	30 Work 9-1	31 Dog Shelter		

Chapter
3

Inspiration
for the
Young
at
Heart

Never Too Late
for Romance

Love Online

Grow old with me! The best is yet to be.
~Robert Browning

Love at eighty-two? Highly unlikely! But two years ago, I found it on the Internet.

I had been widowed two years when a friend urged me to give a dating service a try. "Are you kidding?" I asked. "Who's looking for an eighty-two-year-old woman?"

"You'd be surprised," she responded. "They say there's someone for everyone. Why don't you try eHarmony or Match.com?"

"Don't be silly," I scoffed. "I'm not that desperate!"

But I was.

One night I secretly got on my computer and entered my profile on a dating service: "Looking for someone who enjoys candlelight, soft music and good conversation. Must be between the ages of 75-85 and live within 50 miles of Clearwater Beach, FL."

A few days later, my computer signaled that I had received photos of twelve men between the ages of sixty-five and eighty-five, living in Denver, Tucson and Seattle.

"You must be working from the Sarah Palin book of geography," I complained to the Internet service. "I live in Florida!"

Within a day, I had a new page of Florida men, from both the East and West Coast. I gave them my best, but I struck out on all counts.

A few weeks slipped by, and I was losing heart, when suddenly...

There He Was! "Harvey1926." His profile matched mine exactly. He was born in March, 1926... I was born in February, same year.

Harvey's picture showed that he was tall and good-looking, with a mane of white hair and a smile that hinted at a sense of humor.

We had both lived in Massapequa, Long Island, and both worked for CBS in Manhattan. Harvey was the director of music royalties... I was a songwriter for Fred Waring and His Pennsylvanians on CBS television. Yet our paths never crossed.

He had a player piano... I had a Steinway. We had both read *Bomba, the Jungle Boy* as children. (I even had a pet monkey named Bomba.)

There was just one problem. "Too bad," I wrote. "We would have been perfect for each other, but you live in New York, and I live in Florida."

Harvey wrote back, "We'll meet in Paris!"

Hmm, he had definite possibilities!

He had received responses from other hopefuls and actually had dates with three women in the New York area. In fact, his grand-daughter commented, "Grandpa, you had more dates this week than I did!" But none clicked.

"Tell me more," I wrote.

He had been a widower for six months, had two married children and three grandchildren, had traveled the world, and now was look-ing for someone who enjoyed Broadway shows and sing-alongs with friends around his player piano. The Paris trip would come later.

I painted as dazzling a picture of myself as I could. But then, on second thought... "I have a confession to make," I wrote. "I walk with a cane."

"In which hand?" he asked.

"The left."

"That's good," he answered. "I walk with one in my right hand. We'll fit together perfectly."

After a week, e-mails weren't enough. We exchanged phone numbers and with 164 years of living between us, we had plenty to talk about.

His children had already made reservations to fly him to Sanibel for the Christmas holidays. Two days before they left New York, he learned that they would be renting a car in Tampa and driving south. A quick call to me determined that, yes, he would be welcome to visit me for a few days when he got off the plane.

His family was stoic.

"Can she cook?" queried his daughter.

"An octogenarian Lolita!" sniffed his cousin.

"Get a pre-nup!" counseled his lawyer son.

My family was equally supportive.

"Don't cook for him, Mom," advised my older daughter.

"How do you know he's not an axe murderer?" fretted my younger daughter.

"Get a pre-nup!" warned my son.

So much for the children! We were in love, and we hadn't even met.

A somewhat disgruntled family parted with Harvey at the airport gate.

"Maybe we should wait until you're picked up," they suggested, but Harvey was adamant... they should drive to Sanibel, and he would join them in a few days.

We almost missed each other at the exit. He waited at one door, I waited at another. After forty-five minutes, he was beginning to think he might have to take a bus to Sanibel. At that moment, I realized my mistake and drove a few feet to where he was sitting. We were equally excited to find each other and fell into each other's arms before driving to my condo.

Between moonlit walks on the beach and candlelight suppers in local bistros, our four days together went far too quickly. Every word, every nuance, every touch brought us closer together.

While Harvey spent the holidays with his children, I joined my daughter in Washington, D.C. We were out shopping in her car when her cell phone rang. On the other end, a rinky-tink piano played and an off-key voice sang, "I just called to say I love you."

"He's a keeper, Mom," she laughed. And sure enough, he took a train to Washington for New Year's Eve.

It only took a little time to convince me to return to New York with him to see how I'd feel about living there again.

Once there, I knew I'd found my new home. To suit our grandchildren's college schedules, we selected August for our wedding date. Friends suggested we call an interfaith center to locate an officiant who would marry us in Harvey's Greenwich Village apartment.

We were somewhat taken aback when a young yogi, recently ordained, answered the phone, but he was available on our chosen date, so we moved ahead with plans. He apologized that he had never performed a wedding before. "No problem," we assured him happily. "Between us we've been married six times. We'll walk you through the ceremony."

Harvey's apartment on the fifteenth floor, with a view of the Empire State Building in the background, couldn't have been more romantic for our wedding. My son escorted me to the flower-laden altar in the living room where Harvey awaited us with his son, the best man. Then our minister shared the ceremony with my two daughters, who read my favorite verse from First Corinthians.

In attendance were our five children and their spouses, six grandchildren and three great grandchildren.

And Harvey delivered on his promise of Paris for a two-week honeymoon, followed by a ten-day river cruise on the same rivers where he had fought in WWII during the Battle of the Bulge.

The climax, though certainly not the ending of this fairy tale, is that Harvey and I celebrated our first wedding anniversary at the wedding of one of my granddaughters in a little New England church. This time it was Grandma who read First Corinthians in the ceremony. As I looked across the congregation at Harvey, the words had new meaning... "If I have a faith that can move mountains, but have not love, I am nothing... And now these three remain — faith, hope and love. But the greatest of these is love."

~Phyllis W. Zeno

Damaged Goods

The only sure thing about luck is that it will change.
~Wilson Mizner

When you are over sixty, it is hard to find someone to date. In fact, it is nearly impossible.

I asked my friends to introduce me to their brothers, cousins, neighbors, anyone, but according to them, they didn't know any unmarried men. I didn't believe them and suspected they were hoarding all the single men for themselves.

I had joined clubs, gone to lectures, volunteered for practically everything, tried sports I hated, visited different church senior singles events and checked out the Internet. Nothing had worked. I think the last time I had a date Reagan was President. Okay, I could be wrong about that, but it had been a while.

My friend, Marsha, started dating a very nice man and was annoyingly happy. She said she'd met him at the grocery store between the carrots and green peppers. By the time they reached the checkout, he'd asked her for a date.

Well, that might be fine for Marsha, but I was hoping for something a little more romantic, like meeting him in a field of daisies or seeing each other across a crowded room and experiencing love at first sight.

Sometimes, you can wake up on a perfectly ordinary morning and feel like something wonderful is going to happen to you.

Thursday morning I woke up, went into the kitchen to make my coffee and promptly turned around and hit the left side of my face on a cupboard door that had swung back open. It only took a few minutes before my eye was black, puffy and nearly swollen shut. It also kept tearing up so that I had to keep dabbing at it to keep it from leaking down my face.

I also had a root canal scheduled that morning and the tooth happened to be on the left side of my face. The dentist was so repulsed by the way my eye looked that he laid a paper towel across my eye so he wouldn't have to look at it. He said he did it to protect my eye, but I think it was because he was repulsed.

After the root canal I decided I'd better stop at the store on my way home and get some soft food to eat that night. I was bending over the frozen dinners trying to find something that would require very little chewing when a man stopped beside me on my right side. I glanced up at him with my right eye. He was tall, in my age range, and wasn't wearing a ring.

"It's hard to find a frozen dinner that tastes better than the box it came in," he said. "When you live alone, it really isn't worth trying to cook a meal."

"Yes, you're right," I said. I'm a brilliant conversationalist.

"I get tired of frozen dinners but it's no fun to go out and eat alone. Sometimes it would be nice just to have someone to have dinner with once a week," he smiled.

My mind was racing. He's nice, he's tall, he's mentioned twice he is single. Marsha was right! You could meet a man in the grocery store. This was my lucky day!

"Yes, it would be wonderful to have someone to have dinner with, someone to talk to." I stood upright and turned to face him.

He stared at me.

"Oh, I'm so sorry, were you in an accident?" he asked.

I reached into my purse and took out my compact. My eye was black, swollen shut, and leaking tears. My jaw was the size of a baseball from the root canal and I was drooling just a little from the corner of my mouth because my lips were numb and swollen.

I looked like I should be ringing a bell in a tower. The only thing missing was a hunch on my back and the day wasn't over yet.

"I've had a bad day." I started to explain that I didn't always look like this but he was already backing away.

"Try the roast beef dinner; it's pretty good," he said and pushed his cart down the aisle as quickly as he could.

I decided to accidentally bump into him at the checkout to explain why I looked hideous but he was too clever. When I reached the tea and coffee aisle I saw his abandoned cart. He'd left without his bananas, onions and bread.

Well, his loss. He'd left behind his groceries and possibly the great love of his life. If all he cared about was superficial looks, then he wasn't the right man for me anyway. In another week my eye wouldn't be black and leaking and my cheek wouldn't be swollen and I wouldn't be drooling and even if I ran into him in the store again, I wouldn't speak to him. After all, I have my pride!

I think I'll call Marsha and ask her where she buys her groceries.

~April Knight

The Last Martini
at the Bubble Lounge

Success in marriage does not come merely through finding the right mate,
but through being the right mate.
~Barnett R. Brickner

The whole thing started when my neighbor's son told me he had gotten a summer job at the Bubble Lounge. "What on earth is that?" I asked.

"The new martini bar. You haven't been yet?"

"No, I don't believe I have. It's called the Bubble Lounge? Cute name. The last martini at the Bubble Lounge," I said dreamily. "That would be a good title for a short story."

"Uh, yeah. Well, I guess I'd better get going," he said, not sure where the conversation was headed, but certain he didn't want to tag along.

Of course writing a story to fit a title would horrify my creative writing instructor at the community college's Department of Continuing Education.

"Build your story around strong characters," she said over and over, "and everything else will follow."

But I couldn't get that title out of my mind. So one evening I drove by the Bubble Lounge. It was the latest addition to the upscale shopping village that had established itself in the heart of our historically significant and recently "discovered" neighborhood. I pictured my neighbors, those endlessly energetic, creative, fixer-upper professionals, behind the bar's frosted glass, sipping elegant concoctions. They would be swapping the latest parenting tidbits, I supposed, or sharing landscaping tips and names of decorators before dashing off to the corner bistro or the gourmet take-out for their dinner.

I imagined it all as I opened a package of pork chops and put potatoes on to boil. It kept coming back to me. "The Last Martini at the Bubble Lounge." Why the last martini? A story about the closing of a bar? Set in prohibition times? I couldn't let it go.

My writing instructor says to start with character. Okay. A tortured soul's final toot before heading off to A.A. It didn't work. Maybe it was more symbolic and personal. In the Bubble Lounge of life, I was, after all, close to the last round.

I thought about it one whole afternoon as I strolled with my grandchild through the shops, passing the dark lounge that would come alive like a handsome, seductive vampire when dusk settled on the neighborhood. Plots and characters danced through my head as I chatted with some of the nannies in the park near my house. I knew I was getting obsessive when I couldn't remember the bid at my bridge group that evening. My mind was not on cards. It was at the Bubble Lounge! I had to write the story and be done with it.

The next day I called my husband, Tom, at his office.

"I thought you might want to meet me for a drink after work," I suggested.

"What's wrong with the back porch?" he said.

"What's wrong with a little change? It would do us good. We can grab dinner somewhere."

But the basketball game was on TV. He was tired. Another night, maybe.

Two weeks later, "another night" had not materialized. After dinner, I told Tom about my desire to visit the Bubble Lounge.

"I don't know what you're talking about. You don't even like martinis," he said and disappeared into his laptop.

I loaded the dishwasher, put on some lipstick and my new black slacks.

"Tom, I'll be back in a little while. I'm going to the Bubble Lounge."

"By yourself?"

•••

"Oh, yes, we have drinks other than martinis," said the personable, young bartender who also happened to be my neighbor's son.

I sat at a tiny corner table by the window, sipping a cosmopolitan (vodka and cranberry juice, in case there's anyone left who doesn't know). Cranberry juice for the bladder and vodka for the soul, I told myself. Soft jazz played, candles flickered, and repartee sparkled at the neighboring tables. It was cozy but cool, everything black and glass and retro or deco or something. What a treat to spend an hour or so in an environment completely alien from one's own. And only a few blocks from home.

Home. I thought of Tom, happily lost in Internet Land. We had once cherished an evening in a place like this, away from mountains of responsibility and interrupting children, where we could just be together and talk. Our mountains were all relative molehills now. We finally had the time to go whenever and pretty much wherever we wanted. A ballgame on TV, a good book, a drink with friends on the porch—it was fine, very good, in fact. But no matter how nice the ride, if you take the same route every day, the scenery becomes boring and is taken for granted.

"Excuse me." I didn't realize the waiter was standing by me. "A gentleman at the bar would like to know if he might join you."

"Oh, good Lord," I thought and looked toward the bar. Tom lifted his cosmopolitan in salute, pointed to himself and then to me, his eyebrows raised questioningly.

When I stopped laughing, I motioned him over. My neighbor's son stood behind the bar, cleaning a glass and wearing a quizzical smile as he looked from my husband to me.

"I like this place," said Tom. "Can't believe it's taken us so long to try it out."

He told me about his boss's flaky secretary. It might have been the drinks, but we laughed and laughed. I told him about my obsession with the story of the Bubble Lounge. We made vacation plans and talked about doing some much needed landscaping.

"Last call, folks. Do you want anything else?" said the waiter.

I looked around, and the place was almost empty. Hours had slipped by.

"When was the last time you had a martini?" Tom asked me. Before I could answer, he told the waiter, "Bring the lady a martini."

I watched the young man fill up his tray and serve the other tables. He put the drink in front of me. I took a sip, winked at my husband, and said, "The last martini at the Bubble Lounge."

~Margaret P. Cunningham

Love at First Flight

There is no surprise more magical than the surprise of being loved. It is God's finger on man's shoulder.
~Charles Morgan

I felt good butterflies in my stomach instead of the dread of another lonely day. I fixed my bowl of cereal and fresh strawberries. I sipped my second cup of coffee and tried to recall his face. Two times around a dance floor wasn't enough time to get a mental picture of someone I had just met.

My life was defined by visits to doctors and so much fatigue it took my best effort to get out of bed. Going to a singles' dance the previous weekend was not my idea of fun, but my best friend Sue had dragged me to the Methodist Church event and convinced me to try the electric slide. I was catching my breath and tapping my toes on the sidelines when Charles had asked me to dance.

So why did I agree to meet Charles this day for lunch and a hike? I wasn't the hiking type. Just thinking about a hike made me tired. Since my husband's death, dates had been few and far between. Aren't women over fifty—especially a woman in my condition—more in danger of dying from a terrorist attack than finding another man? I often prayed, seeking God's will concerning a second marriage, but convinced myself that no man in his right mind would date a sick woman.

"Don't lead him on. Tell him the truth right away," Sue insisted on the phone.

"Can't I just have fun and forget about my disease for one day?" I responded.

"Be sure you tell him before it gets serious," were Sue's last words.

I laughed. "Don't worry. Getting serious about a man isn't on my radar screen."

The morning flew by as I showered and selected jeans and jacket, with a turquoise shirt. Native American earrings made the color pop. Nike walking shoes completed my ensemble. I was glad most people couldn't tell how bad I felt by looking at me.

I reread the directions I had scribbled down, then backed my car past the fading yellow daffodils and red tulips in full bloom. Fifteen minutes later, I pulled into the parking lot of the restaurant.

The cool, crisp March day was perfect for a hike. I reminded myself to put on a happy face as I tried to keep up with Charles's long stride. I had to admit his warm strong hand felt good wrapped around my fingers as we walked around the park. Charles pointed out the red bud trees and wild azaleas. The whole world was coming back to life, but I barely noticed.

"Look there's a waterfall," Charles pointed out.

"I'm not too good at this. I have limitations," I said as we climbed a hill before reaching a bridge over a small creek.

Sue's words rang again in my ears. Tell him right away. The sooner you tell him, the less you'll get hurt. After all, he seems like a nice guy and needs to know the truth. But the words stuck in my throat.

"See the rock outcropping up ahead?" Charles said. "Let's sit and rest a while before we turn back." The granite rocks were stacked at just the right height for sitting and, although cold through my jeans, a welcome respite for my out-of-shape body.

"Tell me more about your work." I had learned during our very enjoyable lunch that Charles had retired early from a career as an aerospace engineer.

"Well, I do research for government contracts. After my wife died I didn't want to just sit around. Now I'm thinking about starting my own company." I was impressed, but still cautious. I had been warned there weren't many eligible men with ambition. Or the good ones were already taken. Since I wasn't being entirely honest with him, he probably wasn't being honest with me either.

I glanced at Charles and liked what I saw. He was well built, suntanned and his baseball cap sat at a cocky angle on his head. He was just plain cute as he looked up into the cloudless blue sky. Maybe there was more to him than I was willing to admit.

"Do you want to go flying?" he asked.

"What? You're a pilot, too! What kind of planes do you fly?"

"Small light aircraft."

"Sure!" I said, throwing caution to the wind.

"I'll call and see if there is a plane available."

"Now? I didn't know you meant now!" I said in a shocked voice.

Charles looked amused, "Why not? It's a perfect day for flying."

• • •

From 1,000 feet in the air, my problems took on a different perspective. They seemed as small as the ant-sized cars, *Monopoly*-board houses and white steeple churches that dotted the ground below. The roar of the engine drowned out normal conversation. But an unexpected still small voice seemed to speak to me. Isn't this how an all-knowing God sees your life—viewing the big picture and not focusing on just your daily trials?

As I gazed over the cockpit and focused on the smoky horizon, I recalled teaching that truth to my class members last month. My hesitation and indecision disappeared. I would tell Charles about my disease and my need for an organ transplant, and leave his reaction and my future in God's hands.

"Wheels down! Request permission to land," Charles announced to the air traffic controller.

"That was fun—a great flight and landing," I commented as we walked hand in hand toward his car. "Thanks for taking me up. Let's get dessert—my treat. I have something to tell you."

Charles brags that at age sixty-five, he made two winning proposals. After three weeks of dating, he proposed marriage and, after ten years of widowhood, I accepted. Then the United States Air Force agreed to fund his second proposal, giving him a contract to improve aircraft flying characteristics.

Two years after our marriage, I received a liver transplant. My adventurous life would not have been possible without a generous donor family and Charles' loving support. At age eighty, Charles continues to promote his patents and his ideas for aviation improvement.

~Frieda S. Dixon

The Bet

Why not go out on a limb? Isn't that where the fruit is?
~Frank Scully

At sixty-two I didn't expect to find love. But on New Year's Eve, 1998, when online dating still was considered more risky than routine, I resolved to try Socialnet.com. Long divorced and just returned from a decade overseas with the Peace Corps, I worked in Little Rock, far from my California origins. Dateless for eons, I pictured casual Saturday outings to view Renoirs at the Arts Center or to share fried chicken and a hike at Pinnacle Mountain State Park. Love was for others. I'd settle for companionship.

So masquerading as "Dumpling," I posted my online bio and personal preferences, and prepared to review my matches. My inbox promptly began to fill with a list of potential dates' screen names and the distance they lived from my Arkansas home. To learn more, I'd have to click on the profile. Sometimes I sighed at the quirkiness of the computer matchmaker. One match, Bettor, I left unopened… the man lived two thousand miles away. Not a good bet for Saturdays in the park.

Those nearby didn't always prove to be good bets, either. A Kentucky widower wrote that if I helped him raise his four teen-age sons he'd provide me with a new washing machine. I passed. A Wichita Falls adventurer invited me on a rafting excursion on the notoriously challenging Cossatot River. We'd have to wait, though, until he convinced his wife that he deserved a weekend away. I declined. An Oklahoman declared he loved my moniker, Dumpling. He bet that I was one enticing fat mama. I didn't respond.

I finally agreed to meet one local widower for supper at Cajun's Wharf. The riverside setting, though, reminded him of the seafood dishes his late wife had prepared. Soon he was sobbing into his devilled crab as he recounted her prowess with halibut, trout and flounder. By the time he began to wail about her bouillabaisse, I'd finished with my barbecued shrimp... and our date.

Then one day at work my administrative assistant, Bev, asked how Social.net worked. I pulled up my list, which for months had been headed by Bettor's unopened profile.

I ran my cursor over his name. "I've never written this guy because he's too far away," I explained. "And with a name like Bettor, I suspect he's a gambler. But let's peek."

I clicked on his profile and quickly scanned it. Hmmm. Like me, he appreciated jazz, art, books, dogs, cooking, and travel. What's more... he sounded sane.

I glanced up at Bev. "I've been to the ends of the earth with the Peace Corps, so what's two thousand miles?" I pounded out a quick paragraph introducing myself.

Bev eyed me. "What if he turns out to be The One?"

The next morning I had a response in my inbox.

"My name's Ken and I think I'm in love," I read. "I value a coherent message. Bettor is my Nissan's vanity plate, which amuses friends here in Reno. I deal poker at Circus Circus, but don't gamble myself, as my three boys will attest." He added a link to his domain page, dubbed Sunflower.

I hesitated before clicking on it. I didn't want any kinky surprises. So I was delighted to find that he'd filled his webpage with photos of his three grown sons and assorted grandkids.

"You and your sons each are more handsome than the other," I wrote back.

We corresponded with caution, gradually building trust, and then shared our private e-mail addresses. Eventually we traded phone numbers. Friends warned about axe murderers, but I believed in Ken's sincerity. "I don't even own a tiny hatchet," he'd assured me.

Sunday mornings, home from his graveyard shift, Ken would phone. He e-mailed jokes to start my day, and sent gifts, a wooden car, a casino chip, framed photos. Then one day I opened a small box to find a ring with a diamond sunflower. It had belonged to his mother, he wrote.

In turn, I mailed cards with sunflower motifs and a motion-activated potted sunflower that played "You Are My Sunshine," one of the only songs he claimed he knew the words to. We debated how and where we could meet in person, beginning to realize we were falling in love. "I've never had a doubt," Ken swore.

I decided to attend my high school reunion in California and then visit my father's widow in Napa. Ken drove from Reno to her place to meet me, and we toured the nearby wineries. When we paused for supper that first evening, the waiters all buzzed around after we described our long Internet romance. They produced a bottle of Chardonnay on the house, gazing at us with sappy smiles. We billed and cooed like aging lovebirds.

Weeks later I flew back to Reno for his son's annual mystery party. I sported a feather boa and toted a stuffed wirehaired terrier, and Ken looked dapper in his rented tuxedo, as we impersonated detectives Nick and Nora Charles from the *Thin Man* movies.

I returned for the holidays, suitcase stuffed with Christmas gifts and decorations, and Ken provided a little tree. His son joined us for Christmas dinner and presented us with a mouse pad that featured us in our *Thin Man* costumes.

On New Year's Eve afternoon Ken taught me some poker basics so that I could accompany him to work that night. Because of the Y2K fright, though, the card room crowd was sparser than antici-pated so he got a phone call from the manager offering him the night off. We rushed out to rent videos, grabbed a bottle of champagne and ordered a pizza.

At midnight we toasted the millennium and made a joint resolu-tion to marry. On July 1, 2000, we wed at his son's home in Reno.

Socialnet.com sent us a Waterford crystal photo frame. It holds a picture of us cutting our cake and sits today on the top shelf of a china cabinet in the living room.

Together Ken and I cruised the Mediterranean, the Baltic, and the Alaska Inner Passage. We hoisted steins in Munich at Oktoberfest. We searched for Nessie in Inverness, and pub-crawled in Dublin. We gardened, played a running gin game, watched *Jeopardy!* and spoiled our two dogs and three cats. I never quite mastered Texas Hold 'Em. For nine years Ken e-mailed me those daily jokes. We survived surgeries, spats, falls and fractures. We wandered those art galleries and picnicked on fried chicken, just as I had envisioned. I confess that Ken sauntered, rather than hiked.

After a lingering illness, my sweet Bettor died last spring. But opening his profile proved to be my best bet ever. He indeed turned out to be The One, my sunshine, my love. He's left me with a myriad of precious memories.

You can bet that I adore technology. Who knew that it would lead me to companionship... and to love?

~Terri Elders

5,000 Bachelors and Me

Nothing defines humans better than their willingness to do irrational things in the pursuit of phenomenally unlikely payoffs. This is the principle behind lotteries, dating, and religion.
~Scott Adams

Sixty and single. That wasn't how I'd planned to spend my life. Now I either had to start dating, spend the rest of my life alone, or get a bunch of cats and become the weird cat woman. I decided to start dating.

At sixty, it is nearly impossible to meet eligible bachelors so I tried Internet dating. I saw an ad that promised there were five thousand single men in my age group in my zip code area. This was going to be a piece of cake! I had five thousand lonely men to choose from! I filled out the very long application form online, answering questions about my favorite color, favorite movie and favorite food, etc. When I was finished and submitted my answers, a large banner appeared on the computer screen saying, "We're sorry, but you are incompatible with all of our clients." They refused my membership and didn't want my $29.95 a month dues. I'd been rejected by five thousand lonely, desperate men in five minutes!

Finding someone to date was going to be a little harder than I'd expected.

There was a big community Christmas party coming up. I wanted to go but I didn't want to go alone because there was going to be a dance afterward with music from the 1940s and 1950s and I love to dance.

The only bachelor I knew was Owen. He was a nice man but he was shorter than me and had a very thin, sparse moustache that he filled in with an eyebrow pencil. He also had an artificial knee that sometimes clicked when he walked.

I decided Owen was going to be my date for the Christmas party but I knew he was fairly shy and it would be up to me to ask him to be my date. I hadn't asked a man for a date since I was twenty. It felt awkward when I was twenty, and it felt even more awkward now that I was sixty. At least Owen wouldn't reject me like those other five thousand men had.

But he did.

"Oh, I'd love to take you to the party, but I already have a date," he said.

Owen, with his drawn on moustache and clicking knee had a date.

I'd broken a record. In one week I'd been rejected by 5,001 men!

Two days before the party, Owen called and said the woman he'd planned to take to the party had to attend her aunt's funeral in Texas and now he was free to take me. I was sorry the woman's aunt had passed away, and I was sorry someone had to die before I could have a date, but at least I was going to the Christmas party!

I bought a new red dress, new black heels and a black lace shawl to sling over my shoulder in case I had the opportunity to tango. Before the date I put on make-up, sprayed my hair so it would stay in place, and put on my favorite perfume, called Wicked Woman. I looked in the mirror and decided for a woman my age I looked fantastic! Well, if not fantastic, at least pretty good.

Owen picked me up and when I got into the car I noticed two things immediately.

Owen had not only drawn on his moustache, but in honor of the occasion, he'd drawn on heavier eyebrows too, but he'd arched them so much that he looked perpetually surprised. If he'd connected the line over his nose, it would have looked like there was a giant "M" drawn over his eyes.

Hey, I still had a date for the party so I wasn't going to be picky.

Owen was very impressed by how glamorous I looked. He started breathing heavily as soon as I sat next to him in the car. In fact, I looked so fabulous, I took his breath away!

I really did take his breath away.

Owen gasped out, "Your perfume... allergic... asthma... hospital. Can't breathe!"

We traded places and I put the windows down and drove him to the emergency room.

While the staff was working on him, I went to the ladies room and washed off my perfume and make-up and tried to brush the spray out of my hair. I joined him in his room and sat with him. There didn't seem to be much to talk about. I'd nearly killed him and he ruined my chance to go to the Christmas party.

He urged me to take a cab and go to the party without him but it seemed a little tacky to leave him stretched out on a gurney while he was wearing an oxygen mask.

An hour later he felt well enough to drive me home.

We said goodnight, knowing we would never attempt a date with each other again. Once you almost kill a man, you don't get asked for a second date.

I looked at the clock; the dance would be starting now. I put on some music and danced around the living room by myself.

I won't give up... I want to love and to be loved. I don't want to spend the rest of my life alone. Just because five thousand men rejected me and just because I nearly killed the only man who did agree to take me out (but only after someone else died), that doesn't mean I should give up hope.

I believe every kettle has a lid.

I believe in love.

~Holly English

Distant Promise

To watch us dance is to hear our hearts speak.
~Hopi Indian Saying

After more than thirty years of marriage, I thought our days of romantic secrets were over. That is, until Loren announced, "Don't plan anything for your birthday. I have a special surprise."

On the evening of my birthday, we dressed up and drove into town. We pulled into the parking lot of a strip mall and I scanned the storefronts. Hmm… a costume store, Harbor Freight Tools, the driver's license place, and then I saw it. The sign on the corner building read "Arthur Murray Dance Studio."

Loren wasn't kidding when he said he had a surprise. We had never danced, not even in high school, and I had always wanted to learn. Though he didn't think dancing was manly, early in our marriage he promised, "Someday I'll take you dancing."

Instead, life's well-worn routines took over our days and we never found the time. What followed were years of raising kids and long hours of hard work building a career. Middle age found us changing jobs, helping our aging parents, and busy with seven grandchildren.

Now here we were, more than a few pounds heavier and our hair a little grayer. My girlish fantasy of whirling across a dance floor had faded, long since tucked away in the place of surrendered dreams.

Heather, our instructor, a tall slender blonde wearing a short tight skirt and stilettos, welcomed us at the door of the studio. She showed us to a desk where we had a short interview. Her eyes glistened with tears when she learned Loren was making good on a thirty-two-year-old promise.

"Why now?" she asked him. "What took you so long?"

"I guess I had to grow up," he said, giving my hand a squeeze. "And it's important to me to make her dreams come true," he added, as he looked at me with a love far deeper than the young man who had made the promise decades earlier. I giggled when our eyes met and he blushed with a grin he couldn't contain. No doubt, we seemed like a pair of infatuated teenagers to our twenty-something instructor.

Heather described the various dances taught at the studio. We decided to focus on the waltz for our two introductory lessons. Between Loren's hearing loss, two knee surgeries and a back surgery, and my arthritis, we felt like stiff old broomsticks.

We stumbled through our first awkward steps with enthusiasm while he tried to lead and I attempted to follow. Loren looked forward to our lessons as much as I did. When the trial period ended, we agreed to continue.

We signed up for eight more lessons and chose to learn rumba, swing, and the hustle. Each week became a new adventure. When we walked to the car after our seventh lesson, we turned to each other and said simultaneously, "I don't want it to end." Our laughter rang out across the dark parking lot. We determined then to keep dancing.

Six months later, we dance two or three nights a week. The mambo and cha cha have brought new energy into our relationship. But the best is when Loren turns to me and says, "May I have this dance?" He takes my hand, slips his arm around my shoulder as we waltz across the floor doing an under-arm turn, and I know even forgotten dreams can come true.

~Kathleen Kohler

32

Which Pocket?

It's important to have a twinkle in your wrinkle.
~Author Unknown

Meeting new friends can be quite a challenge, especially when lots of folks my age prefer to stay at home to watch a DVD rather than attend a concert, play, or some other social function. And with the advent of e-books, I don't meet too many people in libraries or bookstores anymore, either.

And then there's the Internet. Where we used to catch up on the local "gossip" by stopping in at the coffee shop, now we just log on to Facebook. I'm still not sure if home computers are a blessing or a curse, but I do so enjoy having a world of information at my fingertips.

So I decided to use the Internet to see if it might be a way for me to meet new people. A little research gave me many different sites to explore. Yes, there were sites for dating, I already knew about those. But there were also sites for meeting others who enjoy similar activities, from kayaking to quilting, and reading to rock hounding. And most of these sites were free!

I set up a profile, posted a few pictures, and began happily corresponding with a goldmine of potential friends. Soon, though, it was time to meet someone face to face. The little naysayer hanging out in my subconscious leaped to the forefront.

"What if he's not at all who he said he was? What if he's using the Internet to meet vulnerable women? What if he's an axe murderer?"

Knowing that little voice always has my best interest at heart, but can also be a very wet blanket, I cautiously set up a meeting with a man I'd spoken with several times on the phone. I picked a very public place and a very daylight time.

I sent my best friend an e-mail telling her where I was going, a copy of his picture, his phone number and e-mail address, and everything else I thought I knew about the guy. "If I turn up missing," I wrote, "make sure he gets the electric chair!"

Arriving at the appointed place a little early, I was pleased to see lots of people milling about. I blended in with them and watched the park bench from a safe distance. My new potential friend arrived, sat down, and waited patiently.

He looked just like his picture. He didn't appear to be concealing a chainsaw under his shirt. I decided to approach him.

"Hi," I said, extending my hand. "Nice to meet you."

We sat and chatted for a while; then he suggested we get lunch at a nearby restaurant. I smiled and reached into my jacket pocket, producing a small water pistol. I playfully shot him with it, and he laughed.

"What's this all about?"

"This means I'd be delighted to have lunch with you," I replied. "I didn't know if you'd turn out to be a nice guy or a creep, and the nice guy gets the pocket with the squirt gun."

For just a second, my new friend looked puzzled. Then he smiled with understanding as we stood up to go to our first of many meals together. "So what, may I ask, is in the other pocket?"

I grinned from ear to ear. "Pepper spray."

Rick breathed a sigh of relief. "Well, then, I'm certainly glad you don't think I'm a creep."

"So am I," I replied happily, and I took his proffered arm to walk the short distance to the restaurant.

~Jan Bono

33

The Price of a Smile

A people that values its privileges above its principles soon loses both.
~Dwight D. Eisenhower

The line moved across the computer screen like some kind of magical Etch A Sketch, erasing only surface wrinkles and leaving the facial features of the model intact, now ten years younger.

Would that be enough? I walked to the mirror and examined my own features yet again. No, there was no way to produce a similar effect without a back-to-the-future anti-gravity device, and I did not have the money for a facelift—or even Botox. My grandmother used to tell me about using a mixture of egg whites and oatmeal applied in upward strokes across the face and neck, then flinging herself backwards across the bed, like some 1920s melodrama heroine slain by an irate lover… head dangling back over the edge as hair swept the carpet, until time could be halted for one fairy tale evening. *That* I could afford. It would have to do.

Thirty-five years of monogamy had ended, and after two years of grief and recovery I realized I wanted to see—once again—the radiant smile of a man as he approached me, that look of delight and desire usually relegated to young boys spying a plate of chocolate chip cookies. Just one more time, I vowed, before surrendering to puppies, flowers and small children.

I had been told as a girl that "pretty is as pretty does," and then I was one of those young women in the 1960s who refused to market her body—focusing instead on trying to change the world while relishing underarm hair and a face free of make-up. It was somewhat of a shock to wake up like Rip Van Winkle and discover that what men really responded to was a beautiful *visual* experience. If there was a mind and a soul under it all, well, that might be okay, too.

If there was anything I had learned, though, it was goal-oriented achievement skills, and this was no different than all the others—total immersion. Observe, visualize, list, purchase, practice, repeat. A friend of mine enjoyed a weekend companion—quite an enviable arrangement, actually. Meeting on Saturday afternoon, they would go out (or stay in), having dinner and entertainment. Did I want that? You bet I did!

A full year older than I, she was healthy, slim, active, well groomed and stylish. Contacts, hair dye, jewelry polish and teeth whitener gave her a youthful sparkle. I could be like that. I enrolled in a yoga class and a gym program. I shopped the aisles for lotions and foot callus removers. Hair dye, contacts, eyelash tint. Check! Three months later, fifteen pounds lighter, I surveyed the results. Not bad! Next step: inside out.

I joined the "Contact Seniors" dating website, turned in my *Economist* subscription for *Cosmopolitan*, and spent time with facial masques reading more than I ever wanted to know about male "preferences." I didn't know how much more I could stand, but dauntless in my determination, I switched from C-SPAN to *Sex and the City*, to learn flirtation by sheer osmosis. Soon I had a date scheduled!

I had one more item on my to-do list, and then I would reap the rewards of my efforts. I made an appointment for the day before the date to undergo the all-important teeth bleaching. Years of coffee had stained my smile into that socially unacceptable yellowish color of dried apples. My perfect friend had teeth that gleamed in the restaurant lights like sun sparkles on fresh spring snow.

The dentist's office didn't have *Cosmo*, so I leafed through the *New York Times* while waiting—Thomas Friedman, Paul Krugman, Maureen Dowd. A forgotten voice in my head ventured to query, "Are there any men out there who still think wild strawberries taste better than gourmet pastries? Who still believe that dandelions are flowers and not weeds?" Maybe, maybe not. But I began to wonder about my own beliefs. Possibly the price of a smile was going to be more than mere money?

I turned the page and found myself staring at an advertisement which read, "Millions of children in developing countries are suffering with cleft lip and palate… The Smile Train provides life-changing free cleft surgery which takes as little as 45 minutes and costs as little as $250"—the exact duration and price of my dental bleaching. I looked at the faces of the children. They were deformed, but the eyes of the one-year-olds were still bright and hopeful, not yet absorbed in the cruelty of a shallow humanity. Their souls peered out in joy. How soon would that gleam die? The eight-year-old already looked inward with self-loathing.

The dental assistant called my name… once, twice. I stared at her, speechless, and slowly shook my head. With no other explanation, I folded the newspaper and slipped it under my arm, rose to leave—and greeted the outdoor sunshine with a brilliant smile.

~S. Ann Robinson

34

The Anniversary Waltz

An anniversary is a time to celebrate the joys of today,
the memories of yesterday, and the hopes of tomorrow.
~Author Unknown

Long, long ago, when we were newly married, my husband and I were invited to a fiftieth wedding anniversary party. The celebrants, Max and Molly, were neighbors of my parents.

We were so young and so impressionable that every element dazzled us: the invitation on fine ivory paper with loops and flourishes in the script—the "half-after-seven" time designation—the discreet notation of "black tie" in the bottom right corner.

I can still remember stepping into the grand ballroom of a city hotel and being dazed by all I saw: chandeliers, women in gorgeous gowns ablaze with bugle beads, and a huge orchestra playing the kind of music one hears in dreams.

But from all the images that evening, one lingers in a far deeper way.

At some signal, the orchestra suddenly struck up the familiar "Anniversary Waltz." And then, with infinite grace and tenderness, Max led his Molly to the center of the dance floor, and they began gliding back and forth, letting the music carry them.

Fifty years!

Such an abstraction to newlyweds. Such an unfathomable number.

But even as a breathless young bride, closer to adolescence than adulthood, I knew that something quite magical and magnificent was happening on that dance floor. It left its mark. And I wanted that for us. Someday.

But ahead of us, waiting in the wings, was life. And we created it together, year by year, experience by experience and, as it turned out, baby by baby.

As the years tumbled into one another, and as children filled our lives with proms, graduations, summer jobs and endless promises to clean up their rooms, we were often distracted. It happens in the best marriages.

Then those children left us. Cars and homes got smaller again. And it was back to just the two of us. After so many balls in the air, it took some getting used to. The quiet seemed to climb the walls, until grandchildren came along and brought with them their joyful noise. How we welcomed it!

Our marriage reached a new plateau, rich with something more permanent, something built on respect and deep, deep connection. My life-sharer and I began to realize that warmth and comfort and the best kind of familiarity—the kind that breeds content—were now ours. Such gifts take on new meaning when you are no longer younger than springtime, and when nights can be long and scary.

In this era, our parents have left us. So have friends. And as we've grieved the losses, we've clung tighter to one another.

While our backs were turned, the decades have passed. There have been high moments—career milestones, a few indulgent vacations, Thanksgivings and Passovers filled with laughter and peak experiences.

We have seen in a new century... together.

We have walked on beaches as the sun was setting and climbed into bed on rainy nights to watch stupid movies together... and wondered how we ever got so lucky.

I make him chocolate pudding—the cooked kind—when he seems a bit down, and he brings me flowers sometimes just because I'm feeling misunderstood and fat.

We still hold hands on airplanes as they take off because we did that on our first plane trip together—and it just feels right.

And now—now it's our turn to mark fifty years.

How can it be? What happened to all those days and nights, weeks and months, years and decades?

Here we are, growing old together. And still making each other laugh.

For our golden anniversary, there will be no ivory invitations to a dinner dance in a ballroom. The gifts we exchange will be meaningful, but we've never been much for lavish.

We surely recognize, at this fifty-year mark, that being married gives us a history that is ours alone, with unique and cherished images that can be replayed in the delicious slow motion of memory. Maybe this fiftieth anniversary will be marked by some family party, small and plain. That's the vibe we'd want.

And then it will be home again, because home is our happiest place now, our shelter from the storms. I say that in joy, not regret.

And if we can possibly find an old recording of "The Anniversary Waltz," maybe we'll play it. And dance in the living room.

~Sally Schwartz Friedman

35

When I'm Sixty-Four

Love one another and you will be happy. It's as simple and as difficult as that.
~Michael Leunig

I am sixty-four, just like in the old Beatles song. And I am in love! It is written that ladies don't find love at this age. Do you realize that the odds for a woman of sixty-four to find a match are about 100 to 1? Is it any wonder that I am giddy as a schoolgirl? I feel as giddy as I did over my first boyfriend, Doug McCoy, when I was fourteen.

Widows my age are doomed to life with a cat. Being allergic to cats, I was doomed to a life alone. But it was not meant to be.

I gave up on men. I'd been married twice. One I ran out and one I wore out. I was widowed for nearly twenty years and quite content. At least that's what I thought. But my friend Norma from square dancing insisted she knew my perfect "mate." When I finally gave in and consented to meet, it was absolutely love at first sight.

I'd always downplayed love at first sight. Even though Dad declared that Mom would be the woman he would marry the first time he laid eyes on her. Did it run in the family? Was I doomed before the first meeting? And why did this happen at sixty-four?

I'm supposed to be an old woman. Yet I feel like I've taken a Fountain of Youth pill. I'm suddenly dressing to kill, or at least to walk out of the house. Exercising! Eating more carrots than chocolate and sharing them with my love. And I am on a high! No drugs are needed! No alcohol, no cigarettes. I'm going to live forever and take care of my new love.

I look across the room at the hairy chest peeking out from the argyle sweater I just bought. Not a word of complaint. I vowed I would never fall for another hairy chest again. God must have laughed at all those times I said "never." He sure did have other plans.

And unlike the Beatles song, "When I'm Sixty-Four," my soul mate has plenty of head hair. No bad comb-over. How could I get this lucky?

And manners. I receive hand kisses that make my knees weak. Who knew the palm of the hand was an erogenous zone? Why wasn't I told? I thought I knew everything I needed to know about life.

Our romantic walks reveal new sights and smells I experience now that I am in love again. It truly doesn't matter where we go. Everything is more exciting when you experience it through the eyes of a lover. We even went to the hardware store to check out a new doorbell and had a fabulous time.

Stingy? No. In fact, the Baptist Church in my neighborhood would be the recipient of several anonymous donations left out front if I hadn't stepped in. After all the Beth Yeshua Messianic is directly across the street, and we do not play favorites.

My family has even come to accept us as a couple. They do, of course, recognize the good breeding and aristocratic demeanor. Our studio portrait is my favorite photo of all.

I believe that men in my age category are looking for Barbie Dolls and eye candy. I'm certainly not qualified in either of those areas. And I admit that sometimes when we are out and about I feel a pang of jealousy when my companion shows interest in someone else. But then, those big brown eyes turn to me with the look of adoration I know so well. That brown mustache can't hide the smile I feel in my heart.

How could I have been so foolish as to think love had died with my late husband? I never knew there was a Yorkie named Lucy that was ready to show me what love at sixty-four was all about.

~Linda Burks Lohman

Sunday	Monday	Tuesday	Wednesday	Thursday	Friday	Saturday
		1 brunch at Smiths	2 Work 9-1	3 babysit Jessica	4 work 9-1	5 Pack
6 Pier 3 at 4 sharp	7 CRUISE!!	8	9	10	11	12
13	14 work 9-1	15 Jessica ☺	16 Work 9-1	17 Dog Shelter	18 work 9-1	19 Golf with Gene
20	21 Work 9-1	22 Dr. Miller - 10:30	23 work 9-1	24 dog shelter	25 Work 9-1	26 Dinner Party 7:00
27 DC trip 27th-29th	28	29	30 Work 9-1	31 Dog Shelter		

Chapter 4

Inspiration for the Young at Heart

New Careers

Hello? Is Anybody Out There?

Radio is the theater of the mind; television is the theater of the mindless.
~Steve Allen

Three years into my early retirement, my friend Heather called. She was the manager of Spoken Word programming at a local radio station.

"Hey," she started. "Listen, I have three Arabic shows and they do not speak English. From the anger when they say Israel or Jews, you just know they're not saying anything good or giving the other side's point of view."

"So, take them off the air," I said, while wondering what her problems at work had to do with me. I was naïve.

"Can't do that. You know, freedom of speech. What I need is a Jewish show for balance, and as you're the only Jew I know, you're the host. You start next Thursday."

"Are you nuts? I don't know enough about radio to do a show like that. Besides, I'm retired."

"Well, it's not like you're doing anything with your retirement other than schlepping your kids around. Where's the purpose and creativity in your life? You need to do something challenging. Think of it as a retirement hobby. I'll help you."

"There's no way I'm doing this," I said adamantly.

"Well, let's have lunch."

Heather is a good talker. She's cheap, too. I paid for lunch *and* took the job.

The following Thursday, at eight in the morning, I was in the ON

AIR room introducing myself to an audience I knew nothing about. Nor did I know what to discuss. I knew no Yiddish or Hebrew, and very little about Israel and the Middle East.

"Boker tov, good morning," I began. "Hope everyone is doing okay today. We've got some Klezmer music for you and recipes for Friday night's dinner."

It was that banal.

At one point the lights on the control board went off. I panicked. Was I still on the air?

I nervously tapped the microphone. "Hello?" I said. "Is anyone out there?"

I tapped the mike again. "If you can hear me, would you call the station to let me know? Thanks."

The first caller was very nice. And very Scottish. "Aw, Lassie, are ye havin' a wee bit o' trouble?"

"Yes," I said and explained what happened.

He was a radio broadcaster from Edinburgh and he talked me through getting the board lit up again.

Four years passed and the show improved. Let's face it. It could not have gotten worse! I discussed holidays, recipes, how to raise a Jewish child, the Holocaust. I even did interviews.

Of course there were occasional glitches. And humiliating moments, like the time I interviewed talk show host, Michael Coren, and the line suddenly went dead. Never could get him back on air. He's never agreed to another interview.

In the year 2000, Yasser Arafat declared another "intifada" on Israel. All of my listeners wanted to know the truth about this war, not the stories they heard from what they felt were anti-Israel journalists, especially the ones from CNN and BBC. I suddenly had a crash course in the Middle East.

My studies of the region intensified as Arafat's war raged on. I read three and four history books a week until I felt smart enough to ask intelligent questions. Serious interviews with scholars and politicians from Israel became the norm. Where it used to take me three to four hours to prepare a show, now it took twenty to thirty. This was no longer a hobby; it was a full-time job.

In 2001, after terrorists brought down the Twin Towers and attacked the Pentagon, listeners demanded to know who these fanatic Islamists were. Why were we targets? More research. More interviews.

Arafat's war on Israel suddenly intensified and many feared there was a connection to 9/11. Suicide bombings in Israel increased and hundreds of Jews were murdered.

All of a sudden my friendly little Jewish radio show changed into the hard-hitting, alternative opinion "balance" show Heather had wanted. I was a war correspondent, talking to survivors of suicide bombings, conversing with people in Israeli towns bombarded with Kassem rockets from Gaza. I now had four and five interviews a show, interviews no one else had, and we explored the hard questions other stations were afraid to ask.

Heather entered the ON AIR room one day with a grim smile on her face. "Congrats, kid," she said. "You are doing an awesome job. People claiming to be Hamas called and they want you dead. Keep up the good work."

Me?

The next week, while on air, the phone rang. "You have a collect call from Osama bin Laden. Will you accept the charges?"

I nearly fainted. "Sure," I managed to squeak out. The young man yelled at me for several minutes about how mean I was to say they had no right to kill Westerners.

I politely said, "You do realize this call has been traced. The Royal Canadian Mounted Police should be at your door any minute."

"Oh crap!" he cried. I never got another death threat.

Fourteen years have passed since that first show. Terrorists are still wreaking havoc in the world, the Middle East remains in turmoil, and I am still on the air.

Heather has moved on to another radio station.

"When do you plan on retiring from this job?" asked my husband the other day.

"When there's peace in the Middle East, honey," I replied.

I'd love to retire from this job. Knitting will be my next hobby.

~Pamela Goldstein

Old Songs, New Life

A good thing never ends.
~Mick Jagger

An unemployed friend recently said, "Looking for a job sucks the life out of you." Agreed, but when you come to realize that you're too old and that your experience and abilities are no longer of any consequence, you are robbed of something every bit as precious—a sense of purpose, self-respect, a reason to care about getting up in the morning. The scene plays over and over in my mind: the elevator ride with our director of human resources, our silent walk down a deserted hallway, entering the basement conference room, three senior staff people seated at one end of the long table, all forcing their best "down-to-business" expressions. Barren cream-colored walls, the smell of hours-old coffee, the only sound a faint buzz from the fluorescent lighting.

They each study a spot on the table, the carpet, the back of a hand. I sit down, the awful truth drifting into my thoughts like dark smoke. My unit director finally makes eye contact. His delivery is flat and rushed, as if he fears that his resolve might fail before he gets the words out. "Your department is shutting down and your position is being eliminated, effective July first." And with that succinct and cold-blooded declaration, I am jobless. My sixtieth birthday just months away and, after nearly twenty years of developing and honing very specific job skills for a very specialized position, my value has suddenly expired. (To add irony to insult, my former work place repeatedly makes the AARP's annual "Best Employers for Workers Over 50" list.)

So, what's an unemployed almost-sexagenarian with a mortgage, car payments, zero prospects, and a three-figure savings account to do? The answer, for me, came from one of the unlikeliest of sources: Rock and Roll.

It's not easy rehearsing the same songs over and over until your calloused fingertips throb and your throat feels like it's coated with loose sand. It's not easy dealing with thoughtless club owners who refuse to return phone calls and who don't always honor commitments. It's not easy lugging bulky speakers and amplifiers to the car at 2 a.m. after a four-hour performance. And I don't like putting personal or family plans on hold in case we're able to schedule a gig for a Friday or Saturday night.

But when I step onto a stage or in front of an audience, a transformation takes place. I'm no longer used up, tossed aside, past my prime. And when our first chord rings out, I'm swept up in a wave of energy and passion that carries me through the night. I'm seventeen again. As I watch other people dance or tap their feet or move their mouths along with the music we're making, I'm soaring on the highest of highs, and I don't begin my descent until I'm home in my bed, hours after the final note of the night has been struck and sung.

Our band is called Reprise '60s. As the name implies, we concentrate on music from the decade of the British Invasion, acts including The Beatles, The Stones, Searchers, Gerry and the Pacemakers, Herman's Hermits, to name a few. I last played in a band when their hits were hot off the record presses. They recorded the songs I grew up with, the same ones I listen to today.

Building a consistent following for our group has been difficult. Younger performers can count on friends and peers to come out for the late-night shows. Our contemporaries tend to go to bed much earlier and are less likely to frequent bars and clubs on weekends. Some nights a place will be packed when we start, with lots of spirit and enthusiasm for the first couple of hours, and then nearly empty by the time we're into our final set.

During one recent job at a local bar/restaurant, we set up our equipment and ran through a brief sound check while the dinner crowd was still bustling. After we did a couple of verses of a warm-up song and set our instruments down, a man approached the stage. In his arms he held a girl of maybe three or four. "My daughter was very disappointed that you didn't play a whole song. Would you be willing to play something for her?" he said.

We played "Thank You Girl" by The Beatles while she bounced and swayed on the dance floor with her dad. As we came to the last few notes of the song, I realized that the entire restaurant had gone still and all heads had turned to face the stage. When the song ended the room erupted in applause and cheers.

It was a great and memorable moment for us. Unfortunately, we were competing on that date with our area's biggest, most popular annual summer event, taking place just a couple of miles away. Once the dinner patrons had gone, the bar and tables never completely filled up again, so our pre-performance number ended up being the highlight of our night.

On another job, we played for four hours to a packed house. Though patrons hung around till the wee hours, drinking and talking, they all seemed to be ignoring the band while we worked harder and harder to entertain them. When we took our break, a couple of them approached the jukebox, dropped in some coins, made their selections. A few others joined them on the dance floor. As soon as we strapped on our guitars again, they all cleared the space directly in front of the stage area and returned to their seats at the bar. Throughout the night I thought, *we're bombing here*. The word *disaster* kept running through my mind.

At the end of the night, the room was still jammed with twenty- and thirty-somethings. As we gathered our gear and started working our way through the crowd to load our cars, people were grabbing my arm, patting my shoulder and shaking my hand. "Great job!" "You guys rock!" "Fantastic!" The effusive praise kept coming at us until we were packed and ready to leave.

Part of the appeal of performing is that we never know what to expect. But then, it doesn't really matter. For us, it's all about making music. And if sometimes people get to enjoy what we're doing, if we can put a smile on someone's face or a song on someone's lips, if we can make a little girl happy for a few minutes, that's just a bonus.

This new venture will not resolve all of my financial issues, but I do feel a sense of accomplishment for the first time in months. When I tell friends that I'm playing in a band, that I still get a kick out of pretending for a few hours that I'm a Beatle or a Rolling Stone, I'll occasionally get that narrow-eyed look that says, *he's probably gone senile*. Why, they might wonder, would somebody's grandpa want to spend weekend nights chasing the rock star dream in clubs and taverns filled (or not filled) mostly with strangers and the occasional drunken heckler?

Maybe those friends are right. Maybe I have lost it.

But if this is senility, I say *bring it on*.

~Gary Ingraham

"Mom I'm not 'ruining my life.' Most musicians
I know joined a band in their early twenties.
Be glad I waited forty more years."

Back in the Catskills

Learning is a treasure that will follow its owner everywhere.
~Chinese Proverb

My husband, Arthur, and I (born two days apart) could hardly wait for our sixtieth birthdays. Some of our older friends were feasting on a smorgasbord of senior seminars at colleges and camps around the country and abroad. I was a retired elementary school teacher, yet anxious to get back to the classroom—on the other side of the desk—a kid again. Finally, in the winter of 1988, we were eligible to sign on. Hallelujah!

To escape New York's frigid weather, we chose a jazz and history program in Louisiana. The instructors were excellent, the courses absorbing, the coordinator hospitable. But the spirit and savvy of fifty Elderhostelers, some of them well into their eighties, were even more impressive. Our classroom dynamic was driven by four thousand years of collective experience.

Dining on po-boys and pizza, we mingled with undergraduates in the school cafeteria, and gathered to share stories and jokes after dinner. Each evening, a law professor from Connecticut pulled out a packet of index cards and delivered one-liners he used in his legal lectures—the most hilarious stand-up routine I ever heard. By week's end, group members were planning a reunion for the spring—the first of many reunions yet to come. Arthur and I were hooked.

Since then, most of our vacations have been learning adventures—discussing Pat Conroy in Georgia, constructing dulcimers in Maine, exploring galleries at the Art Institute in Chicago. While considering a barge getaway in France, I received a phone call from a community college in the Catskills. Would I fill in for a teacher who cancelled out of a writing workshop in their summer Elderhostel program?

Ah, the Catskills—playground of my girlhood. My family headed upstate every summer, escaping the hot city. "For the healing mountain air," Ma proclaimed. My heart was thumping. Could I accept the offer? I'd never been able to speak in public. In all my years as a student, I neither volunteered an answer nor voiced an opinion. In college, I took as many large lecture courses as possible, so I could get lost in the crowd. Yes, I published some magazine articles after I retired. And I taught writing to children. But working with youngsters was not the same as working with adults. My answer was "No."

Still, the idea percolated for almost a week, and a lesson plan developed in my head. With a mixture of dread and enthusiasm I called to say I'd do it. Too late—the job was filled. Whew! A month later, I agreed to an on-site coordinator's position with the college, which seemed less threatening than conducting a workshop. I enlisted Arthur as my assistant, and we've been working there ever since.

So, what does a coordinator do? I tell people I'm the "housemother," but my husband doesn't like that terminology; he prefers "facilitator." For thirteen summers I've been back in the Catskills, busy "facilitating." I barely get outdoors to inhale the famous Catskill air.

As we drive up on the first morning of each program, stopping off at a visitors' center for the latest regional brochures, I feel the buzz of excitement. Another "happening" awaits us. Sessions are held in a resort hotel, and we dash in—to check out classroom equipment, dining room setup, registration area, and refreshment table. Where are the sugar-free pastries? We meet with the program director and survey the student roster. Elderhostelers drift in all afternoon to pick up their folders and name tags. Who are they? Where do they come from? What do they do? I can hardly wait for the evening activity—Orientation.

Back in 1998, at our very first Catskill program, the director, normally the master of ceremonies, informed me that it was the coordinator's responsibility to address the group. Luckily I hadn't known that beforehand.

I do just fine in one-on-one conversations, but in a group even thinking about speaking up makes my heart race and my face turn red. Yet, I'm also a dutiful daughter, and the task at hand is to conduct a ninety-minute forum. So each week at Orientation, my eyes glued to a detailed outline, I clarify the schedule, urge my fellow seniors to rotate seats in the dining room, recommend the potato pancakes, and preside over introductions.

I'm Debra Kerr, in *The King and I*, whirling round and round — "Getting to know you, getting to know all about you."

"I was a bookie," says Sam. "My favorite retirement activity is going to the race track."

"I'm Sybil; I live with Sam. Heidi Fleiss (the notorious Madame) was my boss," says his wife. "I retired when she went to jail." We laugh — another good group.

Participants reveal their ingenuity and diversity: recording for the blind, editing a community newsletter, mediating civil disputes, keeping fit, sleeping late. They are Little League coaches, political junkies, and "domestic engineers." They sing, they act, play musical instruments, and perform as clowns — in nursing homes and children's hospitals. I anticipate lively conversation at mealtime.

Back in the Catskills, experiencing a personal growth spurt each season, Ma's healing air is not the catalyst. As coordinator, I get to sit in on all classes — from Great American Short Stories and Musical Theatre, to Ethical Decisions and Globalization; almost two hundred courses so far. Learning for the fun of it — no studying, final exams or homework, but still taking notes.

When the need arises I turn into an audio-visual and air conditioning technician, health consultant, variety show producer, psychotherapist and crisis manager. My mother called it "helping out." That was her bent — from the time she was a young girl until well into her nineties, Florence Nightingale to all — her parents, siblings, cousins, neighbors, daughter. I did not follow in her footsteps. But here I am — back in the Catskills — and that's my job. It feels so good.

Like a Boy Scout, my motto is Be Prepared. I've yet to help a little old lady cross the road, but I paired a lonely freshman with an upbeat veteran, and the two women laughed together happily all week. "My room is cold," Eric told me. "Turn off your air conditioner," I counseled. He did. George was frantically searching the hotel for his "missing wife." I found her — in their room. I couldn't help Lillian, who called at midnight, complaining about a fly that was keeping her awake. Subsequently, I purchased a fly swatter.

With time, I've learned to relax when addressing a large group. A microphone enhances my voice and empowers me. "Would anyone be interested in an after-class writing workshop?" I asked in my sixth year. The words just popped out of me, without forethought. Seven women and one man signed on; most of them had never written before. They read their stories aloud, surprised and encouraged by the response their work elicited. No one was more surprised than I. So I ran another workshop, grew comfortable with it, ran another. Triumphant.

~Ruth Lehrer

Rewriting Retirement

If there's a book you really want to read, but it hasn't been written yet,
then you must write it.

~Toni Morrison

When the continuing education catalog from my local community college arrived in the mail, I nearly tossed it in the trash along with a stack of junk mail. But I didn't. For some reason it piqued my curiosity, and I flipped through the pages instead. How could I have known at the time that it would be a life-changing moment?

I scanned the course descriptions and stopped when I read: "Writing Small Booklets for Fun and Profit." I'd never thought of myself as a writer, but looking back on the events that had shaped my life up to my fifty-sixth year, I realized that all roads had converged on that very outcome.

An avid arts and crafts person, I began designing needlework and craft projects for magazines more than twenty-five years ago. But I thought of myself more as an artist than a writer, even though writing the instructions for readers to reproduce the project was the most critical part.

As a wedding consultant, I wrote guidelines for brides to help ease their stress during the complicated task of planning a large event. And after becoming an interior-decorating instructor, I wrote handouts for the students in my decorating classes.

For most of my life I've been accumulating knowledge that I

longed to share with others, but until I read that course description, I never realized that writing books was the perfect outlet for my creative spirit. I signed up for the class that same day.

The course was more inspiring than I had imagined. I learned about book printers, International Standard Book Numbers, text layouts and selling products on the Internet using a website. Each new topic called for further exploration.

For my homework assignment, I produced a booklet about interior decorating. The decorating classes I was teaching at the time prompted me to expand that short publication into a 104-page book.

The next continuing education catalog I received revealed a "Creative Writing" course. I signed up for that, too. It helped hone my writing skills and inspired me to launch an in-depth research project on the publishing industry.

I became so intrigued with self-publishing that I started my own company to produce creative how-to books and cookbooks. Armed with nothing more than determination, I hit the ground running. I needed a DBA, a resale tax certificate, a business bank account and a logo.

Soon, I was ordering ISBN numbers, searching for a book printer and designing my own website. As the saying goes, "One thing leads to another." Until that point, I'd been a low-tech, elderly crafter who could barely retrieve my e-mail. Suddenly, I needed to learn software programs for creating book layouts, designing book covers, publishing websites and integrating a shopping cart.

Within a few months, my first cookbook, *Easy Microwave Desserts in a Mug*, was finished and ready for printing. And I was back online rubbing shoulders with the big publishing houses, registering my book with Books in Print. Who knew?

Before embarking upon my new mission, I thought I was content to coast into retirement, idling away the time playing with my grandchildren. Apparently not! I'm relishing every minute of my new career. I had no idea that opening that catalog would add so much joy and fulfillment to my life.

By the time I reached my sixtieth birthday, I'd published thirty-eight how-to books, cookbooks, and humorous short story collections, all drawn from information and personal experiences I'd been gathering all my life. And with today's computer technology, I can offer my books to the world. How great is that?

I've come a long way since receiving that first class catalog. The journey was sometimes frustrating and always involved long hours and hard work. But when you're passionate about your vocation, the hours fly by like minutes and the work seems more like play.

I never imagined I would start a new business this late in life, but my unforeseen career change is living proof that it's never too late to learn something new.

~Gloria Hander Lyons

Unabashed

You are as young as your faith, as old as your doubt; as young as your self-confidence, as old as your fear; as young as your hope, as old as your despair.
~Douglas MacArthur

All I wanted to do was write articles for a new local magazine. I didn't want to actually meet anybody. But one day, it came in the mail. An invitation to their publication party. "How do I get out of this?" I internally screamed, already in full panic mode.

I had nothing to wear. I don't get out much. The straps on the one bra I own are so stretched out that family members compare me to Grandma — whose bosoms ended up around her waist. My belly serves as a sturdy shelf for mine.

I rifled through my closet. Half the things were Woodstock-fringed and beaded. "What's in style?" I asked my husband, Bob.

He picked up a tie-dyed tunic with the words "Peace, Love and Rock and Roll" on it. "Not this," he said.

I went to Kmart for a new bra. I tried several on over my T-shirt before someone said, "They've invented dressing rooms."

Miracle bras, wonder bras, sports, strapless, push-ups. Too many choices. I scrapped my quest. Instead, I safety-pinned the straps on my old bra so I'd be up where I'm supposed to be when I'm out in public.

The night of the party, Bob pushed me out of the car, in front of the fancy restaurant. I opened the restaurant door, changed my mind and headed back.

He made scoot-go-on-now motions with his hands. I went in. He had been invited too but had to go to the bank first.

I was an anxious wreck. The magazine is very elegant. The editors are mature and sophisticated, yet somehow they let me write for them.

The publisher greeted me graciously, then asked, "Where's Bob?"

"Who?"

"Your husband."

"Yes, of course. That's right. He is."

She looked baffled. "Isn't he coming?"

"He's at the bank. We have money in there. And… we need money… where they have it… there."

I darted out to the phone and put in a dime. Nothing happened. Finally, I put in enough money to make it work. Again, I don't get out much.

"What's wrong?" Bob asked from his cell phone.

"Nothing. Could you hurry?"

I hadn't worn earrings in ages. It hurt to poke my gold studs through closed-up holes. My lobes became awfully swollen and itchy.

"I'm Saralee," I forced myself to say to another writer.

"I'm Debi." She was warm and friendly.

"I'm Saralee," I repeated to her, scratching my ear. It was bleeding.

"I love your columns," another writer said.

"What columns?" I forgot I'm a nationally syndicated columnist.

She said, "Excuse me," and went to talk to a sane person.

Everybody loves Bob. I write about him a lot. When he came in, women surrounded him. He stood by me. I hid behind him. He took my hand. It was bloody.

That's when one safety pin broke, and my right side plummeted.

I grabbed someone's full drink glass, snugged my fallen flesh into the crook of my arm, and held myself up, level with my left side.

The woman politely motioned for her drink. I shook my head "No!" and backed away, clutching her glass. Bob whispered, "You're acting like a lunatic."

When I handed her drink back, my right side plopped. I looked down, then up, and explained, "Don't you just hate it when your safety pin breaks and your ear's bleeding?"

She put the glass down and quickly walked away, while glancing back warily.

And so, here is what I learned:

1. The three writers I admire the most were just as insecure as I was.

2. Self-consciousness is normal. I had a great time in spite of it.

3. I had a better time when I stopped thinking about myself and started asking others about themselves.

4. It truly doesn't matter if you repeat yourself out of nervousness, or your hand trembles when you're shaking someone else's.

5. And, well-known writers sometimes talk with a piece of green pepper in their teeth.

~Saralee Perel

Substitute Career

The best substitute for experience is being sixteen.
~Raymond Duncan

"Yes! We've got a sub today!" The grin on the student's face told me all I needed to know. I was in for a challenge and first period hadn't even begun. After years of traveling around the country as a motivational speaker, I had retired and turned to substitute teaching. The advantages seemed numerous. Instead of entering a new school each day, I could settle at a single local high school. The work schedule was flexible; if I wanted to spend time visiting with my grandkids, I could say "no" to teaching. And instead of speaking on the same topic day after day, I could branch out and teach English, Chemistry or Spanish.

Returning as a teacher, however, made me realize just how much of my high school studies I'd forgotten. Was I really smarter than a tenth grader? Pulling algebra and geometry from the recesses of my brain was a challenge. And in history class, what did I know about life in ancient Greece? The kids thought I was old, but not that old!

Students, of course, switched seats as I took roll. Classes attempted to convince me that their teacher hadn't announced the quiz I was to proctor. And of course, I learned never to send more than one student to the restroom at a time.

When Colby saw a large cardboard refrigerator box as he entered Spanish class, he got a gleam in his eye. He enlisted the help of a crony across the room to distract me and then jumped inside the container.

I spotted him, so I moved to the front of the room, stood next to the box and gently pressed my hand on the top flaps, forcing the boy hiding below to crouch down in a cramped position. I turned to the class and announced, "Today we have access to a new classroom teaching tool: the latest version of Xbox 360. The software inside is programmed to give correct conjugations of common Spanish verbs. Each time I thump the side of the box, it will conjugate one of the verbs listed on the whiteboard. Of course, if the box's answer should be incorrect, then you will input the correct form so the box remembers the next time."

Colby thought his crouched position was awkward, but conjugating verbs in front of the entire class made him even more uncomfortable. Out of sight, this class clown was unable to distract his classmates, and by the time I released him from his cardboard casing, he had reviewed all his verb forms. Who says a sub can't teach outside the box?

Next Aidan needed my attention. He kept getting out of his seat in order to talk to his friend on the other side of the room. When I reminded him to return to his desk, he explained, "I speak Arabic and need to get help from my friend."

Pointing at his desk, I pronounced firmly, "Bito d uk ni'ida!"

With a look of shock in his eyes, Aidan turned to his classmates. "She speaks Arabic!"

I don't. Speak Arabic, that is. But since he didn't know the language either, what difference did it make? Aidan never knew my words were from an obscure Mexican indigenous dialect, but he dashed back to his seat. Obviously I still have gifts as a motivational speaker.

Subbing may have advantages but, believe me, it's no job for sissies.

~Emily Parke Chase

Workamping

Travel and change of place impart new vigor to the mind.
~Seneca

"Housekeeping," says the man behind the desk. "Guest room attendant."

"Cleaning rooms?" My voice squeaks. "What about all those jobs listed on your website?"

"Gone." He props his elbow on his desk, chin in his hand. He looks exhausted. "This is the only job left. You want it or not?" His eyes cut from me to my husband Jimmy.

We take it. What else can we do? Here we are in Death Valley. Our big old motor home is sitting out in the parking lot. We need jobs.

Jimmy glares at me as we're given paperwork to fill out. I know, I know, it was my idea to sell the house, buy the motor home, and drive all the way from Indianapolis to Death Valley. I'd been reading a magazine called *Workamper*, about retirees who live in RVs and work at resorts. That's where I saw the ad for this resort. "Why wait three more years until you start collecting your pension?" I had said. "We can become workampers. Get paid for living at a resort. Meet all kinds of fun people. Let's do it while we still have our health."

Death Valley National Park is a vast, starkly beautiful area with desert, mountains, canyons, salt flats, and the occasional oasis. The resort has been in Death Valley since the 1920s. The sprawling lower oasis, with its rows of motel-style rooms, general store, saloon and restaurants, and an eighteen-hole golf course, was once home to employees of the Borax Corporation. The more exclusive inn, on a hill a mile away, accommodated the Borax brass and clients. The resort employs 300-500 workers, depending on the season, of all ages and from many backgrounds. Some, like us, live in their own RVs; the rest live in large dormitories. Most of us are there because we thought it would be fun.

Jimmy is 6'3" and around 250 pounds. No one his size has ever cleaned rooms before at this resort, so the resident seamstress has to combine two uniform shirts to make one large enough. His size is also blamed for his not being able to clean sixteen rooms in eight hours, so he is almost immediately promoted to rooms inspector. He gets to ride around in a golf cart and tell the room attendants how to do their job.

After a couple of weeks cleaning rooms at the inn, I jump at a chance to do "turn-down service." This involves sneaking into each room while the guests are at dinner, turning down the bedspreads, and leaving chocolates on the pillows, while at the same time checking for any desert insect life foolish enough to have chosen the room as its new home. It becomes a game to see if I can service all sixty rooms without running into a single guest. During the afternoon I lend a hand with the triple sheeting, brass fixture polishing, and the general spiffing up. I quickly come to the conclusion that the main benefit to the job, other than getting dibs on all the stuff the guests leave behind and eating my fill of chocolate, is that I can consume as much as I want of the free buffet meals every day and still lose weight. Not bad benefits overall.

The closest town is Pahrump, Nevada, more than an hour away. Pahrump is an intentionally unplanned city of more than 30,000 with a frontier mentality and many casinos, but only one place to buy clothes—Walmart. No movie theater, no mall, no Chili's or Applebee's. There are plenty of mom and pop businesses, a decent winery, and excellent medical facilities for all the retirees who settle here for the desert air and cheap real estate.

Once a month we spend a weekend in Las Vegas, two and one-half hours away, taking advantage of the $25 rooms prompted by the current economic downturn. We shop at Trader Joe's, see movies, eat decent food, play some slots. Las Vegas has become our reality check.

I start whining that I have no one to talk to and nothing to do when I'm not working. "There's no culture here," I complain. Jimmy advises me to join something. My choices are limited, so I join a walking group. Every evening we gather in front of the little museum and head off into the desert. My fellow walkers include a woman with a master's degrees in psychology and religious studies who works the front desk, a man who formerly ran test labs for GM and now clerks at the general store, a retired corporate CPA who is now a bellman at the inn, and an eight-year-old who was born at the resort and knows no other life. The former CPA tells me he considers the resort to be his assisted living facility: "They feed me, they house me, and they give me an allowance twice a month."

After the first of the year, the head of security talks Jimmy into switching to a security guard job and he easily slides into the position. Eighty percent of his job is driving around in an SUV, to give security a "presence." The other twenty percent of his job includes perform-ing CPR on guests and employees suffering heart attacks, staunching blood from wounds until the EMTs arrive, tactfully coaxing misbe-having guests or employees to clean up their act, and chasing coyotes and bobcats away from the guest areas. He grows accustomed to the scorpions that crisscross the walls of his office nightly.

By mid-May the temperature is reaching 110 degrees during the day, my walking group has switched to water aerobics, and seasonal people are starting to head to the Yellowstone properties and cooler climate. Year-round employees hunker down for the duration, scur-rying from one air-conditioned building to another like desert rats avoiding the daylight. The inn closes for the season, but the 240 rooms on the lower resort are sold out for July and August, mostly single-night stays for tours of Europeans. Desert critters reclaim the golf course for all but the early morning hours when intrepid golfers zip from tee to tee. It's time for us to leave. With so few outlets for spending money, we've saved enough for a summer of leisure.

We pull out of Death Valley early in the morning, slowing down only to avoid a lone tarantula creeping across the highway. Heat is already shimmering over the desert and the wind is picking up, a sandstorm in its infancy. We take one last breath of the sweet, dry air and fix our thoughts on lush Midwestern greenery. Ready to leave after almost eight months, we were told by veteran coworkers that we'll also be ready to return come fall. Like childbirth, they told us, you'll only remember the good parts.

It's been wonderful, we say. The experience of a lifetime. Wouldn't have missed it for anything. But fall is a season away, a country away. And there are so many other places, other jobs, other stories to live. So we'll see, we tell each other. Come fall, we'll see.

~Sheila Sowder

I Love My Boss

Nothing is really work unless you would rather be doing something else.
~James Matthew Barrie

After thirty years of working in a high-profile job, I jumped into retirement with the anticipation of a child entering first grade! I was used to meeting deadlines, learning new processes and working long days. My job was an important part of my life but I thought it would be heavenly to retire and have time to leisurely drink coffee and read the paper, develop my artistic side, watch the news, garden, shop, lunch with friends, travel and watch my grandchildren grow from babies to toddlers.

After trips to Norway, Germany, France and Alaska, I did not plan much more long distance travel. And of all things, my grand-children were growing up and ready to start school. I began looking for a job. Retirement was not my bag. I knew I didn't want a perma-nent job so I answered requests to fill in at local churches, non-profit organizations and offices close to my home when there were vacation or maternity leave openings.

My daughter called one day when I had been off work for a few weeks. She owns a successful environmental consulting firm. Without even realizing how fast the business was growing she discovered one day that her long-time assistant was faced with so much work that she couldn't keep up with essential business. Some catch-up help was needed.

"Mom," she said with desperation, "are you working now or are you committed to anyone anytime soon?"

"No," I replied. "Nothing is on the horizon at the moment. Why?"

"Can you come to work for me?" she asked.

"You mean you would be MY BOSS?" I squealed.

"Well, yes," she said, sounding a little fearful.

"What do I need to do?" I queried. "And are you going to pay me?"

"I need you to come in and help us catch up on invoicing, pay bills, do my banking, send out statements and things like that. It will probably only be for two or three months. Just until we get caught up. And of course I am going to pay you!"

I agreed but told her I really didn't want to work more than two days a week. I started the following week. On my first day she explained to her staff that I was her mother but at work she would be calling me "Caroline." That did not happen. She could not call me by my first name. I was "Mom" and she couldn't change that lifelong habit. The rest of the staff adopted a variety of affectionate nicknames for me. Rarely does anyone use my first name.

That was four years ago. I'm still there, working two days a week. A couple of my coworkers are young enough to be my grandchildren! I love it! Working around this young staff keeps me mentally sharp. It's definitely more fun than when I was responsible for the executive office in a large corporation. All I have to do is follow orders. I haven't had a progress report yet and I've only been scolded a couple of times for taking a long lunch. I love my second career. And I love my boss!

~Caroline Overlund-Reid

"I recently began working for my daughter. Well, that's nothing new—but at least now I get paid for it."

My Second Career

The true way to render age vigorous is to prolong the youth of the mind.
~Mortimer Collins

One of the benefits of retirement is that I can indulge myself: I now have time to do many of the things I had to deny myself when working at a full-time job and raising a family.

I began writing short stories and poetry when I was in fifth grade. My mother bought me a typewriter when I was eleven, and by the time I was twelve, I had mastered the skill of touch-typing. But for many years, writing was just a hobby for me, not something I did full-time.

Before my children were born, I taught English. As they grew older, I obtained my MLS degree and began working as an educational media specialist, which is a fancy way of saying school librarian. I became thoroughly acquainted with Macs and PCs. As the Internet became available, I took courses to further my knowledge. The Internet was not easily accessible at that time and there was so much to learn regarding computer protocols and languages. The Internet was a vast ocean, a sea of treasures that were difficult to obtain.

When my husband convinced me to take an early retirement so that I could start writing full-time and also spend more time with him, since he was already retired, I insisted on only one thing: "The condition for me leaving my job is that we immediately buy a new computer with Internet capability for our home." By then, Internet access was readily available.

My husband, who was not computer-literate at the time, agreed with some reservations. "Pick out whatever you like," he said, "but don't expect that I'll ever be interested in using it."

"We'll just see about that!"

"No chance," he said, shaking his head.

"I won't accept your pronouncement. You've offered me a challenge I can't refuse."

"Honey, I've lived all my life without using a computer. Why would I start using one now?"

I knew he was just being stubborn. So I kept cajoling him until he finally sat down with me and learned the basics. Having been a math teacher, he actually took to it easily.

"Since you follow the stock market, let me show you how easy it is to get up-to-the-second info."

"This is interesting," he conceded, finally paying close attention.

Then, because he enjoyed reading newspapers in the morning, I showed him how to access our local ones.

"Okay," he admitted with a big smile, "I'm hooked."

The fact of the matter is that we reached a point where we needed a second computer in our house. My husband, who claimed he would never have any interest or reason to use a computer or the Internet, is totally into it. He reads newspapers from around the world each morning online and communicates with various people through e-mail and message boards. He also follows the stock market through the computer.

We are able to easily keep in touch with family and friends who now live at some distance from us. We also keep in touch with our busy sons, not only by phone, but also via the Internet. In fact, with our younger son traveling all over the world for his job, e-mail is often the best way to reach him.

Through writers' listservs, I can communicate with other writers and discuss common problems. Sometimes, I even ask for personal assistance. For instance, I was able to communicate with a writer in

Australia who happens to live in Melbourne, a city where my son would soon be working. She advised me to tell Dan to "pack his woolies" as the weather had suddenly turned very cold and it was snowing in the city. That information was, needless to say, very useful.

There is no doubt in my mind that the use of computers and the Internet has enriched our lives and will continue to do so. For instance, word processing programs have made it that much easier for me to write and send out my work.

As I grow older, I am more aware that retirement and aging can bring increased isolation. But because of the Internet, it doesn't have to be so. I, for one, feel greatly enriched and appreciative. Because of the information revolution and the easy availability of computers, anyone and everyone can be a reader and writer. We can communicate with people anywhere in the world. The computer has become an invaluable tool and a true equalizer.

My active retirement has given me the opportunity to do what I always wanted to do, namely become a full-time freelance writer. I now have one hundred short stories that have been published either in print publications and anthologies, on the net, or in e-book formats. Eleven of my fiction books have now been published as well. I've won awards for plays, poetry and fiction. My reviews and non-fiction articles have been published by numerous newspapers and magazines. What am I doing today? I'm working on the next bestseller!

~Jacqueline Seewald

Writing My Story

And by the way, everything in life is writable about if you have the outgoing guts to do it, and the imagination to improvise. The worst enemy to creativity is self-doubt.
~Sylvia Plath

I opened the local newspaper, eagerly searching the pages. Did they publish my tribute to my mother? They did! The article was the first thing I had ever published. I wasn't paid for the work, since it was featured in a weekly human interest column. Still, it was encouraging to realize someone thought enough of my writing to publish it for public consumption.

Work, family, and a mortgage crowded out any further thoughts of writing. After completing an MBA degree, I enjoyed a twenty-year career as a Human Resources Director for multinational financial services firms. Although I worked on Wall Street in New York City, global responsibilities enabled me to travel across North and South America and even to Europe.

One of my coworkers had a dream of her own. She was in the middle of writing the "Great American Novel." As we worked together over a period of several years, she would write a chapter and I would provide feedback. Her book was good, and against all odds for an unknown author, it was represented by the first agent she contacted and published by a major New York publisher.

Holding her book in my hand was almost as encouraging for me as it was for her. It validated her effort to follow her dream, and it gave me hope for my dream, too. She honored me by including my name in the book's acknowledgments as one who encouraged her not to give up during the long, and frequently lonely, process of birthing her book.

It was about this time that my husband retired and I left the corporate world. We relocated to another state to begin the second half of our lives. It was finally time for me to start writing. But what to write?

I noticed a small newspaper article announcing that the famous *Chicken Soup for the Soul* series was inviting submissions for its upcoming book, *Chicken Soup for the Working Woman's Soul*. Perfect!

I put pen to paper, or more accurately, fingers to keyboard. I wrote about an experience that happened to me during a morning commute, and submitted "Not Just Another Rat." Of course, I thought they would immediately agree that it was an enthralling and wonderfully written story. I eagerly and naively awaited the letter notifying me of its acceptance for publication.

I waited and waited and waited… for more than a year! I later learned that more than 5,000 submissions were received from all over the world, but my story was chosen!

Wow, I thought, this writing stuff isn't so hard. My friend was published on her first try. My first newspaper article was published. My first anthology submission was published. Maybe all those horror stories about how difficult it is to get published were nothing more than just stories. After all, my experience proved otherwise. Surely an agent or editor would soon recognize the quality of my writing and offer me a book contract.

After I finished patting myself on the back and celebrating publication of my story, I continued to submit short stories to anthologies. No takers. I wrote an inspirational non-fiction book and submitted it to agents and publishers. No interest. I wrote a novel. No interest in that one, either.

In fact, no one was interested in my work for the next two years. The rejection letters kept on coming. It was a discouraging cycle: write, submit, rejection, write, submit, rejection. Or write, submit, then silence. I'm not sure what was worse: rejections or silence. At least with the rejections, I knew where I stood!

I had two choices. I could turn off my computer and quit, or I could grow a thick skin and keep trying despite the painful rejections. Each one felt as if I had shown my new baby to people who said, "Boy, is she ugly!"

One thing that kept me going was learning the history of Chicken Soup for the Soul. The first book in the series was published in 1993 after being rejected more than 100 times. That book went on to sell more than eight million copies and the series is one of the most successful in publishing history.

So I kept plugging away. I joined a writers' critique group and began attending writers' conferences. I had much to learn about writing and publishing. I began writing articles for magazines and continued to submit short stories to Chicken Soup for the Soul and other anthology publishers.

Then, in 2005, I submitted to *Chicken Soup for the Recovering Soul: Daily Inspirations*. I sent in six submissions and three were chosen for publication. A few weeks later I was notified that the *Chicken Soup for the Healthy Living* series would include a piece I had written on diabetes. By the third *Chicken Soup for the Soul* book, I went from wishing *someone* would publish me to wishing someone *else* would publish me! My husband put it in perspective when he reminded me of the days when I would have been thrilled if anyone published me!

Since 2003, I have been published in twenty anthologies, including fourteen *Chicken Soup for the Soul* books. Additionally, I have published more than thirty magazine articles with more submissions in the pipeline.

Best of all, I published my first solo book in 2010 with a traditional publisher, and I've co-authored two children's picture books published by another traditional publisher in 2011!

My corporate career was successful, but I'm having much more fun following my dream. My desire is to use my writing, both fiction and non-fiction, to encourage others. That's my passion. I refuse to be discouraged by obstacles, rejections, or the naysayers who told me I was too old to start a second career. The publication of my story in *Chicken Soup for the Working Woman's Soul* encouraged me to keep persevering, to continue networking with other writers, and to continue learning as much as I could about the publishing industry.

Overnight successes in publishing are rare. For me, the path to success consisted of a series of small steps: membership in writers' groups, attendance at writers' conferences, writing magazine articles and short stories, co-authoring a children's book, and finally, authoring my own book. In the process, I'm becoming a better writer as I find the lessons—and the humor—in daily life.

I don't know how many more of my books will be published. Whether it's one or ten, I'm enjoying the journey!

~Ava Pennington

Sunday	Monday	Tuesday	Wednesday	Thursday	Friday	Saturday
		1 brunch at Smiths	2 Work 9-1	3 babysit Jessica	4 work 9-1	5 Pack
6 Pier 3 at 4 sharp	7 CRUISE!!	8	9	10	11	12
13	14 work 9-1	15 Jessica ☺	16 Work 9-1	17 Dog Shelter	18 work 9-1	19 Golf with Gene
20	21 Work 9-1	22 Dr. Miller - 10:30	23 work 9-1	24 dog shelter	25 Work 9-1	26 Dinner Party 7:00
27 DC trip 27th-29th	28	29	30 Work 9-1	31 Dog Shelter		

Chapter
5

Inspiration
for the
Young
at
Heart

When a Husband Retires

Mending Fences

*The husband who doesn't tell his wife everything probably reasons
that what she doesn't know won't hurt him.*

~Leo J. Burke

I retired to solid ground after twenty years as a captain of small boats, seventy feet or less, but there is still plenty of adventure in my life. I do a pretty good job of always telling the truth to my wife about these adventures, but I've become wise enough to pick my time and place to do so.

It had been five months since the last hurricane. I had been keeping something from Judith and it was time to come clean. I guess I will never learn. Maybe women are right: "Men never learn."

The last hurricane had flattened some sections of the wooden fence between us and our neighbors. It was actually the neighbor's fence. They are friendly neighbors; in fact I helped them put the fence up originally. It had been three days since the storm, this fence was sitting on the ground and I had a problem. I couldn't stand it being on the ground when I had all these tools lying dormant.

Now the catch here is that Judith informed me that I would only be allowed to fix the fence as soon as Rick the neighbor got off work so he could help. "It's not our fence anyway, we don't have to rush. Blah, blah, blah, blah, blah." Now this was Monday and the fence would just helplessly lie there for at least four more days if I had to wait for Rick to be available. TV was awful. I'd finished the old list and Judith had the new list out at the binders. Besides all this she was going to visit her mother and would be leaving me alone all day to look at the fence.

As soon as the car left the driveway I started counting. Through years of testing I have found that if I can count to fifty without seeing the car come back I am pretty sure she didn't forget anything and she is gone, gone, gone. I headed right for the tools.

The major problem was the sections of fence. I could dig the holes, get the old cement and broken posts out, all that stuff. But the fence sections were heavy. Even so, I had it all figured out. The sections weighed about 100 pounds and they were awkward to handle. I planned to stand them on edge and drag them little by little until they were in place.

The project was going great. I set one new post in the front yard and nailed two fence sections back in place. I'd show her a thing or two. Never mind Judith: "You're no spring chicken. You're in your seventies. Wait for Rick." I was halfway there and it wasn't even noon.

I made lunch for myself. Yes, I know some of you may be surprised but I can make lunch for myself.

At 12:15 I was at work in the backyard. I got two posts in and one fence section nailed in place. One section to go and I would be home free. It was only 2:30 p.m. I didn't expect the inspector until 4:00!

I had the last section in place and I noticed it was not level because it was sitting on a rock. When I bent down to pull out the rock a gust of wind blew the fence section in my direction. There I was trying to remove the rock and little by little the fence slowly fell over on top of me. It caught me off balance. It was like slow motion—there was nothing I could do. I didn't have time to get out of the way. There was a tree behind me that made a perfect place for the fence to wedge itself, and to add to this trifecta there were bushes at each end of the section and the fence posts at the base.

I was lying on my back, the fence on top of me. Funny but I remember it being rather comfortable and there were no white lights. That was reassuring! I couldn't get my arms up to push the fence off because it had flattened me against the ground in a spread eagle position.

Then I started thinking to myself. Judith was going to be home any minute and find me under the fence. The more I thought about this the harder I laughed, to a point where I had to muffle the laughter because I didn't want the neighbors to hear and rat me out to Judith. I lay there peacefully for a few minutes and then I started to squirm. I guess it's something to do with a primal survival thing. Within ten minutes I had wiggled my way out.

Judith came home; the fence was up. I went through all the "What did you do that for" crap. Because of quick thinking on my part I was spared the "I told you so" lecture and certain banishment.

Months went by. Everything was fine. Until about an hour ago.

Yes, I finally told her today. I figured enough time had elapsed. I figured I must be beyond the statute of limitation for this offense.

That's why I am here on the computer. It is quieter here.

I learned a lot today. A statute of limitation does not apply if the "I told you so" lecture is combined with the "can't leave you alone for one minute" lecture. In retrospect, I suppose it's for the better. I had no idea until just an hour ago about the vast number of men who "don't listen" and are squashed by fences in this country every day. Eye opener for me! All in all I made out rather well. There was a moment I thought I would be forced to wear my shirt with the scarlet letters AH embroidered on it.

In a way I'm kind of glad I told her. I needed a reminder of how stupid we men are. We have a tendency to forget this fact. And for the life of me I can't imagine why any man would see a benefit in keeping a secret or lying after reading this. I also now firmly believe that God intentionally planned that men lose their hearing early in life to relieve them from the din.

Now you women may have something going with the "Men never learn" thing, but contrary to your belief, something must be getting through. I know that if I take her coffee in bed tomorrow morning everything I said and did prior to that moment will be forgotten and I will be clear to start anew. I can hardly wait.

~Robert Campbell

Teddy's Tunes

Follow your passion, and success will follow you.
~Terri Guillemets

My husband, Ted, is a number of years older than I, although I won't say the actual number. As he was nearing retirement age, Ted suddenly decided to do just that — retire.

Well, actually, he didn't exactly retire... he just quit his job to pursue his muse. Ted had always wanted to be involved in music. I could recognize this passion, having aspired to be a great pianist decades earlier.

Our living room slowly but surely began to resemble a recording studio loaded with mixing boards, computers, speakers, microphones, microphone stands, and various other pieces of equipment that are still mysterious to me. Was I a supportive wife? Definitely not at first, as I watched my home becoming an electronics circus.

Then Ted started getting jobs as a karaoke jockey (KJ). His new business grew as he started building a following of friends and groupies. I even attended a gig or two. Yes, we had to start talking in KJ language, which included "gig." In those early years of his new passion, Ted's song collection grew slowly as he incrementally purchased karaoke discs and even more equipment. We went through reams of paper and cases of ink cartridges as Ted printed his song lists each time new selections were added.

Ted's clear happiness in what seemed to me to be a ton of work for little money (not to mention the expense of the equipment) was contagious. Who was I to deny him the opportunity to be involved in something that he had always dreamed about? I'm not sure a karaoke jockey was exactly what he had anticipated but it did involve music, although certainly some performances were questionable! I found myself encouraging Ted and trying to do what I could to help him.

One night I made up a flyer for an upcoming event. The proprietor of the establishment that had hired Ted was anxious for a large turnout. So I thought that an advertising flyer might help get the word out. Jokingly, I dubbed the event as karaoke by "Teddy's Tunes." I only printed one flyer, thinking that certainly Ted would not go for his new name. Surprisingly, he did and even more surprisingly, the name took off. Calls came in asking for "Teddy's Tunes" and Ted began being recognized out and about as "Teddy's Tunes." Some friends even made up a little jingle about "Teddy's Tunes" to the tune of "Spider Man."

As Teddy's Tunes' followers grew, even more humorously he became known for "Old People Karaoke." There was an abundance of Rat Pack singers and crooners, a few country folks, and even some that preferred to display their musical ability singing old Broadway show tunes. He typically scheduled his gigs in the early evening, to be finished by 10:00 p.m., while most entertainment doesn't even start until then.

Little by little this karaoke cult took on a personality of its own. Egos abounded and there were disputes amongst singers allowed to sing out of order from the original line-up, preferences being made for audience requests and the like. Some of the singers even branched out to create singing groups and requested Ted as their sound man. Ted went back and forth between enjoying his passion for music and his dislike of the drama.

And I, alas, found myself with a second job instead of slowing down toward retirement. I was keeping track of his schedule to coordinate with family events, and tracking the revenue and expenses for taxes. I even acted as a roadie, lugging the heavy equipment in and out of our van at times when some health issue or minor injury prevented Ted from lifting things.

I was also put in charge of what Ted dubbed a "customer appreciation" party annually. Thankfully, this was held as a backyard barbeque over the summer months, but nonetheless, it required quite a bit of cooking, coordination, set-up, clean-up and all the other chores that hosting a large party brings. Thankfully, we always invited our neighbors and they actually loved the "Old People Karaoke!"

Somehow, Ted's semi-retirement became quite a bit of fun for both of us as we occasionally spent an evening together singing in our living room. And our daughter, Elizabeth, has had many a fun-filled get-together with her friends in that same living room, while our other daughter, Amanda, proudly brings her friends to Ted's gigs. We even have managed to make Ted's new career fit with my work with not-for-profits. Ted has provided sound, music and entertainment for a variety of fundraisers that I am involved in. Even Ted's ninety-three-year-old mother comes out to see her son perform.

I continue to clean around Ted's cords, microphone wires, and speaker stands, and I tolerate coming home from work to find a recording session underway in my home.

Would I ask that Ted give all this up? Absolutely not! I'm planning my revenge for the day that I decide to "retire."

~Lil Blosfield

A Room of One's Own

The happiest of all lives is a busy solitude.
~Voltaire

I had mourned the loss of the occupants of the three smaller bedrooms of our home in Phoenix, Arizona. One by one our sons established lives not centered in our home. Their former spaces were kept as "theirs" for several years, mini-shrines to their place in our family, through college, through graduate school. But then there came a day, when, without any drama or tears, I put the remnants of their lives in a box and I moved in.

I do love having "a place of my own." Giving my room a name has been a problem. Office sounds a bit pedantic, while studio sounds a tad grandiose, so it's just "my room" for the time being. It was a long time in coming. Most of our lives involve sharing space with a sibling, and then there's the college roommate, quite frequently followed by a spouse. Private turf can easily escape one's experience entirely.

My room is just down the hall from my husband's special room. We pass each other in the hall or even stop in for a visit on occasion. If Bill's door is closed I will knock before entering. This is not something he has asked me to do, but privacy seems a nice gift to give. Especially when relationships have entered the 24/7 stage of retirees, having four walls to provide some separateness in our togetherness seems wise.

My room is a quiet room. No television. Sometimes there's a soft background of instrumental music, but more frequently just the sound of an overhead fan to accompany my thoughts. I have my desk and computer. I have my drafting/painting table from which I can look out on a well-tended backyard—a focus of my labor and object of my love. There is a comfortable chair and reading lamp. I have my files of genealogy research and my cabinet with all my art paraphernalia. My room is filled with things that make me happy as well as defining who I am these days.

Bill and I have talked about downsizing. Sometimes I feel like those passenger-less drivers of SUVs—a sort of moral guilt for using more of the earth's bricks and mortar than I have a right to. But the neighborhood is a quiet enclave right in the heart of Phoenix and we count the neighbors as our friends. And, just as we would miss those neighbors, we would miss the house that has been our home. The print of our hands, in small or large ways, is in every room. The trees planted to mark milestones in our life now provide generous buffers from the omnipresent Arizona sun.

So I imagine we will continue to enjoy our place and the space it provides us—a place to be together and the space to be "as ships in the night."

~Maryann McCullough

"Your father and I converted your former bedrooms into our own spaces. If we'd known about half the stuff we found in there, you both would've been grounded a lot more often."

Another Mega-Sized Idea

Three wise men — are you serious?
~Author Unknown

As a baby boomer, I find myself inundated these days with attractive offers for the perfect retirement location:

"It's Baja for Blue Hair, Bingo and Beans."

"Rise Again in Phoenix's New Viagra Timeshares."

"Retire in Witness Protection Program, Arizona. We Have Great Sicilian Food."

"Arkansas: Trailers welcome."

But just recently I found the perfect retirement location that has everything a guy could possibly want.

"Welcome to Costco. I have an opening right here in the middle."

"Thank you," I said to the sales guy. Then I eased my butt down into a Galaxy D3000 Acupuncture Point Deluxe Air Massage Chair.

"Remote?" I asked.

"You bet." The sales guy handed me the throttle to decadence. I fired it up. A groan of ecstasy instantly escaped my now vibrating torso.

"Yeah, you got that right," the guy beside me said. He was fully reclined in an Eclipse D4000 with built-in MP3 player.

"Nice slipper socks," I said. "Get them here?"

"Of course," he said. "I spotted them when I was looking for the forklift guy, to see if I could get that television moved closer in time for the game."

He pointed at the humongous plasma TV, which now featured a commercial advertising something that required a close-up of more-than-ample cleavage.

"Ever do any rapelling?" another guy asked.

"No and I've always regretted it. Maybe when I retire."

"My wife wants to travel when we retire, which always screws up my digestive system."

"I know what you mean," someone said.

Two new guys moved into the chairs to my left. When they got the speed set properly, they passed around a pillow-sized bag of pretzel nuggets and a cheese block the size of a foreign car.

I was thinking about retirement and the odds of getting a massage chair. My wife's not big on furniture that requires extension cords. I found that out when I tried to pass off a refrigerated wet bar as a coffee table.

"You know," the guy beside me said, "it's too bad we couldn't just retire here."

"What? You mean in Costco?"

"Sure. Think about it. This place has everything." We were interrupted by a saleslady passing out free barbecued mesquite chicken wings. "See?" the guy said.

Another guy agreed. "There's enough beer and wine here for the entire baseball season, plus they must have three hundred pounds of tri-tip steaks. Not to mention desserts up the wazoo."

"We could take turns cooking. They've got a gas grill over there could easily hold enough for a dozen of us at once."

"I do a mean charbroiled fish," one of the new guys said. "And they just brought in a truckload of tiger prawns."

I reversed the kneading function on my Galaxy D3000 and turned up the back heat. "What about recreation?" I asked.

"They got a twenty-foot inflatable water slide that looks like a lot of fun, plus we could clear a few aisles and easily set up a tennis court."

"Or put down a couple hundred throw rugs and make a fairway."

"Plus, we could set up a couple of tents and sit around one of those tables with the fire pit in the middle and play poker."

"The wife says you're supposed to get cultural stimulation when you retire," one guy said.

A group of purple-haired teenagers walked by followed by an Asian couple, a family of Pakistanis and two large women speaking Russian.

"No problem."

"Maybe we could buy, like, timeshares."

"Wow!" we all said.

"We should pitch this idea right now," I said. "See if we can get a group rate."

We called the chair sales guy over and told him our plan and he immediately left to talk with management. We began planning.

"First we should set up a computer so we can download all the sports schedules, then get some beer and start in on some rotisserie chickens. Maybe drag in some patio heaters for when it cools down later."

The sales guy returned. "The manager loved the idea of you wanting to spend more time here," he said. "So he gave me these."

He handed us all job applications. There was a huge sound of deflation, as if the air was being let out of the Goodyear blimp.

"You know," one guy said, "I've heard good things about Baja."

"And Arkansas," I said. Then I shut off my Galaxy D3000 and headed home.

~Ernie Witham

Fourth Place

A long marriage is two people trying to dance a duet
and two solos at the same time.
~Anne Taylor Fleming

I snuggled in the crook of Ray's arm as we planned our day. Monday, the first day of his retirement. I'd worried about how all this togetherness would work out. After four years of marriage I still loved him to distraction and looked forward to more time together. But, as a freelance writer, I was used to scheduling my own days while he worked. Now I'd need to be in partner mode all the time. I wasn't sure how good I'd be at that.

"Think of it," Ray murmured in my ear. "Time for the things I want to do, and a wife who likes to do them with me." His arm tightened around me. "How about loading our bikes and riding the scenic highway from Lewis Park to Multnomah Falls today?"

"Meow." Naomi, our eight-pound black kitty, jumped on the bed and climbed up my chest to peer into my face, reminding me that I was late with her breakfast.

"Hi, Kitty," I told her, rubbing her soft cheeks.

"So, what about the bike ride?" Ray asked.

"It's a great idea. I'll pack a lunch."

Thud. Annie, our eighty-pound Golden Retriever, plunked her large, red-fawn body on the throw rug near our bed. Her collar jangled as she reached back to chew a spot near her tail.

"The whole family's here," Ray said.

I hoped I didn't hear a trace of impatience in his voice. To me, the animals were family members and omnipresent in my days. "Guess I'd better feed everyone. Want a veggie scramble? Breakfast in bed for your special day?" I asked Ray.

"Sure."

I turned and glanced at the clock on the nightstand. "8:05!" I cried, bolting upright.

"It's okay. We're on retirement time." Ray reached for my shoulder to pull me back down.

"The ferrier will be at the barn at 9:00. I forgot."

"The ferrier?"

"The man who trims my horse's hooves."

My stomach knotted. All my life I'd wanted a horse. Now I had an Arabian beauty and I rode her several times a week while Ray worked. With him home all the time wanting to do things together, when could I go to the barn without hurting his feelings?

"Can't she get trimmed another day?" Ray asked.

I propped myself on an elbow. "It's too late to reschedule. I'm really sorry. We could do something this afternoon."

"Cat, dog, horse. I can see I'm number four." Ray's tone of voice was teasing, but I read disappointment in his eyes.

"Number four? Never," I assured him. An image came to mind of an old-fashioned balance scale with Ray on one side, and the animals on the other. I could see his point. I wanted my second marriage to be a good one, so I had to change that perception and fast. But how? "You're the only male in the house and you offer things they can't," I insisted, kissing him soundly to prove my point.

He didn't look convinced.

I chewed my lip and wracked my brain. I could see him adjusting to the cat and dog. Evenings the cat often stretched the length of his chest as he read in bed, her gravelly motor running. Retirement could bring more stress reduction of the purring kitty variety. The dog's boundless enthusiasm for all things active would make her delightful company on many of our outings. But what about my horse? I thought about the one time Ray had ridden with me. Afterward he'd stated flatly that he'd rather play golf.

Golf. I had an idea! "What if every time you see me grab my barn boots you head for the golf course?" I asked hopefully.

Ray's brow furrowed. "How often do you go to the barn?"

"Three times a week."

"Three times a week? I could hit balls some days, get a game or two together with friends?" The furrows in his forehead smoothed.

"That's what retirement is about." I slipped out of bed and pulled on a T-shirt and jeans.

Ray stood and made a few practice swings. "You know, hon," he said, looking over from his golfer's stance. "I don't expect you to give up your life now that I'm around all the time."

I startled. I hadn't let myself put my fears quite that way.

"I may whine from time to time," Ray went on, "but I don't really mind the animals. And I know you need to write, go to the barn, whatever else. If you'll just tell me when stuff is going to come up, I can plan to do something else. Golf, a gym workout, lunch with some of my buddies."

"You're the best," I said, putting my arms around him. "We can still join the mid-week bike club like we talked about. Take the Tuesday ski bus to Mt. Hood Meadows this winter."

"We'll figure it out. We always do." He pulled me close.

I relaxed against him. We did always figure things out. When we married we successfully blended his six adult children and my three, his love of golf and my love of cycling, his long hours as a restaurant owner and my erratic hours as a writer. We could keep a joint calendar and I could do a better job of letting him know, often, how much I appreciated his good-natured, giving ways. He wouldn't feel like number four again.

~Samantha Ducloux Waltz

No Place Like Home

Forgiveness is the fragrance the violet sheds on the heel that has crushed it.
~Mark Twain

"Mom, where is your pepper?" I ask, searching the usual spot.

"Who knows!" she answers with a sigh, rolling her eyes. "I can't find a thing. I came home yesterday and your stepfather rearranged all the cabinets."

"Why?"

"He joined a cooking class. Lord help me. He said he needed everything within arm's length of the stove." She shook her head.

Explanations for various things have become commonplace since my stepfather retired. Such as why the TV is now programmed to turn on via remote only after turning on the DVD player, having the channel set to five, the VCR turned on, and the microwave in the kitchen running on low. My mother has threatened to go from working part-time to full-time.

My phone rang. "Judy..."

"Yeah Mom?"

"My bushes are gone!"

"What do you mean, gone?"

"I mean. I just got home, pulled in the driveway and all my bushes are gone!"

"How could they be gone?" I was baffled. Her bushes lined the driveway, providing a border to the yard. This enclosed a quaint flowered yard with two beautiful apple trees.

"They're GONE! I gotta go." Click.

My stepfather discovered the most harmful tool ever given to a retired man. The chainsaw. Once a man experiences the power of cutting there is no stopping him. No wonder they call them power tools.

I drove to the house. Sheer void. I sat in my car staring at the emptiness that was once a mass of beautiful bushes. Just like I once pondered the meaning of life, I asked myself, "Why?"

Stepping inside, I simply raised my hands and my mother answered my unspoken question. "So he could see the garage." Hmmm... wasn't blocking that view the reason the previous owners planted them in the first place?

Unfortunately, no wood was safe from the new Paul Bunyan. Except of course for the wooden fence that escaped its fate merely due to the blisters that formed on my stepfather's hands. I'm certain these were caused the day he "pruned" the apple trees.

Ring....

"Judy! He hacked the apple trees!"

"He chopped them down?"

"No. He cut all the branches into stubs! No tops, no ends, no leaves!"

I tried to picture this. No, I couldn't envision it, even with my vivid imagination.

Arriving at the house, I stood in the kitchen gazing out the window into the backyard. There before me was a tree trunk with stub branches and no top. Times two.

I saw the tears in her eyes. "They were so beautiful."

I contemplated buying him yarn and knitting needles. Then I glanced at my mom. The needles could also double as weapons. I changed my mind.

He's now a member of a men's singing group. He spends hours walking around the house harmonizing. My mom chooses this time to recharge her hearing aid batteries and reads a book in silence.

I love my stepfather dearly, but it is evident his retirement is talking its toll on my mother. I meet her for lunch. Somewhere away from the house. This has become our custom on her days off. I talk as she combs the want ads.

I don't think she'll ever retire. She'll get that second job, and after that find something for weekends. My stepfather will spend a month experimenting with various computer programs until he finds the perfect one necessary to create an attendance sheet for sixteen singers.

I'll wait for my phone to ring. I can picture it now. I'll answer.

"Judy! Did you see it?"

"Yes Mom, I did." This time there would be no panic, just excitement. "I have it right here in my hand." There she will be, my mom, Donald Trump's new CEO on the cover of a leading magazine.

Guess you can do just about anything when you work 24/7.

~Judy A. Weist

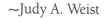

"The woman interviewing me for the job is about my age. When she asked why I wanted the position, I said, simply, 'Because my husband just retired and is home all the time.' She made me an offer right then and there."

The Reluctant Triathlete

If God invented marathons to keep people from doing anything more stupid, the triathlon must have taken Him completely by surprise.

~P.Z. Pearce

"How shall I spend my retirement?" I said, thinking out loud in my wife's company, a frequent error on my part.

Retirement would mean earned relaxation. Absence of exertion. Gentle challenges like crosswords. Time to remember, to reflect, to meditate, to ponder. A chance to put competitiveness to one side.

"Triathlons," she said.

"What?" said I, dumbfounded by the non sequitur, but not that dumfounded—wives specialize in non sequiturs, as anyone who has been married for more than a few milliseconds well knows.

"Swimming, cycling and..."

"I know what a triathlon is," I interrupted, lying, but knowing that whatever it was, it would hurt. "I just don't know what relevance it has to my retirement."

"Something... to... do," she said, enunciating the words as if my age were closer to six than sixty.

"I have plenty to do." She had given me a list of what seemed like several thousand things to do around the house, things that had been pleasant suggestions while I was working, but now hung over me like menacing threats to our continuing relationship.

"I mean a real challenge, something to aim at, something to achieve," she said.

"I can't swim."

"Yes, you can."

"I mean I can't swim more than a length without getting exhausted."

"If you can swim a length you can swim a mile," she said—no, she declared as an uncontestable fact, like a proven theorem—a veritable Pythagoras, my wife.

"I can jump in the air a few inches. Does that mean I can fly to the moon?" I said, waiting to see how Pythagoras would handle an encounter with W. C. Fields.

"With practice, I mean," she said, reverting to the talking-to-a-six-year-old-tone.

"With practice I can fly...."

"With practice you can swim a mile!" she interrupted, before I could complete my lampoonery, the smirk dying on my face as I began to feel uneasy, cornered, threatened.

And that's how it started. She threw down the gauntlet, and down is where it stayed, on the floor of my mind, ignored; until three days later I found myself Googling "triathlon," and that, as they say, was that.

"Elderly man dies doing first triathlon!" screams the tabloid headline I imagine whenever I consider my own death being reported in the press—not that it ever will be, but one can at least aspire to posthumous fame even if one never manages to acquire any of the prehumous variety. "He should have known better—says medical expert!" the fictitious press account continues. "He might just as well have taken up Russian Roulette—exciting certainly, but inevitably short-lived."

"I Googled 'people dying in triathlons' and got 24,000 hits," I told my wife.

"People die doing anything. Reading. Having sex," she said. We looked at each other for an uncomfortable few seconds. I don't know why it was uncomfortable, but I suspect it wasn't related to reading, and before I could work it out she carried on talking.

"Think of all the people who'll live longer because they're getting fit to do triathlons," she said.

"Do you want me to live longer?"

"Of course."

"Longer than you?" I asked.

"Yes," she said. "One second longer."

I had to think about that one too. Did she mean that she... I stopped myself. Don't go there. Stick to the subject.

And I did. In fact I stuck to it so effectively that a month later and $2,000 poorer, I was the owner of a wetsuit, updated running shoes, a carbon fibre road bike and endless other accessories and bits and bobs I didn't know existed until I entered the world of triathlons.

Don't ask me why I had to have a carbon fibre bike rather than an any-old-other-fibre bike; people just told me I did. Ditto this wet-suit rather than that wetsuit. Ditto just about every item I would have chosen, which needed to be replaced by what someone else suggested, the one common denominator amongst the replacements being they were more expensive, a lot more expensive. It was like joining an esoteric cult where "all will be revealed" at some future time, that is, during your first triathlon, when you'll understand all your own, uninformed choices of gear would have proven idiotic, laughable, disastrous, fatal even. Thus it is you blindly follow the advice of the cognoscenti.

Like many of her gender, my wife finds the act of buying cloth-ing, any clothing for any person, as stimulating as eating chocolate. She accompanied me when I went to buy my wetsuit, which serves to illustrate the strength of her addiction.

"I didn't know your stomach stuck out until I saw you in that," she remarked, helpfully, after I had levered myself into the first suit I tried on.

"Well, there's not exactly anywhere to hide it," I quipped, "unless I can squeeze it up to my chest."

"Yuck, don't do that. You'll look even more grotesque."

Her remark didn't offend me, which only goes to show either (a) how close we are, or (b) how little we value each other's opinions.

At this point the shop assistant yanked up the zipper to complete the fitting process. Garroting couldn't be more painful.

"He's gone purple," my wife said. "Is that normal?"

"Only if it doesn't go away in five minutes."

"I think it's too tight," I managed to wheeze out of lungs compressed to the size of shriveled lemons.

"It has to be tight," said the assistant. "You only want a thin layer of water between you and the suit to keep you warm."

"But I can't move," I managed to groan. "How can I swim if I can't move my arms and legs?" Ironically, as if in a taunt, the shop began to swim before my eyes, and as I tottered towards a faint the assistant yanked the zipper down. An elephant had stepped off my chest.

I tried another. Comfortable, but too loose. And another, which nearly cut my testicles in half.

"I've had enough," I said, panting. "Let's come back another day."

"How do you expect to do a triathlon if you haven't even got the energy to buy a wetsuit?" asked my wife.

"It's you who expects me to do a triathlon," I told her, not sure what point I was making.

"I do," she said. "You will." No doubt the point she was making.

Fast forward a year. I have completed four triathlons. They weren't easy, but they weren't that hard either, once I'd decided I was going to complete them. My wife is proud of me. I'm a little proud of myself. I'm still alive and convinced that despite age, even the most absurd challenges can be met if you (and your partner) think you can make it—particularly your partner, because she has no incentive to fail and, however mysteriously she acquired it, no reason to doubt your aging body still has life in it.

We live by the judgments of others, so why not let them set our challenges from time to time? Perhaps they know us better than we know ourselves, particularly as we grow old together.

~Brian Staff

Living with Retired Spouse

Retirement: That's when you return from work one day and say, "Hi, Honey, I'm home — forever."

~Gene Perret

It was hard to see beyond the excitement of that memorable day when my husband and I would begin a new stage of our lives called Retirement. His company had finally come through with a great incentive package for early retirement and we agreed the time was right.

When we talked about really "living together," my only request was, "Please don't invade my space," to which I received a polite grunt that I took to mean "I won't." I had read articles stating that the drastic changeover from valued working employee to retiree could be traumatic, so I silently vowed to be caring and sensitive. I would tread lightly.

Soon, however, my life became defined in terms of "before retirement" and "after retirement."

Before retirement, I had a comfortable routine — I ate a quick breakfast, straightened up the house, and then spent as much time as needed in my home office. I could do errands in the afternoon... if I felt like it. I owned my time and space, as much as I wanted and could grab for myself.

After retirement, I lingered over breakfast, enjoyably at first, to chat with my spouse. Following our breakfast conversation, the new retiree spread out numerous reading materials on the kitchen table so that I had to clean around him or send him to another room. Minutes before I finished my morning chores, he finished his reading material and settled himself comfortably in my office, where I found him scrutinizing rows and columns of figures on my computer's monitor.

"How long will you be?" I asked him cautiously, aware of his possible fragile psyche. "I need my computer to finish up some work I didn't get to yesterday."

"Oh, sorry," he replied, his gaze fixed on the computer screen. "I'll only be a few more minutes. Can you give me another five or ten? This is really important."

I saw the newspaper open to the stock market pages and thought, "Hmmm. The rest of our retirement could depend on these figures." I acquiesced.

It was several hours before I could reclaim my office, now newly cluttered.

I began to leave the breakfast table earlier and earlier each morning, purposely shortening our breakfast chats.

The goal was to be first in my office. If I could clean the kitty litter while hubby loaded the breakfast dishes into the dishwasher, I could make substantial headway; that is, if precious minutes weren't wasted mopping up the cat's water that I knocked over in my haste. I gauged my time by keeping my eye on his dishwasher progress and then on how his pile of reading material was dwindling. I saved the laundry for the evening and discarded the Windex in favor of smudged bathroom mirrors. No matter, he was always in my office before me, by only seconds, it seemed.

Psyches are fragile and it was mine that was about to implode as I realized that the trauma of hubby's retirement was all mine.

I approached him at my desk with a wide smile and gritted teeth. "Remember, dear, that second computer we've been talking about purchasing? Why don't you go out and price one?"

The second he was out the door, I removed his clutter of papers from my desk and organized them into a portable file. The forty-year-old, barely-used sewing machine table became a desk wannabe (we could buy a modern one later). With a little rearranging of the furniture in our spare bedroom, an office awaited the retiree's return.

A few hours later he trudged up the steps carrying a large carton. "Honey, guess what I bought? Think there's room on your desk for another computer?"

"I don't think there's room on my desk, but why don't you try it in your new office?" I replied.

By the end of the day, he was comfortably settled in his new quarters, columns of figures glowing on his computer screen; social security comparisons for ages sixty-two, sixty-five and seventy; potential IRA distributions stretching far into our very old age. Oh yes, I could see that our retirement was in a good place—a nice, cozy, converted spare bedroom.

Is my "after retirement" finally as pleasant as my "before retirement?"

Well, let's just say that my psyche's fragility is on hold until I confront a certain pile of reading material that has morphed into several stacks of non-touchable, non-discardable coffee table embellishments.

~Linda J. Cooper

My Husband, The Sculptor

Youth is the gift of nature, but age is a work of art.
~Stanislaw Lec

"**S**o what will you do now?" well-meaning friends asked my husband when he retired as a New Jersey Superior Court judge.

Vic would smile, shrug and answer that for a while he might just "float." Decompress. Rest his brain and senses after a lifetime in law.

I worried. A lot.

I was fearful that this man with whom I had shared my life would be bored or lonely or lost. I was concerned about how he would fill days that had once overflowed with important concerns and challenges. I suppose every wife of a newly-minted retiree has those dark-of-night anxieties.

"I think I'll take a sculpture course," my husband announced one day as we were having dinner. I almost choked on my chicken—he might as well have said, "I think I'll train to be an astronaut."

Never in our forty-four years together had Vic shown or expressed any interest in sculpting. Never in all that time had we actively sought out a sculpture exhibit.

But in this brave new world of retirement, I was to learn that lives are reinvented, and deeply buried yearnings burst forth. And thus it was with Vic—and sculpture.

My only involvement was to suggest a few likely venues for courses. As a longtime arts writer, I thought I could provide at least that much. As it turned out, it was Vic himself who finally identified the local arts center where his new venture would unfold.

I admit it was slightly weird to watch my husband, most often seen poring over voluminous law texts, as he gathered sculpting supplies, from planing tools and tiny sculpting knives to a simple bucket for his clay.

And there was a slight déjà vu about the September morning when my beloved student went off to art school for the very first time. In other years, I had stood by the kitchen door to watch each of our three daughters march into that big world out there, lunch boxes and backpacks in place.

This time, it was a taller person with silver hair, a man dressed in jeans and a plaid shirt, not his former suit-and-tie/briefcase ensemble, who was off to school. I admit I got a bit misty watching him leave the house.

I spent the morning of Vic's first sculpture class worrying. Would this absolute artistic novice feel intimidated? Would his fellow students be latter-day Michelangelos with limited tolerance for the new kid on the block?

As it turns out, I needn't have anguished.

My husband came home from that first class with obvious exhilaration. For starters, he'd gone and done something unexpected. Score one for a new retiree willing to "try on" a brand new experience.

Vic also discovered, over the next several months, that he had some talent for figural sculpture. Mind you, no museums have come begging for his works, which include a pretty decent female nude (yes, a live model did the posing) and my favorite, the profile of a young man.

By winter, my husband was also taking a drawing class, buying charcoals and drawing paper, and finding that there was, indeed, life after law. Fortunately, the class didn't conflict with the second semester of sculpture.

The astonishment: a man who had never ever done more than doodle was exploring a whole new part of himself. Torts, dockets, motion days and sentencings were receding, and human anatomy and perspective/proportion were on the ascendancy.

Vic is quiet about his life in the arts. He talks about it only when asked. And for now, his artistic efforts are stashed in an upstairs room, not yet ready, he believes, for prime time display.

But as my husband flexes his art "muscles" and takes those first tentative steps into brave new endeavors, I'm standing by the sidelines cheering him on.

After all, Michelangelos are born in every generation.

And who's to say that they can't be retired judges?

~Sally Schwartz Friedman

55

Deposing the King

A retired husband is often a wife's full-time job.
~Ella Harris

My husband and I have been married for thirty-seven years. We met in high school, were college sweethearts and just knew we were meant for each other. After college we got married, and he got a wonderful job. He quickly rose through the ranks to become a high-powered executive. I stayed home, raised our kids and was in charge of the home front. I made all of the decisions: where to vacation and when, when to paint the house and which colors to use, when to buy new furniture or new appliances, and all decisions about schools for our children. I even bought his clothes for him. I was in charge of everything except his job. Division of labor—you get the idea. I didn't tell him how to do his job and he didn't interfere in mine.

And then he retired. He stayed home... with me. He had no other places to be... except with me. He no longer had employees to direct... he only had me. He no longer had a professional life.... so I became his focus and things quickly deteriorated.

For thirty-seven years I was the one who made coffee in the morning—whether he was home or not. The morning after he retired I went to the kitchen and couldn't find the coffeemaker. Where was it? I looked and looked and then finally found it in the family room—right next to my husband. He hadn't actually made the morning coffee but he was looking very pleased. "Why is the coffeemaker in the family room?" I asked, thinking this whole thing was kind of cute. "Well," he said, "we drink the coffee in here so it only makes sense to have the coffeemaker in here too." It didn't make the best sense to me since the water, the coffee beans, the sugar, the milk, the cups and the spoons were in the kitchen, but I let him have his way. No big deal.

After breakfast my routine was to straighten up the house, make the bed, check e-mail messages and get ready for my day. Suddenly my husband seemed to be connected to my hip. If I turned around, I'd bump into him. If I went into the living room, he was right there with me. When I gave the dog her breakfast, he was there, too. When I loaded the breakfast dishes in the dishwasher, he watched and then he moved them to a different place.

"Why are you putting the cups on that side?" he asked.

"Because that's just where I always put them. Why?"

"Well," he said, "they would be better over here."

Not true, but not wanting to get into a confrontation about the stupid coffee cups, I let it go.

Time to go to the grocery store—oh, joy! Since he didn't have a life he was going to go with me. Ah—togetherness. I always went up and down each aisle when I shopped. That didn't seem to suit the King of Direction. He only wanted to go down the necessary aisles although he was not sure which ones those might be. And he asked questions about each thing I put in the cart. He asked why I bought a certain brand of tomatoes rather than an alternate brand. He asked why I needed the stinking tomatoes in the first place. Excuse me but why was that any of his business?

Time to put the groceries away. The King of Kitchen Arranging decided that all of the cupboards needed to be rearranged and that the items in the pantry needed to be in alphabetical order. Never mind that the pears didn't go with the pasta or the rice didn't go with the raisins, they started with the same letters so now they were together. Same thing with my spices. It didn't matter that there was a method to the way I had them arranged. They were not in the order that the King of the Alphabet wanted them in so they were put in new places. I had only one thing to say to him after this fiasco… "Get out of my kitchen!!!"

Thank goodness, when I had lunch dates with friends, he knew he couldn't come. But... he could call. Every twenty minutes! Just to check in with me. He'd call to ask if I had ordered, what I had ordered, had it been served yet, was it good, and on and on and on. And I know what you are thinking—why didn't I just NOT answer the phone? I only tried that once. But then, thinking something could be wrong with me, he came rushing to the restaurant to be sure I hadn't choked on a chicken bone or something like that.

Suddenly nothing that he did was cute anymore. Everything was annoying and dumb. My life as I knew it was over. He was micro-managing my life and I hated it. I hated him and his smiling face and our togetherness and I hated making coffee in the family room instead of in the kitchen. But then came the straw that broke the camel's back. He wanted to know why we needed two cars since we were always together. Why didn't we sell one of them? He thought we could get along just fine with only one car.

That was the last and lowest blow. I had never thought about getting a divorce before but now I was looking up divorce attorneys in the Yellow Pages. Of course in order to do that, in private and by myself, I had to do it in the bathroom because that was the only place I could ever be alone. Then I realized that what he really needed was... a life. Of his own. He needed a purpose, something to do. So I found projects to keep him busy and new hobbies that interested him. Pretty soon he was finding things to do all on his own. And best of all, he was doing them by himself and leaving me alone!

You'll be happy to know that things have settled down now and we are both enjoying his retirement. We have made adjustments in our routines, compromises in our expectations and have found new, fun things to do. We do lots of things together but we also have our separate interests and things to do alone. That's the way it should be. But every now and then, when I least expect it... the King of Micro-managing reappears and I have to put him in his place.

~Madison Thomas

Sunday	Monday	Tuesday	Wednesday	Thursday	Friday	Saturday
		1 brunch at Smiths	2 Work 9-1	3 babysit Jessica	4 work 9-1	5 Pack
6 Pier 3 at 4 sharp	7 CRUISE!!	8	9	10	11	12
13	14 work 9-1	15 Jessica ☺	16 Work 9-1	17 Dog Shelter	18 work 9-1	19 Golf with Gene
20	21 Work 9-1	22 Dr. Miller - 10:30	23 work 9-1	24 dog shelter	25 Work 9-1	26 Dinner Party 7:00
27 DC trip 27th-29th	28	29	30 Work 9-1	31 Dog Shelter		

Inspiration
for the
Young
at
Heart

The Privileges of Age

56

You're Doing What?

The trouble with retirement is that you never get a day off.
~Abe Lemons

There are many pluses to living in a retirement community. One of the most beneficial is that since we are all of an age when our health is starting to wane, we are experiencing the same problems. If we are concerned about an ailment, there are fifteen friends who can give us advice on how to deal with it.

At a time when we are battling arthritis, preparing for knee and hip replacements, or having cataract surgery, we take great comfort in knowing that many others have been there, done that and are now tackling the next problem with a little help from their friends.

Because growing older and living with ailments is so common among us, we begin to laugh at our plight and ourselves.

When friends say, "What?" or "Speak up," we know they are experiencing the same hearing loss as we are.

We laugh when most of us in our golf foursome need help seeing where our ball has come to rest.

We walk into a restaurant with our shoulders square at a fairly brisk pace. But when we get up from the table after sitting for an hour, arthritis keeps us bent over. We waddle and wobble to the door with baby steps until the pain has subsided. We look at each other's posture and laugh together.

When our friends start a sentence and then say, "Now… where was I going with that thought?" or, "What's that word I'm trying to think of?" we breathe a sigh of relief that maybe we are not in the first throes of Alzheimer's after all. We can't *all* have it!

Our children think it must be awful to live in a retirement village. "Mom, I can't imagine you and Dad being with a lot of old people. You are just going to curl up and die there."

At first they have a hard time understanding why they can never reach us when they call… why we don't return their calls until days later… why we're not home after 10:00 p.m.… why we don't have time to read that book they recommended.

Then they come to visit. "You're doing what?" they yelp when we tell them we're going skydiving.

They look at our calendar with disbelief. "You're golfing three times a week, Dad? How do you guys get this many dates for bridge in one month? You're in a musical, Mom?"

They see that we are relaxed and happy and surrounded by many friends. They see us fulfilling lifelong dreams. By the time our children leave the village, they have decided that retirement cannot come soon enough for them. They envy our new lifestyle. And they decide that retirement most definitely does not have to mean slowing down.

When the children leave, we glance at each other with a grin and make a mad dash to the phone. There are golf tee times to be scheduled, tickets to order for an upcoming play, confirmation for a party next week, and finally a quick call to our best friends. "Get the cards out. We'll be right over."

Those youngsters have slowed us down and now it's time to get back into circulation!

~Kay Conner Pliszka

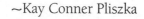

"I recommend increasing your iron...
namely your 3-iron, 5-iron, 7-iron and 9-iron."

Sixty Doesn't Suck

Retirement is wonderful.
It's doing nothing without worrying about getting caught at it.
~Gene Perret

They say that sixty is the new forty, but I'm not buying it. After all, at age forty, I was knee-deep in work responsibilities, family duties and a long-term mortgage. If I'm looking for a proper comparison with reaching my seventh decade, I sure wouldn't choose forty.

Fifty doesn't work so well, either. When the big five-O hits, chances are you're still immersed in all those work, family and home-related chores. Plus, hitting fifty has a way of concentrating your mind and cruelly pointing out that you're over the hill and rapidly descending the down slope on the other side.

If I were going to describe sixty, I'd say it's the new twenty. Not because of the constantly aching joints and back, mind you. But otherwise, it's a pretty fair comparison. At least that's the way it's working out for me. Turning sixty wasn't some drawn-out pity fest with me longing for the days of my youth. Rather, it signaled all kinds of great things.

First of all, turning sixty meant I could retire from the federal public service with no penalty on my government pension. Getting out of the federal government these days is reward enough. But to get out with an unreduced pension that just happens to be indexed to the cost of living is enough to make one jump for joy. Subject of course to any jump-restricting arthritis in the knees and hips.

On top of that, escaping into retirement feels much like being in university at age twenty. That long list of seemingly never-ending duties and responsibilities starts to fade away into the far recesses of memory.

No more dragging one's butt off to work every morning. No more churning out reports, plans and recommendations destined to be shelved or ignored. No more home mortgage and far less time spent raising children. At this stage, any interaction with older children is generally brief and primarily centered around handing out money.

Like my twenty-year-old self, I am pretty much able to do what I want. Granted, that no longer includes indoor Frisbee, recreational pharmaceuticals or beer chugging contests, but I am now free to play my own age-appropriate games such as golf, yoga and limited wine consumption.

Before I hit sixty, I had some sense that this was going to be a golden age. But now that I've passed that marker, I've found that there are all kinds of hidden treasures that I knew little or nothing about.

For example, the other day I was wandering the mall (one of my new pastimes) and discovered that the local barber has a reduced price of $10 for a haircut for those over sixty. Not only that, without even being asked, he seems quite happy to cut off additional hair in other locations for no extra charge.

But the cornucopia of riches that is sixty doesn't stop there. A recent visit to a drugstore chain alerted me to the fact that one particular day every month is Seniors' Day, with a generous twenty-percent discount tacked on for me and my boomer buddies who are now seventy-bound.

This is nothing to sneeze at or cough at or scratch at, for that matter. Although I'm loving sixty, even I realize that it comes with an extra load of salves, ointments and medications to keep the body lubricated and mobile. But the good news is that your stash of pharmaceutical supplies now comes at a significantly reduced cost.

It seems that everywhere I go these days there's someone waiting to give me a discount. Department stores have special days for seniors, travel companies offer savings, and even insurance companies apparently think my failing eyesight and slower reflexes make me a better and cheaper candidate for auto insurance.

My older friends tell me this is just the beginning. "Wait till you hit sixty-five," they say. "You ain't seen nothing yet, kid."

So with visions of candies, sugar plums and reduced-price prosthetics dancing in my head, I can hardly wait to add another five years to my age and see what awaits me. If sixty is the new twenty, I'm guessing that sixty-five may be the new fifteen. Without the facial blemishes, of course, but with considerably more back and ear hair.

And for those afraid of facing seventy and beyond, I say, "Bring it on." If eighty is the new ten, eighty-five the new five and so on, I can't wait to get back to those carefree days when all you had to do all day was play and someone else would do all the work.

~David Martin

Shifting Sands

Old age, believe me, is a good and pleasant thing.
It is true you are gently shouldered off the stage,
but then you are given such a comfortable front stall as spectator.
~Confucius

"Be careful!" our daughter Jill commanded as her father and I climbed the semi-daunting outdoor steps of a Long Beach Island, New Jersey stilt house where Jill and her sisters were spending a week with their families. "These stairs are tricky."

The admonition could seem a perfectly ordinary caution, but was actually a bit more. Slowly, inexorably, a shift in roles has been taking place. And it boils down to this: increasingly, we're now perceived as the led instead of the leaders.

How many summers had we been the ones saying "Careful!" countless times to three little beach-going daughters as they scrambled down steps and ramps and dunes to get to the Atlantic Ocean? How many times were we the guides/fearless leaders to that joyous destination, the deep blue sea?

Throughout a deliciously long visit at a crowded rental beach house with cutesy wall hangings and seashore colors, my husband and I were under the watchful eye of our daughters. It's not that we're feeble. It's just that they are increasingly vigilant about how their father and I maneuver the world.

The role reversal they seem bent on initiating makes us smile, sometimes, because we see ourselves thorough a vastly different lens. We generally feel the same vigor and zest we have always had. Only the number—our ages—is new, and yes, startling.

But our daughters see us differently.

These same three who used to toddle behind us while we carried the buckets and shovels, the rafts, the towels, the umbrellas and sunscreen, now forge ahead insisting that we need not carry "the heavy stuff."

Huh?

On our recent visit, these sisters who once seemed incapable of sharing a blouse, let alone a beach house, showed a generosity of spirit—and an amiability—that both stunned and delighted us.

"I never thought I'd live to see this," I whispered to my husband when all three leaped to their feet to clean up from a very messy, noisy lunch that involved seven kids and eight grown-ups.

What came rushing back were the chore charts I used to make at these seashore cottages when there were endless squabbles about whose job it was to clear and stack, and whose turn it was to sweep.

Now our daughters, all mothers, make those charts and attempt to make sure that the three "smalls"—Danny, Emily and Carly—get the easy chores while the big kids pitch in with the harder stuff.

And the grandparents?

We're asked to sit out on the deck and enjoy the breezes.

It takes some getting used to. But to protest might seem a rejection of their abundant good will and solicitude. So we submit to the spoiling, even though we know perfectly well that we can still navigate the world more ably than they seem to think.

We let them believe that their view is the clearer one. It's a small, harmless deception.

It was just yesterday when we were in full charge, even if that meant very little relaxing on this wonderful island. But there we sat on the beach on a golden summer afternoon and didn't once get up to chase a child on the run, or to scan the ocean every third second for the one old enough to be swimming with a buddy.

While I never thought I'd miss those unmistakable markers of parenting, I did.

We were invited to dig a huge hole and to help create a few sand castles, complete with towers made of dripping wet sand. And while it was undeniably harder to get down on the sand—and get up again—we wouldn't have missed it for the world.

We were observers at a spirited game of Frisbee, and a few rounds of touch football as the day waned. But we were definitely not participants. We do have some sense—who needs muscle sprains?

Yes, it's a new era. We're not on the front lines. We felt it keenly on that day at the shore. Not with bitterness, but with good humor.

In the endless dance of the generations, we seem to have arrived at a new destination, as our adult children see it. Our own interior monologues tell a different story. We are who we were—just seasoned.

After a dinner on the deck, prepared by the family's premier chef, son-in-law Michael—after watching our grandchildren chase one another around that deck with the boundless energy of the young at the seashore—we rallied ourselves for a departure. Home was just over an hour away—but it felt like another planet.

We walked down those outside steps again, this time by the light of a flashlight that Amy, our middle daughter, insisted upon holding for us.

Then the whole clan stood in the driveway to noisily wave us off.

"Be careful!" warned a chorus of voices as we pulled away.

We smiled at one another, and waved to our protectors as we turned the corner to return to our quiet world.

And yes, we were careful.

~Sally Schwartz Friedman

Batter Up!

Baseball fans love numbers.
They love to swirl them around their mouths like Bordeaux wine.
~Pat Conroy

With nothing else to do on a lazy spring afternoon, Richard flopped on the sofa, television remote in hand, zipping through the channels and watching ten seconds of every show before moving onto the next. Frustrated, I got up to go read a book.

"Don't go," he pleaded.

"Then find something to watch," I insisted.

A baseball game popped up on the screen. The Tampa Bay Rays versus the New York Yankees. I was surprised when the channel surfing came to an abrupt end.

No one would consider my husband or me a sports fan. Richard usually worked on the weekends and I simply wasn't that interested. We would watch an occasional televised sporting event but usually had a game of *Scrabble* going at the same time.

And then we retired.

I'd come from a long line of baseball fans. Every Sunday afternoon my father parked himself in front of the television with his cigar to watch a game. If I wanted to spend time with Dad, I had to watch baseball. Curious, I would ask questions. Eager to teach me, he explained every play in great detail while puffing cigar after cigar. I studied the players' names and positions while memorizing the teams and their cities, never minding that I reeked of smoke by the time Mom called us to dinner. Sitting in front of the television that day with Richard, my long forgotten love of the game sputtered back to life.

Richard had no such childhood experience. As a kid his mother enrolled him in swimming and tennis lessons. He knew virtually nothing about how baseball was played. His childhood memories didn't include hot dogs, peanuts and cotton candy while listening to the roar of the crowd in a major league baseball park.

And still he watched.

"What's a double play?" he asked.

I explained.

"Home run!" he screamed.

"No, it's not," I shot back, wondering how he could be so ignorant about our national pastime.

"Why isn't it?" he pouted.

"It bounced off the wall and back into play. It's a ground rule double."

The next day we settled in to watch another game, my eyes glued to the television.

"What do they mean by the seventh inning stretch?" Richard asked.

"Seriously, you don't know what that is?" I asked in disbelief.

"No, I don't."

I explained about President Taft getting up to stretch in the middle of the seventh inning. He was very overweight and found his seat increasingly uncomfortable. Since he was the President, the fans also stood up in respect. Thus the seventh inning stretch was born.

"Interesting story." He immediately got right back into following the action of the game.

I fell in love with watching the Rays. The crack of the bat, players sliding across the field to steal a base or leaping at the wall to catch a ball, mesmerized me. I cheered for each run scored and sulked when the opposing team hit a ball that rolled through the infield. Out of the corner of my eye I could see Richard dozing off on the couch.

How could he be losing interest in what had become my favorite pastime?

"I'd forgotten how much I loved baseball. It's so exciting." I commented while shaking him back into consciousness.

"It's too complicated." He reached for the television remote. "I don't understand all those statistics the announcer keeps talking about."

"Give it a little more time. You'll get the hang of it." I grabbed the remote from his hand before he could turn to his favorite cops and robbers program.

"I'm tired of it," he said. "Let's watch something else."

I loved being able to show off by answering Richard's baseball questions but maybe I'd been a little too smug. I thought we'd finally found something we could enjoy together, but my enthusiasm overwhelmed him along with his lack of knowledge of the sport. While I dusted off what I remembered from childhood, Richard grappled with whether or not he wanted to learn it too. Each night I turned on the game. And each night Richard tried to turn on something else.

"The Rays are only a half game out of first place today," I announced while reading the paper one morning over my cup of coffee.

"That's nice," Richard grumbled.

"How about we go to Tampa and see a game for your birthday?" I raised the question to see if he would bite. Richard's June birthday was only a few weeks away. Tropicana Field was a two-hour drive from home.

His eyes lit up. "Will you buy me a program?" he asked. "I want to learn more about how this game works. That'll be in the program, won't it?"

"Of course."

"Let's do it." We gave each other a high five.

"Happy Birthday. I'll make the reservations." I spent hours planning our perfect baseball adventure. First I picked seats behind the Tampa dugout. After a lengthy deliberation, I selected a hotel close to the beach with a stop for the shuttle bus that would take us to the stadium.

Arriving at the ball field early, we wandered around examining every nook and cranny of the stadium that until now we'd only seen on television. I joined the frenzy in the shirt shop, eventually settling on a dark blue one with the number eighteen for my favorite player, the amazingly versatile Ben Zobrist. Richard got in line at the concession stand and plunked down a twenty-dollar bill for two hot dogs and sodas in souvenir cups. With the game about to start, we made our way to our seats in time to sing the national anthem.

The Boston Red Sox came up to bat. The crowd cheered as the players struck out, one, two, three. The Rays came up and went down the same way. During the bottom of the third, the Rays got a man on first base. The next batter came up. The pitch was thrown and his bat came down, bunting the ball along the third base line. The runner slid into second and the crowd went wild.

"Did you know a sacrifice bunt doesn't count as an at bat if it's solely to advance a base runner?" Richard said.

"Really? Who told you that?" I was curious where he'd gained this unusual tidbit of baseball information.

"It says so right here in the program," he proudly answered. "I bet there's a lot of stuff in here you don't know."

Richard clutched the program to his chest to watch the Rays hit a home run. As soon as there was a break in the action, he returned to studying the lineup. He carefully examined each page, searching for some bit of trivia to share with me. With each swing of the bat, and each turn of the page, I watched the sparkle in his eyes return.

Our Tampa Bay Rays lost but it hardly mattered.

"That was great." Richard commented as we were leaving the stadium. "Can we stay another night and come back again tomorrow?"

Without a minute of hesitation, I turned around and walked back to the ticket window. We were, after all, baseball fans.

~Linda C. Wright

A Sense of Order

Growing old is a bad habit which a busy man has no time to form.
~Andre Maurois

We were encouraged to join the fun. Throwing caution to the wind, we entered our early sixties and the palmed gateway of Monte Vista at Mesa, Arizona in the month of January.

We didn't think we had yet achieved the prime age required for entrance. Friends, albeit a bit older, were enthusiastic in their descriptions of golf, hiking adventure, softball games and elderly camaraderie. We didn't think we were ready for shuffleboard, yet we headed out after Christmas.

The roads from Minnesota to Arizona are busy at the start of each new year, as snowbirds find their way down from Iowa to Kansas and on into New Mexico. At nearly eighty miles per hour, one reaches the Arizona border in two long days. As first-time travelers to the land of enchantment, we were filled with anticipation as we hurtled down the highway.

For the first time, my wife and I had left our home of thirty years, situated on a frozen lake covered with ice houses and fishermen, to venture off for several weeks of lemon trees, blue skies and thirty-six-hour-a-day activity. What was to become of our house and family and lifestyle of frozen days and warm hearts? How could kids and grand-kids survive without a daily dose of parental guidance? Would there be anyone at the desert end who knew or cared about our arrival or about our impending days of lonely life in a tin-covered camper?

Upon arrival on New Year's Day, we were met at the gate by a gracious guard who called security via a handheld radio to escort us to our home site. We were pleased to have such personal attention and were overwhelmed by the beauty and order of the 1500-resident community. Household keys and engraved name tags were there for us on the dining room table, along with instructions on procedures and a packet of activities that would get us started on the adult schedule of frenzied relaxation. We were soon engaged in classes and golf and exercise and daily bike rides to visit new friends and locations. Afternoon social hours and evening concerts entertained us. Saturday night cards in the Social Center with a dozen semi-permanent residents brought us into the loop. There was fresh lemon pie at every turn.

We soon began to enjoy the order, safety and security of it all.

The cool pre-sunrise desert mornings — with moon and stars and quiet — and anticipation of another seventy-degree day made rising early easy. At 5:30 one morning, half an hour late for me, I sat on the small patio. My solitude was interrupted by the occasional thump of a newspaper being thrown toward residences subscribing to the *East Valley Beacon*.

On Sundays, the thump was louder, as the contents of the paper were heavier. Today, as I sat on the patio, the sound was quieter, yet similar. But something was missing. There was no car. The quiet thumps moved closer to our home. As I looked out, I spotted an elderly gentleman in Bermuda shorts walking toward the neighboring house. He bent down, picked up the paper under the footlight and carried it a few feet away from the address sign at each residence. He walked to the driveway, took a step toward the house and cast the paper ten feet or so up toward the home's entry. He walked on to the next residence with a paper in front and repeated the maneuver. He repeated the procedure for each of the houses he came to until he reached the corner and turned — thus the thump!

Talk about a sense of order. Wow! This was the quintessential move of the day toward order. Of course, there were no cigarette butts on the street. Even I had taken to sweeping the street in front of the house as I saw neighbors doing—and as I had seen being done in the small villages of Germany on Saturday mornings when I visited there. This was clean!

But to have your paper moved into a more exact space was beyond Germanic. It may have been at the least manic—or possibly a compulsive disorder. Was it the resurrection of the paper-thrower's early morning paper route of youth? Was it a sense of order endemic to his heritage on the farm—or an external expression of his accounting background and zeal for alignment? What was the driving force?

We adapted slowly to the desert chill at sunrise and sunset, to the continuous warmth of people and to sunshine throughout the day. The exceptional cleanliness and safety of the Monte Vista environment and our new, comfortable Adoba home made it "so nice to come home to." Security was present, the staff was helpful and friendly, and everything was clean and cared for throughout the days. Although missing the wind-chill factor of home, we began to thrive.

We would start our days with a ride on our lemon-colored bikes to the post office or the fitness club, to a game of pool at 6:00 a.m. or an aerobics class at 7:15 or a pancake breakfast at 7:30. From that point on, our days were filled with silversmith class, writing a life history, yoga, seminars, "Lunch with Luigi," square dancing, pool and spa, happy hour and social events that abounded. We hadn't even begun to touch the full-time schedules of tennis and softball and shuffleboard and pickle ball.

On Sunday, we dressed up, walked to church for a great ecumenical service, and met more of our neighbors for a cup of coffee. Evening entertainment was provided throughout the week, with a choice of cards or theatre, steak fry or community dinner. On occasion, we got into our ever-so-clean car, with no trace of road salt, to visit the mountains, stub a toe on a desert rock, wander the open-air market or enjoy a beer and burger at Tortilla Flats.

Golf courses have felt our wrath, as we sent missiles off to the left and to the right. Apache Sun, Sunland Springs and Painted Mountain all felt the shock of our clubs gouging new channels in their greenery. The best drive I hit went over 200 yards and abruptly hooked to the left to implant a cactus with a new, white growth. Newfound friends were kind with their comments on the golf course.

Kids and grandkids will just have to survive. My partner in life wants to extend for another month.

Standing under the lemon tree and viewing the blue sky on this seventy-two-degree day, I think, "There must be a reason to return to Minnesota, isn't there?"

~Kent O. Stever, Ph. D.

Contentment

Life begins at retirement.
~Author Unknown

There were two lounge chairs nestled under the trees in our backyard that had been gently beckoning me for some time. I was always too busy to lie back and relax on the soft blue cushions and listen to the quiet. The only sound there is the chirping of the little brown birds that nest in our trees. Finally, though, I have retired and I have that precious commodity—time. Why do they call it retirement? Why not replenishment, enjoyment, or fulfillment, or how about contentment?

What a joy to finally sit in one of the lounge chairs and play a game of *Scrabble* with my husband on a weekday afternoon! Or to read a book with our dog snoozing on the lawn a few feet away! What a joy to check the paper for the timing of the tides and to drive over to Dog Beach during low tide! My husband and Molly and I walk up and down the shore, soaking in the beauty, and enjoying the happy faces of the owners and their dogs.

How delightful to pick up our little granddaughter at the end of her day in kindergarten and walk her home to our house. We get to listen to her tell us about her day and explain the papers in her folder. Then we go outside and ride bikes together.

It is such a pleasure to have time to write stories and memoirs that have been simmering in my soul for years. What a challenge to peruse the current issue of *The Writer's Market* for possible publishers for my work. What a pleasure to get ideas from my writing group!

After years of walking wistfully past the piano in our living room, I finally have the time to practice and at long last I can play John Lennon's "Imagine" fairly well. After some lessons, I can occasionally hit a golf ball in a straight path down the fairway. My husband is particularly proud of my prowess on the green, and I've actually heard him bragging about the putts I've sunk!

We work very hard throughout our lives to fulfill our responsibilities and to achieve our goals. Now I wake up in the morning and I can do the things I have always dreamed of doing and have always had to postpone. I am so grateful to at last be able to spend as much time as I want with those I love. This time is even more fulfilling and rewarding than I ever imagined. Yes, I think instead of retirement, it should be called contentment.

~Virginia Redman

The Cell Phone

For a list of all the ways technology has failed to improve the quality of life, please press three.
~Alice Kahn

"I'm mad as hell, and I won't take this anymore!" That line came from an old movie called *Network*. And that's what I mumbled yesterday as I followed a woman driving her car and weaving all over the road. She was talking on her cell phone!

Was she calling her mother? "I'm headed to the grocery store and wanted to see if you need anything."

Next, I noticed a kid walking along the road with a gizmo stuck to his ear. What important call was he making?

I've had it up to here with those cell phones. They are everywhere!

So now, here I am, retired and sitting in my recliner chair. Nearby, sits my remote controls—one each for the VCR, CD player and the DVD. And next to them, is my cell phone. Yes, that's what I said—my cell phone! My daughter purchased it for me. She said that I might need it in case I get a flat tire at two in the morning. I'm never on the road at two in the morning!

So far today, I've received three phone calls. The first was at morning mass. The phone chimed "The Hills Are Alive with the Sound of Music." Father Peter gave me a dirty look. Thank God the lady next to me knew how to silence it. "You are supposed to turn it off before mass starts," she whispered.

"Sorry. Only my daughter knows the number and she's out of town."

The second call came as I was driving to the mall. Not a good idea to answer it while driving, so I pulled over. This time, it was a girl trying to find Jason.

"Wrong number," I snapped.

At the mall, it seemed like everyone was talking on their cell phones—people walking around, shopping, sitting on benches or eating in the food court.

Suddenly, my phone rang. Might be my stockbroker or the President. I answered the dang thing.

"Hey man, is Jason there?"

"Yeah, this is Jason. Can't talk now," I said, as I punched the off button.

I purchased an ice cream cone and sat down on a bench to eat it. Talking on a cell phone is starting to be fun. Let's see—who can I call?

Suddenly, a woman slipped and fell in front of me.

"Help," she cried. "I think I broke my leg."

Without hesitation, I pulled out my phone and dialed 911.

"I'm at Countryside Mall—at the food court. A lady just fell. We need assistance immediately."

As I finished my call, another lady rushed up, identified herself as a nurse and went to aid the injured woman.

"I called 911 on my cell phone. The ambulance is on the way."

"Thank you," the nurse responded. "I'll take it from here."

Within a short time, the paramedics arrived, put the injured lady on a gurney and started to wheel her away. The nurse pointed toward me. "That gentleman called 911 on his cell phone."

I smiled at the group. "I never go anywhere without my cell phone."

~Raymond P. Weaver

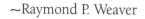

Adventures in Retirement

Retirement has been a discovery of beauty for me. I never had the time
before to notice the beauty of my grandkids, my wife, the tree outside my
very own front door. And, the beauty of time itself.
~Hartman Jule

My husband Pat and I retired the same day six years ago, celebrating with our family and several of our good friends. We have never looked back.

Yes, we did hear good-intentioned comments such as, "Now that you're retired, you should think about a part-time job or you'll be totally bored." We just smiled. That wasn't the route we intended to take. After all, we had just spent a combination of seventy-eight years working full time and raising a family of four girls. A part-time job was certainly not on our agenda. It was our time now. No more waking up every weekday, jumping to a fast-paced schedule, spending the best hours of the day at a desk or in a factory, with the sun shining outside while we were stuck inside.

One of our more pleasant outings is taking a car trip, maybe just for one or two days at a time, sometimes with no destination in mind. Ending up in hamlets we didn't even know existed was like a new adventure. Each village was unique and charming in its own way. Antique stores, century-old mills transformed into bookstores, or maybe even a picturesque waterfall not mentioned in any travel brochure. Mom and Pop restaurants with that good old home cooking and baking are always irresistible.

My camera and notebook are my companions whenever Pat and I decide to take off. A note of caution: check the area before taking a shot. I had a close call with a Rottweiler when I infringed on his territory. Apparently he didn't like my bright red jacket. On one occasion I had the misfortune of slipping into a swamp, due to looking up and walking simultaneously. At the last second I heard Pat shout "look out," with, I think, a hint of laughter. Next trip, I made sure I brought a change of clothes, just in case.

Traveling the country roads has led us to entrances for hiking and cycling trails, which we take advantage of regularly. Cycling on old, well-maintained rail beds provides a scenic experience you can't get when driving. The many rivers, remnants of pioneer homes, and historical iron bridges are just a few sights that are awesome. Pack a cheese and lettuce sandwich and a thermos of whatever you like and you're on your way for the day.

Winter arrives and off we go with cross-country skis to beautiful places you can only see on ski trails. Traveling deep into the forest on groomed trails, trees thickly laden with a new snowfall, has to be the best. Also, outdoor skating is, I believe, the most enjoyable way to skate, so we make sure the skates are in the car in case we spy a frozen pond on one of our journeys. Our next venture is to try snowshoeing so we don't have to wait for just the right temperature for skiing. That should lead us into some interesting predicaments.

When at home, we busy ourselves with our flower and vegetable gardens, each year experimenting with different varieties. This year we planted everything that rabbits seemed to relish. Where did they come from anyway? I hadn't seen a rabbit for many years. At harvest time, we ended up with a handful of tomatoes and a family of six rabbits. Our project for this fall will be erecting a fence around the area to keep the fluffy bunnies out.

The other day, while doing some de-cluttering, I came upon several old piano lesson and theory books that the girls had used when taking, as they say, "the dreaded piano lessons." About fifteen years ago I had taken basic lessons, but due to work, I never found the time to practice and so it fell by the wayside, as so many interests did.

At my own pace, I started brushing up my piano skills. It's so delightful to know that you don't have a deadline by which to learn a song.

Pat, on the other hand, is the inventor in the family. Whenever he goes to the shed I know something is going to be rigged up, either a streamlined way of obtaining rainwater and using it for the garden or perhaps a new method of composting. It's always been quite interesting, and ninety-nine percent of the time it really works.

Cold winter nights or dreary dismal gray days are just as interesting as bright sunny warm times. Our library has grown quite extensively over the past years from attending book fairs and garage sales. There's nothing better than sitting by the evening fire, surrounded by books and having a good read.

There has never been a day when I wish I wasn't retired. The freedom of no time restraints is invaluable. Also, if we wanted more excitement, all we would have to do is check on our six grandchildren and their predicaments. They are so creative at getting into the most unbelievable situations. Emergency babysitting and school events keep us close.

What can I say? Retirement has been a complete joy. I highly recommend it.

~Christiana Flanigan

Rock, Roll
and Retirement

An inordinate passion for pleasure is the secret of remaining young.
~Oscar Wilde

I hadn't planned on retiring early, but not a whit of regret has crossed my mind in the past eight years. The loyal, dependable, likable worker shed her duty suit and flew the coop to embrace the world and its endless adventures.

First, since it was October, a Welcome Fall/Retirement Party was in order. Why not hire my favorite band to send me on my way? The Swizzle Sisters band (a seven-piece band including three fabulous female vocalists) was the perfect topper to a terrific party. It was wonderful to have family, friends and coworkers of twenty-three years share such a special time.

The first day of retirement was like a strange new birth, a newfound freedom. Time was mine. I took my gift money and bought a digital camera, which has been at my side ever since. My photos grace walls and gift cards, are on display in a local hospital gift shop, and now crown the cover of a new poetry book.

The need to get out and exercise sent me to yoga classes and I began tap dancing. Both of these help stave off the onset of dementia, falls, depression and a myriad of other maladies, not to mention increasing my agility and balance.

I took up writing again too. I'd done a lot as a child and longed for the day I could just sit down and write to my heart's content. Signing up for poetry and creative nonfiction writing classes soon had me back where I wanted to be. I've been blessed to have publications in three books, several magazines, newspapers and newsletters.

Now that I had more time on my hands, I decided to finish up a tattoo tribute to my family and Scottish/Irish heritage. Once I had the last of the twelve tattoos in place (I started this in 1972 at age twenty-seven, when women with tats were not considered nice), I had photos taken, wrote an article about why a woman my age would choose body art and surprised our three children this Christmas with a photo collage of mom's tats.

Singing has always been a love of mine. Listening to my mother and her four sisters sing together around the house and at family gatherings began my lifelong love of four-part harmony. I sang with the Sweet Adelines for about five years when our children were young but got sidetracked with other activities. Several years ago I learned of a Doo Wop group in town and found my old tenor voice again, belting out the golden oldies.

These are all things I do regularly to this day, but another love I share with my husband of forty-four years is travel. We are unconventional travelers; by that I mean, if we can go by raft instead of boat, we will. If we can go by rattletrap bus instead of an air-conditioned van, we will. If we can stay in a tent or hut in the Amazon, we'd rather do that than stay in a five-star resort; we've done all that and more!

Growing up, I was about as far from a daredevil as a person can get, but now I'm up for anything. Among my adventures: parasailing in Bonaire (in the Dutch Antilles), racing through the mangroves in Belize, zip lining through the forest canopy in Costa Rica and horseback riding through its rich, tropical forests of monkeys, snakes, exotic birds and butterflies. Snorkeling through the Eastern Caribbean, most of the Hawaiian Islands and parts of Mexico and Honduras opened up a whole new underwater world of mystery and beauty for me. Swimming with nurse sharks and manta rays was like meeting new underwater friends.

Vacations in Guatemala, Mexico and Peru have provided us with the unique experiences of being with and sharing cultures with some of the world's most beautiful people. Especially rewarding was time spent at a research lodge in the Amazon. Hiking though the jungle at night in snake boots, looking for poisonous frogs, turning off our flashlights to listen to the night noises and see the night sky constellations upside down (since we were below the equator) was thrilling. Night canoe rides looking for caymans, gazing excitedly into their eyes glowing in the distance were awesome. Our guide even brought a small one aboard, held it in front of anyone who wanted a photo taken with it. Did I? You bet I did!

Back home in California I experienced snow falling for the first time in my life. In Sequoia, I caught that first snowflake on my tongue and made my first snow angel. Snowshoeing to a frozen waterfall was like time standing still.

White water rafting on the American River has been a yearly outing that sends shivers of fun up and down my spine. Along the river are huge outcroppings of rocks adventurers can climb and jump off into the river. Did I? Well, why not! I've even had to encourage youngsters to look out over the beautiful river and just jump. Why miss out on the fun?

Closer to home, last spring I decided to cross another wish off my bucket list. I headed to Lompoc Airport and suited up, was strapped to a gorgeous British gent with our parachute, flew to 13,000 feet and jumped out of a tiny airplane. I've never felt closer to God in my life. The exhilaration was like nothing else. I'd do it again in an instant.

Retirement is not only going and doing, but staying home and doing as well. I love gardening, photography, scrapbooking and reading, among other hobbies.

I'm proud to be the block coordinator of our Neighborhood Watch Program. I have five fabulous captains to assist me in keeping the neighborhood safe. It's a great way to get to know all the neighbors and form a united community.

I volunteer as a conductor for the Pacific Southwest Railroad

Museum in Goleta, California and especially enjoy seeing the excitement in the eyes of children taking their first train ride.

Retirement has provided the opportunity to see and do things I never thought possible. You just have to get out there and make things happen. Each day is a brand new chance at a miracle. You can make them happen, I know!

The greatest joy of retirement and closest to my heart is the time I can now spend with our children and grandchildren. Nothing is more precious than family and friends. We are lucky to have all our family here in California, so visits are frequent and dear.

I cringe when I overhear someone say, "What will I do in retirement?" What won't I do in retirement is what I say!

~Ann Michener Winter

We Late Bloomers Are Right on Time

Only Robinson Crusoe had everything done by Friday.
~Author Unknown

I helped my husband heft four trays of perennials we had just bought at the garden center. As we put them on top of newspapers lining the back seat of our car, I noticed the look on his face. It was a giddy excitement at the prospect of creating his garden. He's had the same goal for more than thirty years. During the entire spring, summer and fall, there should always be flowers in bloom. That is his definition of the perfect perennial garden. "Now that I'm retired," he said, "I am definitely going to make this happen."

Of course, he has yet to achieve his ideal display. But I have recently learned something. He has been growing a perfect garden all along, flowers or not. He just doesn't know it.

"So what if the lilies leaf out and there are no flowers for a few weeks until the hydrangeas bloom?" I said.

He carefully arranged the flats on the back seat so that no tender plant would be crushed. "That is not what a perennial garden is," he said. "In a perfect garden, there is always successive color."

I thought about this goal of his. How we all bend to pressure to have everything bloom and happen in our lives at the "right" time.

So often I have felt that I wasn't in sync with what was

expected—with the norm—with what everybody else was doing at the age when they were supposed to be doing it.

I had such anxiety by age twenty-four, when I hadn't figured out what I wanted to do with my life, and at twenty-five when I didn't have a husband, and at twenty-six when I didn't have a child.

By the time I was thirty-five, my well-meaning friends warned me. "You won't have the energy to play with your kids if you wait much longer." But I wasn't ready to have a child. Then demons haunted me with images of nursery school where I'd be sitting next to twenty-five-year-old moms. This didn't happen but even if it did, it wouldn't have mattered. That's what I needed to realize.

And so, one recent afternoon I was sitting on the bed reading, for the third time, a dear friend's invitation to a cookout on the beach. I've always kept secret the fact that I am afraid of water and therefore can't swim. And it was certainly, in my mind, too late in the game for me to do anything about this problem.

With resignation, I put the invitation in my top bureau drawer. I could hear my diligent husband out back working in the garden. He was trying some new fertilizer in his relentless pursuit to have the lilacs, the roses, the phlox and the rhododendrons bloom at the right time in the right place. It was then I was struck with a life-altering question. "Whose schedule are we keeping to?"

Often what turns our lives around happens in a single moment. I thought of my sixty-seven-year-old friend who decided she wasn't past her prime, whenever that is, and went to college. And another pal who bought a piano so that she could learn to play. And others who took up oil painting, horseback riding or yoga at the age that was right for them.

It was at this magical instant on that sunny afternoon that I took the invitation back out of the drawer and internally declared, "The schedule we choose should be our own."

Before I could talk myself out of it, I found my old bathing suit. With my husband along for support, I drove to the beach. Tentatively, I waded in the warm waters and in slow increments, went up to my waist. And bit by bit, over the course of the afternoon, I eventually reached the stage where I could propel myself along in a crazily splashing dog paddle. It was one of the best days of my life. It wasn't the task of swimming that was so important. It was what it symbolized.

As it often happens, the positive results built upon themselves. I made other plans that I had always thought were too late and untimely. I decided to set it right with an estranged relative when, at this stage of our lives, I had figured it could never happen. I found three new meaningful friendships that I had assumed you could only have with women you've known for years. All of these things happened according to my schedule, at the right time for me. Our lives and our gardens don't always bloom in neat orderly succession.

Maybe there will come a time when my husband will rejoice in the world of our backyard. The garden is his creation, with buds and leaves and blossoms growing at their own pace, glorious in their individuality. No two gardens are alike. No two lives need to be.

Timing isn't everything. When all is said and done, it won't matter if we did things according to popular timetables. It will only matter that we tried. We late bloomers have our timing just right.

~Saralee Perel

I Have Become
That Woman

The other day a man asked me what I thought was the best time of life.
"Why," I answered without a thought, "now."
~David Grayson

I have become that woman
who smiles at children and they smile back.
I smile again and make funny faces.
I accept that I remind them of their grandmothers.

I have become that woman
who jiggles along with too-big jewelry
and too many colors on her shirt
and who wears flip-flops into October because it still feels right.
And it is all too much for some friends who used to know me.

I have become that woman who talks to strangers
at the checkout register, and the drive-thru and the car wash.
And they don't smile because I'm a crazy woman;
they laugh out loud because I am authentic
and we connect and laugh together.

I have become that woman

who cares more about fewer things,
who disobeys the clock—and the calendar—
who sees miracles and not coincidence.

I have become that woman
who is full of gratitude and mischief
and who uses words like spectacular and fabulous every day
because they are the perfect choice.
She is happy and I like her.

It took a long time for her to get here
and I didn't even know I was missing her.

I thought my mother had taught me all the secrets of retirement
—until now.

~Mitchell Kyd

A Princess Hostage

Everyone has the impulse to be elite.
~Alfre Woodard

I don't ever want to take another Princess Cruise. I really don't. I've been on every one of their ships at least twice. I sailed on the Pacific Princess in 1976 before it was the Love Boat, and now it's soliciting me for a world cruise in 2011... same old name but a new ship. I'm reminded of that little old lady who said, "I sailed around the world last year. This year I want to sail someplace different."

But here's the point. I'm a member of the Captain's Circle. An Elite Member of the Captain's Circle. Do you know what that means? I've taken a Princess Cruise more than sixteen times. I just got off the Star Princess to the Greek Isles, and I was one of only thirty-four Elite people on board who got to eat lunch with the Captain and have my picture taken with him. Do you know how meaningful that is in today's impersonal cruise format? Did you know that captains stopped shaking hands with passengers when norovirus became a health threat? But we Elite Members of the Captain's Circle on Princess are immune to any communicable diseases, so we get to shake hands with the Captain and have our picture taken at the same time.

And we get an invitation that reads, "I look forward to the pleasure of your company at the Princess Grapevine Wine Tasting," in italics. We only have to bring our Elite Key Card to ensure our complimentary place. That means there will only be thirty-three others who don't have to mix with the hoi polloi on board while tasting God knows how many wines.

But here's another reason I have to go back on a Princess ship. I get free laundry and dry cleaning. Do you know how those bills can add up if you change your underwear three times a day? It's such a benefit I even throw in the bedspread!

And listen to this... as if I didn't come on a cruise to get off the ship and visit all of the magical destinations... I can spend 250 free minutes on the Internet just like I'd do if I'd been staying at home. That way Aunt Myrtle will never even know I'm gone.

And do you think I have to wait in line to get off the ship? No! I'm so Elite I can beat all of the 2,599 passengers to those carpet salesmen waiting for us in Kuşadasi who'll gladly trade two camels for one of my blond daughters.

Then there are those eight complimentary mini-bottles of Courvoisier, vodka, gin and Canadian Club in my mini-bar to say nothing of Sprite, Coca-Cola and bottled water to keep me afloat for the next ten days. How could I pass that up?

So even though I yearn to take a Holland America cruise some-where... anywhere... could they offer me such enticements?

Wait a minute! I just read Holland America offers all of this and shoe polishing as well?

Does that mean they'll polish my wooden shoes?

~Phyllis W. Zeno

"I considered trying another cruise line,
but the elite status perks I've earned with this one
are hard to pass up. They even pick me up
at home. In the ship."

Having a Senior Moment

Men do not quit playing because they grow old;
they grow old because they quit playing.
~Oliver Wendell Holmes

Lately, I've been wondering what retirement will be like. My days now are so full of things like going to writer's lunches, writer's seminars, writer's conferences and, of course, e-mailing other writers, complaining about how there's never enough time to write — I can't imagine the emptiness without all that.

My concerns about retirement began when my sister-in-law, Sally, who had just retired, came for a visit and shared some of the projects she was involved in.

"I've started collecting fruit peels," she told me. "I have three jars full already."

Quickly, I closed the windows so the neighbors wouldn't hear. Then I explained to her that statements like that could earn her a one-way trip to a country estate where the music is soft and the walls are quilted.

"You don't understand," she continued enthusiastically. "See, after I have enough fruit peels, I'm going to turn them into candy and send them out as gifts."

"Right..." I said. I had an urge to put all the sharp knives on the upper shelves. Instead I just handed her an orange to keep her amused until my brother-in-law, who's also recently retired, came back.

"Where did Bob go anyway?" I asked.

"To get another book on genealogy. He wants to be the first person to trace his family roots back to the Neanderthals. Isn't that exciting?"

I thought about the word exciting. If I looked it up in my *Funk & Wagnalls*, would it say: "The art of collecting fruit skins for fun and profit?"

I figured this was something I should talk to my wife about, so I waited until Bob and Sally had gone to bed, turned off the evening news, poured us each our nightly drink, and made up a plate of anti-aging supplements. "Is tonight the night we take gingko biloba?" I asked.

"I can't remember," she said. "Is that a Rolling Stones T-shirt?"

"Yup. Found it in the bottom of the closet. I think it shrunk a little."

"Yeah, about three decades worth. What's this all about?"

"I think we should start preparing for an activity-filled retirement. You know, take rock climbing lessons, things like that."

"Rock climbing? You don't even like to stand on a chair to replace a light bulb. Now you want to scale cliffs?"

"Okay, maybe not rock climbing. How about competitive sailing? Or scuba diving? We could dive with the manatees and swim with the sharks."

She tossed back a couple of vitamin E tablets. "I think you should stop watching the Discovery Channel."

"I'm serious. I don't want to end up accumulating cats or becoming vice president of a bonsai pruning club. I want to live life to the fullest. Explore exciting new horizons. Throw caution to the wind. Are you going to finish your herbal tea?"

"No, you go ahead," she said.

I gulped it down, belched, and then ran my forearm across my lips in a manly fashion. This was a situation that called for a proactive approach. I slammed down the teacup, turned my International

Wine Festival cap around so the visor was in the back, and hiked up my relaxed fit, extra-room-in-the-seat jeans.

"Where ya going?" my wife asked.

I managed to put on a hardened look. "To search the Internet until I find a fitting retirement lifestyle," I said. "Don't wait up."

The next morning I was up early studying some of the websites I had bookmarked the night before, featuring rogue horse round-ups, wilderness survival schools, and parachuting lessons, and I had just opened one on river rafting when I heard a voice behind me.

"That's a good one," said Sally. "Especially in the spring when the rapids are really churning."

"And dangerous," said Bob. "We tipped a few times."

I turned around in surprise. "You guys have done this?"

"Sure, and next month we're going whitewater kayaking."

"But what about that fruit peel thing?"

"We like doing stuff like that, too," said Sally. "Matter of fact, today we're on our way to a quilt show. Just wanted to say goodbye."

Later that morning I was just finishing a bowl of warm Mueslix when my friend Rich called.

"Golf?" he asked.

I thought about my new commitment to an active retirement lifestyle, then I said: "Okay. But, today—no carts."

I'm feeling better already.

~Ernie Witham

Sunday	Monday	Tuesday	Wednesday	Thursday	Friday	Saturday
		1 brunch at Smiths	2 Work 9-1	3 babysit Jessica	4 work 9-1	5 Pack
6 Pier 3 at 4 sharp	7 CRUISE!!	8	9	10	11	12
13	14 work 9-1	15 Jessica ☺	16 Work 9-1	17 Dog Shelter	18 work 9-1	19 Golf with Gene
20	21 Work 9-1	22 Dr. Miller - 10:30	23 work 9-1	24 dog shelter	25 Work 9-1	26 Dinner Party 7:00
27 DC trip 27th-29th	28	29	30 Work 9-1	31 Dog Shelter		

Chapter
7

Inspiration
for the
Young
at
Heart

New Passions

No Second Fiddle

The age of a woman doesn't mean a thing.
The best tunes are played on the oldest fiddles.
~Ralph Waldo Emerson

"Did I interrupt your dinner?" my friend Naomi asked when I answered the phone.

"No, I was just practicing my violin," I said.

Naomi was amazed that at eighty years of age I was learning to play. She thought I was heroic.

"There's an old violin in my garage," she said. "Oh, never mind."

That's weird, I thought, but let it pass.

The following week Naomi picked me up on the way to a friend's house for lunch. When we arrived, she opened the trunk and pulled out a gorgeous silver box filled with candy, and to my amazement, a very battered, somewhat dirty, old violin case.

"This is for you," she said, pushing the violin case toward me. "I don't know where it came from; it's been collecting dust in my garage for years."

We entered our friend Cynthia's immaculate home and Naomi looked for a place to put the disreputable violin case. She finally set it on a table outside on the patio.

The latches were rusty and hard to open, but we persevered. Inside was a very old, neglected violin surrounded by bright red velvet. Where there should have been a violin bow there was an incongruous red satin ribbon. Out of four requisite strings, three were slack and the fourth, along with its peg, was missing. The wood was dry and dull. What would it sound like? A cigar box? A Stradivarius? It would need a lot of work before I would know.

Once home, I got to work. The covering on the handle of the case was peeling off, and although Naomi had removed the dust, it was sheathed in a film of dirt. The case was strong and cleaned up very well. The violin's dried wood sucked up the Fiddlebrite oil, revealing beautiful amber areas shading into dark brown. It looked like a pretty good violin by the time I finished, although it didn't have modern fine tuners and it was very difficult to turn the pegs since they hadn't been turned for a long, long time. It still needed new strings and a peg. I tried to string it up with my extra set of strings, but with two pegs stuck and one peg missing, it seemed hopeless. Remarkably I was able to install the "G" string. When plucked, it resonated throughout the entire violin, my heart reverberating right along with it.

I called my teacher, Jefferson, who also happens to be a whiz at fixing violins. When Jefferson arrived at my home we were both excited about the potential of this violin. Carefully he held it in his lap and inserted the fine tuners, but none of the pegs he brought fit. In desperation I pulled out the junky violin my grandkids played with and, lo and behold, one of the pegs fit. He gently held the violin between his knees and began stringing it. When everything was in place, he started tuning it. We looked at each other in amazement. Its tone was incredible. After much peg turning and adjusting, it was finally tuned. Jefferson started to play part of a Beethoven symphony. I was transported to Carnegie Hall.

We decided I'd take my lesson on the "new" violin, even though it had a very different feel. Sure enough, I had a very hard time with the "D" string. I couldn't position the bow properly and produced scratchy off-key sounds.

"This bridge is an old style," Jefferson said. "Let me see if I have my sander in the car. I'll sand it down to be more like what you are used to."

What a difference! I played the rest of the lesson and was delighted with the results.

When Jefferson left, I forgot it was lunchtime, and just started playing music — any music. I played everything I could get my hands on: my husband's songbooks, each with 100 popular songs from different time periods, music that had once belonged to Cynthia's daughter and husband. The sound of the violin was intoxicating. Its deep tones were lush and sensuous, its high tones sweet and flute-like. Feeling a little light-headed, I finally had to stop for lunch, but immediately picked up the violin again.

When my husband came home from his volunteer job I grabbed his arm and dragged him into the living room.

"Sit down and listen to this," I said, wanting him to hear the wonderful sound. We compared it to my other violin, and there was no comparison. The house, the garden, nothing got done — I just kept playing all afternoon and into the evening.

The "new" one was exquisite and the "old" violin was rapidly playing second fiddle to the "new" one. What a conundrum! My "old" violin was my dad's, the inspiration for starting lessons and my connection to him, yet the "new" violin, with its mysterious background, was the one that called to me. Funny, Naomi thinks I'm heroic, but it isn't bravery that stirs me to play; it's the desire to continue to make music. When my once lovely soprano voice became as rusty as the latches on the violin case, no one wanted to hear me sing anymore and a part of me seemed to die. Now, at eighty I'm finding a new voice through a reinvigorated violin.

Violins resonate more beautifully when played regularly because it opens up their voice. I guess it's not such a conundrum after all, I'll play them both and our voices will all sing again.

~Joy Feldman

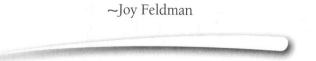

Surfing into Retirement

Retire from work, but not from life.
~M.K. Soni

I've got it bad, seven days a week bad, a dozen boards in the garage bad. To put it another way, I love surfing. I would rather get up at 5 a.m. on a Saturday to ride atop a several-ton chunk of liquid energy than sleep in. I'd like to surf every day, but I never seem to have enough time. My job keeps me going from dawn to dusk. When I arrive home after work, I'm usually tired, too exhausted to even zip up a wet suit.

That's about to change, though. I'll be retiring soon, and I plan to spend my golden years on the waves.

The surfing fever swept over me just last year, when I crouched thigh-deep in broken whitewater and paddled out toward my first wave. The moment I stood up on my board, I was hooked. I felt like a climber at altitude getting a hit of bottled oxygen; like a runner crossing the finish line at the Boston Marathon. That's how much I enjoyed it.

Much of the blame, I suppose, can be placed on the area in which I live. Northern California is one of the most scenic places in the world. It has a beautiful shoreline and some mighty big waves. The kind of waves that have the strength to rip your board out from under you, toss you around like a jellyfish, and slam-dunk you back into the surf much in the same manner that Dorothy's house was slam-dunked onto the Wicked Witch of the East.

Why would a soon-to-be retired sixty-year-old want to risk life and limb in such dangerous waters? Actually, I can't think of a better thing to do.

There's a lot to like about surfing, regardless of your age. First off, you don't have to be King Farouk to afford it. Once you buy a board and a wetsuit, there are no further expenses. The waves are free. And so is the scenery.

Surfing is loads of fun, too. It doesn't matter where you ride or what time of the day you do so. When you're on the water, you're having a blast. Sometimes there are other surfers around, but most of the time you're completely alone.

That's the best part—the solitude. Surfing is a great way to learn the importance of spending time alone. It's a way to find inner peace, a lightness of spirit. It's a way of holding, for a short time, the small personal Holy Grail that each of us seeks in our daily lives.

Like most "elderly" surfers I ride a long board. Short boards are light, thin, and more maneuverable. On a long board you make the board move by running to the back or front, causing it to accelerate or decelerate. Because of the width and weight, a long board doesn't go as fast as a short board does. But waves can be caught quicker and with more fluid efficiency. And that means more waves can be ridden.

I guess you could say surfing has become a religious experience for me. But not one that's easy to describe. It's like a church you walk by a hundred times. It never registers on your emotional seismograph until the day you step inside and have a look around. It's the same with this sport. You have to climb on a board and paddle out into the ocean to experience it for yourself.

So if you're ever up this way, stop by at the beach and squint out over the water. You'll probably see me sitting astride my board, waiting for the next wave to break. One more wave, one more in a lifetime of waves for a passionate surfer like me.

~Timothy Martin

Sweet Torture

A teacher affects eternity; he can never tell where his influence stops.
~Henry Brooks Adams

The bell rang and kids clamored for their classrooms, pushing and shoving their way through the halls. "Walk!" a teacher reminded an overzealous fourth grader as he rounded the corner and plowed into a kindergartener.

It was nearing the end of the school year and the students weren't the only ones counting the days until summer vacation. The office staff was more cheerful than usual when I stepped in to add my name to the volunteer list. It was the final session for math and reading tutors, and the last time this school year that I would see the first graders I had worked with since school began last September.

"Hi, Mrs. Lilly," Nathan waved as I made my way toward Mrs. Connelly's class. He had been one of my students the year before and still stopped for a hug whenever he saw me. Although he was a soon-to-be third grader now, it was nice to know he didn't consider himself too big to acknowledge me, even in the company of his friends.

This was the third year that I had shared a few hours each week with someone else's grandchildren. While I educated them on the basic principles of reading, vocabulary and spelling, they taught me the value of time spent nurturing a fertile soul rather than in my garden or on my golf handicap. Teaching a child to read with emotion and inflection is gratifying, but investing in their search for significance is extraordinarily rewarding.

"Good morning, Emily," I said to my first student as we left the classroom and made our way to the conference room, where we would spend the next twenty minutes together. She slipped her tiny hand into mine and smiled in a way that reminded me of my granddaughter who lives nearly 3,000 miles away. It may not be possible for me to see my own grandkids weekly, but lavishing an overabundance of love on Emily and the others gives me something to look forward to every Thursday morning.

Allen was my last student of the day. He was the most reserved of the five, but a gentle spirit whose determination to overcome a mild stutter earned him the "Super Reader" award. I presented it to him and urged him to read what was inscribed on the ribbon.

"This super reader's award is presented to Allen Barton," he read slowly, then looked at me and smiled. "For out stand ing effort and a chieve ment."

"Great job!" I said, encouraging him after he correctly sounded out the big words.

"For outstanding effort and achievement," he repeated, "in Sterling Heights' reading torturing program."

I burst out laughing. "Torturing program? Honey," I said, pausing to wipe my eyes, "it's tutoring program, not torturing program!" Allen blushed, then giggled, obviously quite pleased with himself.

School is out now and summer's arrived. I am sure that Emily, Allen and the other children I have had the privilege of loving this past year will tuck the memory of our tutoring sessions back into some corner of their long-forgotten yesterdays. As for me, I am looking forward to this fall when I'll subject my new victims to the stretching of minds and twisting of imaginations. I never realized that inflicting torture could be so sweet.

~Dawn Lilly

I'm Following Floyd

Those were good nights.
~Roger Waters

I don't know what most folks intend to do when they retire, but I'm going to sell everything I own, jump in my pickup, and follow House of Floyd around from concert to concert.

I'll become a "Floyd Head."

House of Floyd is a Pink Floyd tribute band from northern California. I've been a big fan ever since I saw them perform in Eureka on my sixtieth birthday.

I wasn't the only old-timer in the audience that night. There were lots of other flower-children-gone-to-seed present for the concert, including a number of bald men with beer bellies and love beads, and barefoot, gray-haired women in granny dresses who looked like they belonged at a Woodstock reunion.

I wondered if they were all as pleasantly surprised by House of Floyd as I was.

It had been almost four decades since I attended my last rock concert, and a few things had changed. For instance, back when I was a fresh-faced young man in bellbottoms and Birkenstocks, concerts involved drunken long-haired men, and braless women with flowers in their hair holding suspicious-looking hand-rolled cigarettes.

They often involved the police, emergency rooms, and courtrooms, too.

But those in attendance for the House of Floyd concert were light years from those ganja-inspired hippie days. There were no alcohol or drug problems that evening. Nor was there any hanky-panky, since a large portion of the audience was probably on blood thinners and couldn't hanky a panky even if the spirit moved them.

The concert was solely about reliving the music that meant so much to all of us.

Pink Floyd's music moved me more than any other band in the 1960s because they were way before their time. They wrote cool experimental material and played some of the catchiest classic rock I ever heard. Their music was spookily brilliant. In my humble opinion, there have been few groups in rock history who could touch them.

House of Floyd recreated the music of that famous band perfectly. Their songs had a way of making you stay in your seat, despite acid reflux discomfort and/or persistent bladder problems. The band was every bit as good as the original, and with no seizure-inducing ticket prices.

The night I saw them, House of Floyd played to a full house, which consisted of people from age twenty-one to sixty-plus, proving that future generations will probably be into the Pink Floyd experience as much as my generation was. Even my fourteen-year-old son, Tyler, came along for the concert. I expected it to be about as much fun as dental surgery for him, but I was wrong. By the time the show was over he was talking like a pilgrim who had just returned from the Holy Land.

I was pleased to see his appreciation for the greatest band in the history of rock and roll. And so was House of Floyd band member Sheri Showalter.

"It always inspires me to look out and see several generations of families coming to a concert together to enjoy the same musical experience," she said. "When our own children join us on stage, I can't help but smile and feel like this is what music is all about. In this day and age there just don't seem to be enough opportunities for families to come together and enjoy the same musical experience. I love being involved in making that happen."

One thing that separates House of Floyd from other tribute bands is their computer-generated light show, lasers and video screens. They run laptops and video mixes, and have current events clips so they can inject a few of those good old political views, just like the original band did.

They also had some footage of Pink Floyd from throughout the years. It took House of Floyd several hours just to set everything up.

The band played entire albums that evening, like *Animals* and *Dark Side of the Moon*, plus most of the hits from *The Wall*. The coordination of the laser show, vocals, video, fog, guitars, drums, sax, and keyboards were simply astounding. It was a multi-dimensional experience for the entire audience.

As the opening notes of "Comfortably Numb" rang out I was transported back to my late teens, and I began to relive the music all over again.

So anyway, I'm not passing the rock and roll torch down to the younger generation quite yet. Instead, I think I'll use it to light my way to future House of Floyd concerts.

~Timothy Martin

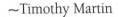

Reaching a Dream

A man is not old until regrets take the place of dreams.
~John Barrymore

Five children, with the oldest fifteen when the youngest was born, kept me on the go for more than three decades. Carpools and doctor appointments, piano lessons and Little League games, Cub Scouting and helping in the classroom. I did them all. And loved it. (Well, maybe I could have done with a little less carpooling!) Early in our marriage, my husband and I decided that I would remain at home with the children. I'm grateful that I had that choice.

Now, with our youngest child having graduated from high school and my husband and myself officially empty nesters, I have time to indulge in a few interests of my own. Writing had long been a dream of mine, most especially writing for Chicken Soup for the Soul. With the publication of its first collection, I had eagerly read the inspiring books.

Could I write a story for Chicken Soup for the Soul? The idea tantalized me, a much-cherished dream that propelled me to take a chance. I wrote a story, submitted it, and waited.

Mine was not an overnight success story. My story was rejected. I tried again. And was rejected again. And again.

I kept writing, kept submitting. When I saw a call for stories about what I had learned from my cat, I knew I had to try once more.

Several months later, I received an acceptance. My story was going to be published.

My pleasure over the sale knew no bounds. I had sold a story to Chicken Soup for the Soul!

I continue writing, submitting to different publications as well as other Chicken Soup for the Soul collections. I receive rejections on a depressingly regular basis, but I persevere. Writing is my passion, my avocation as well as my vocation. To my joy, one of my children also enjoys writing and we encourage each other, sharing successes and rejections.

Writing for Chicken Soup for the Soul has changed my life as I realized the power of reaching for a dream.

~Jane McBride Choate

Dancing Through Life

You don't stop dancing from growing old,
you grow old from stopping to dance.
~Author Unknown

Dancing keeps us happy, healthy, and young at heart. My husband Bill and I began ballroom dancing in our forties, long before we thought about retirement. We envisioned it as a fun activity to do together, welcoming the diversion from demanding work schedules. Soon we were hooked.

We were drawn to the variety of dances and styles, with something available for every mood. We devoted considerable time and energy to learning steps, patterns, and technique, and participated in practice parties and showcases. We had not foreseen the joy we would feel, or the benefits we'd gain as the years passed.

The thrill of dancing is like a writer's pen poised at the blank page, like a runner ready on the mark. Dancers step into their shoes, hearts fluttering and faces glowing with anticipation, as the band strikes up, sending melodies floating through the air. Eager dancers fill the floor, joining their partners to move with the beat. Feet caress the floor, interpreting the music. Spirits rejuvenate. Worries and regrets are forgotten.

After the basic lessons, Bill and I checked out the historic Lake Robbins Ballroom, a charming place nestled in the Iowa countryside near Woodward. Billed as "the finest dance floor in Iowa," the magnificent wood floor was indeed impressive, and so was the camaraderie and hospitality of the staff and the dancers. After such warm greetings, we felt right at home.

We were younger than many of the couples. As we became regulars on big band nights, the longtime dancers advised us, "Whatever you do, don't stop dancing!"

We observed their obvious delight—smiles on their shining faces, the spring in their steps, the fun and laughter they shared. These dancers lived the wisdom they offered us. With the emotional pull of dancing, how could we not follow their seasoned advice?

Although we didn't plan for dancing to do so, it turned into a sound investment, the perfect activity for us to take from our working years to retirement life. By the time Bill and I retired in our mid-fifties, dancing was in our lives to stay, so much so that we had created a personal motto—"dancing through life." By then we knew firsthand how a consistent dancing routine provided social, physical, and mental benefits. We chose to slow our pace as we settled into retirement, trading the rigor of ongoing dance lessons and performance events for more time to enjoy the hospitality and social aspects of dancing.

People asked, "Are you still dancing?"

"You bet we are!" we'd say, with smiles and dreamy looks in our eyes.

We continued to dance at Lake Robbins Ballroom and also joined several area dance organizations, for which we previously could not commit the time. These opportunities widened the circle of friends we've made from a mix of backgrounds, all of us sharing a passion for the fun and artistry of dancing.

Dancing has helped us stand tall, stay active, and remain limber. During a few periods over the years, health issues kept us off the floor—though in our hearts we never stopped dancing. Convinced that dancing fitness boosted our recovery, we returned to the floor ready to waltz, swing, and tango.

Although Bill and I protect our time and energy, we save room for dancing. On top of its positive outcomes, dancing gives us a sense of spiritual unity, a way to express our unique souls. As we have aged and accrued experience, we think of ourselves as dancing ambassadors, as people who keep the magic of dancing alive.

We extol the pleasures of dancing, offer hospitality, and encourage others. We do our part to pass on the culture of dancing, the bliss of donning dance attire and joining a community of dancers on the floor. The delight of dancing is not the number of steps learned or the execution of perfect patterns. It's the heart put into dancing; it's the spirit set to motion.

Now we're the ones who say to young or new dancers, "Keep dancing! Enjoy it, have fun!" Their excited energy invigorates us all the more.

Currently, at barely past sixty, Bill and I watch dancers in their seventies, eighties, and even nineties, who still swing, glide, and polka. They inspire and motivate us, much as they did when we were younger. The difference now lies in our seasoned experience; we dance with grateful hearts, understanding more fully the commitment, the pay-offs, the pure joy that dancing brings.

Once under the spell of dancing, the magic stays. When the music starts our bodies and spirits respond: "dance time!"

We have no doubt that dancing keeps us young at heart, no matter what our age.

Our plan? Dance through life till death do us part.

~Ronda Armstrong

Lessons
from Sir James Galway

Music is moonlight in the gloomy night of life.
~Jean Paul Richter

M y mother used to say, in her southern voice that soothed like the rose-scented lotions she rubbed on her hands, "Life begins at forty, you know." Sophie Tucker's recording of a song by that name had certainly made an impression on her, and as I moved into my fortieth year, Mother enjoyed reminding me that it would be true. "Just wait and see." It was. I found my calling as a teacher and university instructor after I turned forty.

The years raced on and then I was facing my sixtieth birthday, and a look in the mirror reminded me that life certainly didn't begin at sixty. I would be retiring soon. So, what kind of life awaits us after the retirement party? On limited incomes, how many of us will travel extensively, start a new business, or buy a vacation home? What can we carry into our later years that will bring us contentment? What do I already have that might bring me renewed pleasure?

Then I remembered the flute. When I turned forty-one I had purchased an inexpensive flute because I wanted to play an instrument. I took lessons, but I was a terrible student, allowing anxiety to undermine my ability to concentrate. I became discouraged and put the flute away. Why do it if I couldn't be good at it? I had experienced a kind of perfectionism that doesn't work well for us as we age.

Now, two decades later, I dug through my closet, behind boxes of photos still not put in scrapbooks or scanned into the computer. I shoved them aside, those mementos from the first sixty years of my life, and pulled out the hidden flute. I felt a small ripple of excitement as I opened the case and ran my fingers over the keys. I could begin again and bring music into my days. I began to practice, but experienced once again the disappointment of not being good. I continued anyway even though I could feel the tension fill my body.

One day I received the news that my musical hero, the great flutist, Sir James Galway, would be giving a master class at the university for free. All I had to do was show up with my flute.

Walking across campus that March day I felt foolish, but I kept putting one reluctant foot in front of the other until I reached the music building. Students were hurrying in and the seats to the small auditorium were filling up quickly. Still I hesitated. At last I opened the door and slipped into a seat at the back. Everyone was holding a flute in readiness for the great master's class. I assembled mine and waited. To enthusiastic, but respectful applause James Galway came on stage, with his famous flute in hand. On either side of the stage large screens had been set up so that we could see musical scores, and he invited us to stand and play the music.

I had forgotten my glasses and I couldn't see the music. I tried to play anyway, listening intently to the student beside me, but I couldn't keep up. I felt my eyes start to fill with tears, and I wanted to flee, but I was trapped by the arms of people holding up their flutes. Finally the music ended and we took our seats again. I slipped a tissue from my pocket and dabbed my eyes. No one was looking at me. They were riveted to the words and actions of James Galway as he described ways to play better.

When he gave us a break, rather than slip out the back door, I decided to boldly walk up to the stage. He stepped to the edge and reached out to take my outstretched hand in his and warmly greeted me. I told him that I was trying to learn to play the flute, but that

I wasn't very good... that I was probably too old to do it. His eyes twinkled with good humor and wisdom and he reminded me to keep practicing and most of all to have fun.

Fun? I whispered the word as I left and let it skip around in my heart. Fun! That's what I had been missing. I realized as I walked to the parking lot that I had treated my flute like something to be conquered. At sixty it was time to set my ego aside and simply have fun with the endeavors of my life.

In my bedroom, with the door closed, I play my flute with great gusto rather than skill. This is the time to spread my sometimes stiff fingers over the keys and feel the pure joy of making music. Sir James Galway gave me permission to find what was needed... fun. That was six years ago, and now that I'm sixty-six years old, my little grandson toddles around me with his plastic flute and we make delightful music together.

~Caroline S. McKinney

Mollie and Me

Scratch a dog and you'll find a permanent job.
~Franklin P. Jones

I heard the garage door open and knew it wouldn't be long before my husband Paul would come through the door. I dreaded his arrival. Don't get me wrong—I love him dearly, but recently he had started to ask too many questions. He was really getting on my nerves.

"Hi babe, I'm home," came his booming voice. "Where are you?"

"In here," I replied. I was lying on our bed watching the five o'clock news in my pajamas.

"You're still in your pajamas, again? You would feel better if you got dressed."

"Why? I'm not going any place," I replied testily.

He just sighed and started changing his clothes.

"I suppose there isn't any dinner again tonight, either."

"No, it's 'make-your-own' night," I said.

"I thought you said when you retired you were going to make me dinner every night and do all the other things you were dying to do."

"Well, I lied," I said and popped the volume on the television up a notch.

Paul just walked out of the room shaking his head. We weren't fighting but we weren't exactly getting along famously either.

My early retirement had come unexpectedly and although it was due to health issues, they weren't severe enough to warrant staying in pajamas all day. I could still do a lot of things on my "good" days and rest on the "bad" ones.

If this was what people looked forward to their entire lives, they could have it. I was bored out of my skull. My father had instilled in me a strong work ethic. Time was to be spent in useful endeavors, not frivolous ways, and I loved being a career woman. All my life I had worked at challenging jobs... for a city councilwoman, CEOs and presidents of Fortune 500 companies. Now I was reduced to a depressed zombie who couldn't even get dressed by dinnertime.

Not that I hadn't tried to pull myself out of this blue funk. I tried shopping as a diversion, but without my discretionary income this was a bad idea. My best friend asked me why I was hiding from her, but truthfully, getting dressed up and doing lunch was just too tiring. I tried reading... I had an entire bookshelf of goodies just waiting to be devoured, but how much can one read? Working in my craft room also took up part of my day. Somehow these activities didn't hold my interest for very long and I would find myself wanting to sleep. I missed the challenge of deadlines, meeting new people, and a sense of accomplishment. Some days I would be as tired when I woke up as when I fell asleep. This wasn't working out the way I planned.

Everyone kept telling me it took time to adjust, that I would be very busy if I gave myself a chance. I didn't want to be just busy; I wanted a purpose. I just hoped it involved something I could do in my pajamas.

Meanwhile, as I searched for meaning in my life again, my husband stepped in and suggested we get a dog. Ever since my beloved dog had died the previous year, I wasn't sure I wanted to experience that heartache again. But Paul was relentless.

The next Wednesday morning he said, "Hey, get dressed. Today we're going to the shelter."

"Oh, no... I can't."

"Why not? You going somewhere?" he asked.

"Well, um, I'm not ready for that commitment," I replied.

"Sallie, we're getting a dog, not adopting a baby!" Little did he know.

We went to the shelter and returned with a cuddly Beagle-Doxie mix. I named her Mollie, spelled with an "ie" just like my name.

I bounded out of bed the next morning, eager to see what Mollie was up to. I was greeted by doggie kisses and unconditional love. Mollie didn't care that I didn't have a career or that I have health issues. She just needed me.

I began her regime of training. I fed her, bathed her, and started our daily routine of walks. I taught her to catch the ball and bring it to me. Mollie and I were two needy souls who had found each other.

A funny thing happened: my energy returned. The pile of laundry disappeared; my house got cleaned and I tried cooking a couple of homemade meals. I found cooking wasn't really my thing and since my hubby loves to cook, I let that one go.

Instead, I decided to return to my writing and artwork. With Mollie at my feet, I sat at my worktable recently and began to once again design my own greeting cards. Friends came over to meet Mollie and soon we were making lunch plans. My life became meaningful and busy but Mollie and I don't miss a day walking or playing ball. Paul doesn't come home and find me in my pajamas.

I have experienced some losses in the past year—my health, my career, my own income—but I am determined not to look back, only forward.

One recent winter evening Mollie and I took our usual walk. As we crunched the crisp leaves on the sidewalk with each step, I marveled at how my life had turned around since retirement. My heart was full and the stars twinkled as bright as my future. I thought this is how life goes; you just keep putting one foot in front of the other until you reach your destination. Sometimes you need a little help along the way.

I looked down and whispered, "Thank you, Mollie, for coming into my life."

Just then Paul drove by on his way home from work.

"Hi girls! How're you two doing tonight?" he yelled.

I realized who really knew just what I needed. I couldn't wait to get home and thank him.

~Sallie A. Rodman

Younger by Association

Children make you want to start life over.
~Muhammad Ali

No matter how my day is going, when I walk into their classrooms, I immediately feel better and happier. I'd like to think I'm also a little younger, well, at least at heart.

Health problems forced me to retire early from my work in public relations. After several years in a high-pressure environment, I felt a little lost without the day-to-day busyness that accompanied my work.

I began doing freelance writing from home, but something was still missing. That is, until I began reading to four delightful classrooms of preschoolers. The children I read to are between the ages of two and five and come from a variety of backgrounds.

Each week when I arrive in one of their classrooms, I am greeted by happy calls of, "It's Miss Jeannie!" or "Story Lady is here!" I'm nearly tackled by ten or more small bodies giving me "knee hugs" and ten or more voices excitedly filling me in on their latest "owie" or other events of their week.

As we sit together in a circle, there are wiggles, a few pokes, and then we all snuggle together to enjoy two or more books. They delight me with their laughter, their questions and their innocence, as we explore topics from the world around us and share the wonder of imagination. They teach me to return to the simple joys of childhood.

I hope that I am helping them see the wonderful things that can be found within books and that books will become their friends. I know that they are giving me much more than I could ever give them. For a few minutes each week, I am transformed. I put aside my aches and pains. I clear the stuffiness out of my brain, and I look at the world through children's eyes.

The magic of this association does not stop there. Out in the community, I feel a sweet pull in my heart when one of them recognizes me, tugs at his or her mother or father's sleeve and happily declares, "It's the story lady!"

Before the wary parent can pull the child back, I am quickly wrapped in a joyful knee hug and though my body is growing older, my heart grows younger.

~Jeannie Lancaster

Back to Our Future

Every day is a journey, and the journey itself is home.
~Matsuo Basho

What were we thinking? Clearly, we weren't. Thinking that is. At least, most of our friends and family believe we didn't think everything all the way through.

My husband called from his cell phone one day: "I was in Old Town this morning and thought you'd be interested to know the Johnson place has a For Sale sign out front."

"Really!" I squealed. "Did you get the name of the real estate agent?"

"Well, yes. Why?"

"I want to see it, that's why. Who knows when it will be on the market again? Let's snoop."

Of course, that's all it would be—merely an opportunity to tour one of our town's most historic homes. Who knew my spur-of-the-moment suggestion would change the course of our lives?

Oh, sure, we talked it through before we abandoned the happy haven where we had lived and loved for a quarter of a century. Where we'd nourished our four children, made cherished memories, planned to retire. We took time to investigate similar properties and contemplate the huge change this would mean. And we returned again and again with the agent as we mulled the decision.

"This is nuts," I pointed out. "People our age are downsizing. Moving into condos and townhouses." One couple we knew had sold or given away nearly all their possessions to live in a fifth-wheeler, touring the country to visit their children.

"Look at the size of this yard," Norm mumbled. "Neither of us likes to mow or weed."

"And this kitchen!" I shook my head in disgust. "Why would I trade our huge, open one for this skinny galley?"

"No insulation," he muttered.

"Only one bath," I complained.

It was a giant step backward, we both agreed.

"The carriage house sure would make an amazing photography studio. The lighting is perfect. I'd even have a camera room." His eyes gleamed. "And you. You'd get a terrific home office to work from."

Ignoring caution and common sense, we bought the stately place. We sacrificed covered porches, an attached garage, multiple bedrooms and baths, and a finished basement in exchange for an imposing 1887 Victorian Italianate with a musty cellar and steep, seventeen-step staircases.

I found out just how steep, during the move, when I broke my foot from an awkward fall and spent weeks navigating The Matterhorn on my bottom. That initial accident was only a precursor to a series of wild adventures.

Within a matter of weeks, we learned the prior owners had trained neighbors, mail carriers and deliverymen to use the side door, avoiding pigeon droppings that piled up on the front porch. Two years of our lives were dedicated to eliminating those pests in our gables—installing plastic owls, netting, spikes, electronics, even repellents. Do you know pigeons breed year-round? That the best way to get rid of them is to cage them OUT?

About the time the last feather floated away, we discovered bats, dozens of hair-raising bats, flitting from our attic in search of dinner each evening. I gritted my teeth and called pest control. Again. Do you know bats are protected? That some years there are harems and others only stag parties? That they can squeeze through a space the size of a quarter? A massive, five-year undertaking, but Bat Man assures us we've fully sealed the chimneys, eaves, and bricks.

He thinks.

Over time, we've dealt with other home invaders, as well. Wasps, mice, and a felonious raccoon charged with breaking and entering through the laundry room window. Do you know you can tell a raccoon has distemper by his paw-frayed ears? But more so by the deranged look in his eyes.

Our thirty-eight-year-old marriage has gone through as much renovation as our lovely old home. While our peers dine in fine restaurants and luxuriate on cruise decks, most of our romantic dates are spent poking through architectural salvage, hiking the aisles at Lowe's and Home Depot, and leafing through the pages of *Old-House Interiors*.

We've perfected the art of living with a deplorable lack of wall outlets, unreliable light switches, and windows sealed shut by layers of paint. We've adjusted to preparing meals side by side within the constraints of a galley kitchen. We're resigned to toting groceries from garage to house, no matter the weather.

We have, at long last, leveled the grandfather's clock so it keeps good time, the dining room table so the peas on our plate don't roll into the gravy, and our other furniture (well, most of it anyway) because it's immensely easier than fixing slanty hardwood—which, incidentally, provides hours of entertainment for the grandkids. Do you know you can place bets on which direction a marble will roll when it's dropped on the parlor floor?

As serious guardians of our historic home, we are determined, dedicated partners, with paint under our nails and plaster dust in our hair. Why, we've even gained an appreciation for yard work and landscaping. Norm mows The Park; I weed The Woodlands; together, we dream about a grape-entwined pergola, a rustic garden shed, a restored front porch, and a Victorian kitchen garden. Someday.

We've survived seven years in this wondrous place; we're hoping to eke out at least twenty before our kids declare us incompetent. A pipe dream? Perhaps. But our To-Do List is endless. We can only hope our energy and enthusiasm are, too. Do you know bats migrate back to the same "safe houses" each summer?

~Carol McAdoo Rehme

You Can Be the World

Act as if what you do makes a difference. It does.
~William James

On a hot June day in 2004, as I held that letter in my hands, my eyes focused on the return address. I gasped as I read "Carsemu Brown." "He is alive! He is alive!" I said loudly enough that the man standing in the post office beside me stopped and stared. I did not bother to explain as the story would have only confused him and I was too anxious to see the contents.

With trembling fingers I opened the wrinkled envelope. The words were typed by what I thought must have been an old manual typewriter, which caused me to wonder if the letter had been written years before and maybe Carsemu had, as I had feared, died in Liberia's years of civil war. I soon discovered that, indeed, Carsemu was alive and he had recently written the letter. The letter was dated June 5, 2004, exactly forty-nine years from the date Glenn, my late husband, and I had married.

These were Carsemu's words: "I have shed tears upon hearing of Mr. Henderson's death and of your health conditions. My family and I always remember you in our daily prayers. Keep courage and have faith. Thirty years ago both you and Mr. Henderson taught me at Ricks Institute and I have always been thankful that you treated me as your own, giving me a job and paying all of my school expenses. During Liberia's fifteen years of civil war, I have been unable to contact you. Just staying alive has been only through God's care."

He went on, "We have spent twelve years fleeing from one refugee camp to another and watching our friends and family falling in death all around us. My wife even died in a cold wet camp with no medical attention." He went on to tell me of his children, a total of six that he was caring for. Much of the time there was no food and his meager salary was twenty dollars per month.

Carsemu told me of his twenty-two-year-old daughter who was in constant danger of being raped and/or killed. He asked if Lombeh might come to me and be my caretaker.

My life had changed so much since Glenn, our daughter Cindy, and I had returned from Liberia in 1973. Glenn had died and I was several years past retirement. My widow's income was very limited.

Just a few days before the arrival of Carsemu's letter, I had read these words and they had found a home in my heart: "To the world you may be only one person but to one person, you may be the world."

I replied to Carsemu with these words: "I cannot tell you how happy I was to receive your letter. I am so anxious to hear more about your family and the horrors you have endured. I am happy to tell you that, thankfully, I do not need a caretaker. But I want to assure you that, beginning today, I will begin to search for a scholarship for Lombeh and, I promise you that, with the help of God, I will provide for Lombeh, not as my house help but as my daughter." I continued, "Lombeh will receive an education in the U.S. and she will be safe from rebels and soldiers. I also promise you that there will always be rice for your family."

I believe God gave me this mission just as surely as He gave me a teaching mission in Liberia, West Africa, almost forty years ago. In the fall, Lombeh will enter her third year at Lindsey Wilson College in Columbia, Kentucky.

To the world I am one seventy-year-old retired person. To Lombeh, I am the world.

~Margery M. Henderson

Sunday	Monday	Tuesday	Wednesday	Thursday	Friday	Saturday
		1 brunch at Smiths	2 Work 9-1	3 babysit Jessica	4 work 9-1	5 Pack
6 Pier 3 at 4 sharp	7 CRUISE!!	8	9	10	11	12
13	14 work 9-1	15 Jessica ☺	16 Work 9-1	17 Dog Shelter	18 work 9-1	19 Golf with Gene
20	21 Work 9-1	22 Dr. Miller - 10:30	23 work 9-1	24 dog shelter	25 Work 9-1	26 Dinner Party 7:00
27 DC trip 27th-29th	28	29	30 Work 9-1	31 Dog Shelter		

Chapter 8

Inspiration for the Young at Heart

Who're You Calling Old?

Call Me Madam

Nobody can make you feel inferior without your consent.
~Eleanor Roosevelt

Even though I've had my AARP card for many years, I see no reason for clerks, heads of business, bank tellers or others to treat me with a certain amount of measured superiority, as though I am slightly addled or deaf. It's true that on my recent birthday we had to open the door after the eighty candles on my cake were lit, so the smoke alarm would stop sounding. It could happen to anyone who has reached his or her golden years.

I want to tell these people who serve the public that respect is a high priority for seniors. So is dignity. I am well read, do the crossword puzzle every day, have even almost finished one Sudoku puzzle, and I still wear only a size eight. I also walk every day, take an interest in politics, and my husband and I have been married sixty years.

Now let's get to the crux of this complaint. This is the straw that broke the camel's back. I saw an ad in the Sunday paper for a product that I use. The price was great and there was also a rebate. On Wednesday I went to the drugstore that offered it.

I asked a clerk where the product was when I couldn't find it in its usual spot. "Oh, we moved it, dear," she said, and took my arm and pointed me to the right aisle. I smiled a little and said, "Well, I'm glad you moved it. When I couldn't find it I thought I must be growing old."

I looked and looked, but no product. Another young woman

asked if she could help me. She said she'd look. "You're, right, honey, it isn't here," she said. She then said she'd go and find someone. I waited ten minutes and soon a very superior person came who said she was head of the department.

"What's the problem?" she asked.

"Where's the product?" I responded.

She gave a sigh so long and sad that it was worthy of an Academy Award, or at least an Emmy, and pointed to piles of cartons in the aisle. "It's all in there," she almost sobbed. "I haven't had time to unpack it."

"But the ad was in Sunday's paper," I countered.

Now I had hurt her feelings. But she decided to be friends. "I'm going to do something special for you, dear. I'm going to give you a smaller box of the product and prorate it so the deal will be the same. Do you understand, dear?"

I longed to say, "No, speak slower. I am a senior citizen and it's hard for me to grasp this big math you're talking about."

But I tagged along. When we got to the checkout, she said, "Even if you're going to shop somewhere else in the store I must check you out here, honey, because I have to do a special override for this transaction." She almost flexed her fingers the way concert pianists do before performing.

"Dear, do you have cash or a credit card?" she asked, putting the product in a bag with a flourish. I handed her my credit card and she went into her routine again, gave me the bag and said my least favorite farewell: "Have a good day, dear."

I said, "Where's my credit card?"

"I gave it to you," she parried.

"If you had given it to me, it would be in my wallet," I said, looking her right in the eye.

But she was right on her toes: "Did you look in your pocket, honey?" I told her I had no intention of looking since she hadn't given it to me.

A moment later, she said, "Oh, here it is after all," handing it to me. Here's the clincher, the part where I decided never to enter the store again. She smiled across the counter and said, "Each night when I go home from work, I ask myself, 'Did I do my very best today?'"

"No, you failed," I answered, and swept out.

~Nancy Allan

Chronologically Blessed

The minute a man ceases to grow, no matter what his years,
that minute he begins to be old.
~William James

"How old would you be if you didn't know how old you are?" were words once spoken by the great Satchel Paige. How would you answer that question? Would you base your answer on physical condition, mentality alertness, energy level, or yet other criteria?

I often ask myself that question. How old am I, really? Chronologically, I am seventy-five years old, but if I didn't know that... my answer would have to be a very different number—a number much, much lower than seventy-five.

All my days are busy and productive. What do I do? I do anything and everything that I can cram into the hours between waking up and bedtime. When I say my nightly prayers, I always thank God for yet one more "good day" in my life.

I'll tell you a secret. To be perfectly honest, I don't measure my accomplishments by any yardstick other than my own, so everything measures up to my expectations. I don't pressure myself to achieve beyond my limitations, my abilities, or compare my efforts to anyone else's. However, everything I do is my very best or, as they say in the sports world, "my personal best." My ambition still burns as brightly as it ever did when I was young.

I do not fret over not being able to accomplish what I did when I was younger. Instead, I "rejoice over all the things I am still able to do" and that's a lot. I maintain my home quite well, prepare healthy, tasty meals, keep the laundry up to date and the finances in good order. There has been no noticeable decline in that part of my life.

Housework and chores are only a small part of the everyday routine that everyone has to follow. I do not find these chores the least bit boring because of a sense of accomplishment I feel when I am finished with them. And too, I know that when the chores are done, I will have time left to play (and play I do).

Of course, my health is very comparable to a much younger version of me. Good health helps a whole lot when it comes to working through my day. I have a memory like a "steel trap" and I believe I am still quite sharp. Believe me, I do everything in my power to safeguard both of these gifts that I have been blessed with.

I try to exercise, eat well, and get plenty of rest and relaxation to slow the aging process. I have a lot of hobbies that keep me busy during my rest time. I seldom notice the aches and pains of an aging body, such as arthritis, because I am so focused on something other than the "physical" me. I heartily recommend this "trick" to anyone who has chronic pain. I have relied on "keeping busy" for many years to distract me from my discomfort, and it works. I can testify to that fact, as I feel great!

I keep in close touch with my friends and see them as often as practical. Some of my friends are much younger than I. I welcome their new ideas and their fresh approach to life. I keep an open mind, realizing that what I might think of as "the way it should be" may not be practical anymore. Times change. With enough new evidence, I have often changed my mind on many issues. I am willing to listen and to mull things over, which is good mental exercise.

Mahatma Gandhi once said, "Live, as though you were going to die tomorrow. Learn, as though you were going to live forever." This is my mantra. There are so many things to learn and I enjoy filling my mind with new information. Most of the time, I read for information, but I also enjoy curling up with a good novel. I love structured classes and have plans to enroll in some online writing classes. There is lots of information available in electronic form so that it is not necessary to physically attend classes. However, I thoroughly enjoyed the in-class, ten-week Tax Preparation class I attended at our local college last year. I found it exciting and challenging to master a new skill. Besides, it will save us more than $300 in tax preparation fees each year.

I've always heard that "busy hands are happy hands." During the past year, I kept my hands "happy." One of my pet projects was to knit and crochet fifty-two stocking caps and a dozen long scarves, which I donated through my church to a group in need of warm clothing. It felt wonderful to offer all those warm hats and scarves to people who needed protection from the winter cold. I made them while I was watching TV for a couple of hours in the evenings. I don't enjoy sitting hours on end with nothing to do with my hands. This project kept me busy.

Of course, writing is probably my favorite hobby. After retiring at seventy-two, I began writing short stories. It is so much fun and it is as though I am writing my memoirs—one story at a time. I have enjoyed a modest success and have been pleased and honored to be published numerous times. My writing success has far exceeded my expectations. In my wildest dreams, I never thought of being a writer. It is just something wonderful that came into my life after forty-six years of working in the business world. Writing is truly a blessing.

I am active in our church choir. I dearly love to sing and be a part of the music ministry, which adds spirituality to my participation in our church service. The choir shares prayer and fellowship through music, as we "pray together in song."

Last but not least, I love spending time with my husband of fifty-seven years. We now have the time to sit over coffee, for hours, and chat with each other about absolutely everything. We never had that luxury in the earlier years. There were too many other things that required our attention, such as raising our children and indulging our grandchildren. It is as though we have found each other again. You know what? We still like each other after all these years. We have fun together and love having copious amounts of time we never had before, to do the things we love to do.

Revisiting my original point about age… right now, I feel more like I am ageless. On a conscious level, I know that I am seventy-five, but as I go through each day doing things I love to do and feeling at peace with the world, age never crosses my mind. "Living and being" are much more to the point than a birthday number.

Life is good and each day is a new beginning.

I regard each day of my life as a gift from God, wrapped in peace, and tied with a ribbon of love.

~Joyce Sudbeck

Sixty-Two and Better

Old age is like everything else. To make a success of it,
you've got to start young.
~Theodore Roosevelt

I couldn't wait until my sixty-second birthday, but my husband wasn't overjoyed by the prospect. I would work part-time from home as a freelance writer and enjoy this new phase in my life reserved for those "sixty-two or better." Money wouldn't be as plentiful, but we'd manage.

When this turning point finally arrived, I planned food, clothing and household purchases for those times designated by stores as senior citizen's days. I was delighted when salespeople asked to see proof of age and made such remarks as, "I can't believe you're over fifty!" Or occasionally, "You can't be more than forty-five!"

Once the clerk wanted to know, "What have you done to deserve ten percent off at such a young age?"

I smiled and said, "Raising kids should qualify."

However, my husband objects when I request the fifteen percent senior's discount when we go out together to eat.

"Why do you have to advertise your age?" he wants to know.

Recently I told him to ask for the customary senior discount on a repair bill when he picked up my car.

"I feel uncomfortable asking," he complained.

"It's all right for me to save money as long as you don't have to get involved," I retorted.

Later I smiled and told him, "We only received the discount because the mechanic thinks you're over sixty-two."

John is four years younger than I am. He wasn't amused.

I enjoyed my new status as a "golden girl" until one day a family member accompanied me to the post office.

As I was paying for the stamps—no discount requested—the clerk asked, "How old is your grandson?"

Joshua immediately replied, "I'm fourteen and she's my mother."

"There's another at home and he's sixteen," I said.

I think the postal clerk waned to apologize but didn't know how.

I felt embarrassed for my son, as he's always proclaiming that I look ten years younger than his father, who has the gray hair.

Now I began to wonder whether this experience at the post office was only an anomaly. Surely those nice people who looked at me and my identification card were sincere in their compliments.

Soon my sixty-third birthday would arrive. To celebrate the event, my husband took me to a new and pricey restaurant. When it came time to pay I didn't ask my husband to request their courtesy discount.

The cashier looked straight at my husband. "Would you like the senior's discount, sir?"

There was a long pause. Then John looked at me.

"No, thank you," I said. The waiter had made my day very special.

Until John can appreciate the advantages of being married to an older woman, I will continue to collect my social security check, receive courtesy discounts and enjoy going out with a younger husband who eventually will catch up with me.

However, I won't be seen with my son Joshua as often.

~Pat Jeanne Davis

Not Yet

There is a fountain of youth: it is your mind, your talents,
the creativity you bring to your life and the lives of people you love.
When you learn to tap this source, you will truly have defeated age.
~Sophia Loren

A delightful man, a retired metropolitan newspaper editor, recently sent me an e-mail commenting on an essay of mine he'd seen. His words were kind and affirming. And even after many years of writing columns, I loved the praise, because we writers are never completely comfortable or confident.

And then John added one of those cute little "smiley faces" to his note and impishly asked, "But isn't it time for you, too, to retire?"

Hmmm.

It's a question I get a lot, especially since I've passed the traditional "finish line" for work, the big 6-5 that dominated my parents' generation.

I wrote back that it was indeed time — if we looked back to that yardstick. But for me, the "R" word is fraught. Just plain fraught.

I don't want to retire.

I don't want to stop doing something I love, something that for me is as natural as breathing.

I want to write about my life, my family, other people's families and lives, my view of all things familiar and exotic. I even want to keep on meeting deadlines, because I find that an exhilarating challenge.

I want to do it for as long as I have thoughts—and a serviceable computer.

But there's a certain stubborn streak in society that seems to demand endings. It suggests that there's something vaguely unseemly about working beyond a certain age.

I'm troubled by the raised eyebrows I get from young journalists, the ones I encounter at conferences and occasionally in newsrooms where I meet with editors half my age to pitch story ideas. And yes, I'm old enough to be their mother or even their grandmother, but pitch I do.

To their credit, most of these "baby editors," as I think of them, do listen to me. They even assign the stories I yearn to write some of the time.

To add fuel to the retirement fire, however, my husband has been retired for ten years, and is living large. He loves the freedom he feels. He rejoices in the lack of structure of his days and nights after an extremely structured life, first as a lawyer, and then as a judge.

These days, court is in session... without him. He no longer has the awesome responsibility of making decisions that have a profound impact on other people's lives, to say nothing of plowing through mountains of paperwork, endless phone calls and meetings.

Mind you, this is a man who loved his work, honored his title and seldom missed a day in the courthouse where he served for twenty-two years.

But now, he insists, it's his turn to be on the sidelines, doing whatever strikes his fancy.

He had expected me to be his playmate over this last decade. But he also knew and understood that I'd gotten a later start than he had—that there had been almost fifteen years of sticking very close to home when there were three little hostages of fortune to care for.

I did that full-time mothering gladly, but always heard the distant siren song of other things calling to me, things that would ultimately follow diapers, then play groups, then nursery school carpools and endless cries of "She hit me first!"

It was not until Nancy, the baby of our family, walked off in that crooked kindergarten line that I dared to pull out the old electric typewriter and start telling it my thoughts.

It seems fitting that the first piece I ever sold to a newspaper was about walking Nancy to kindergarten—and wondering what I'd do with the rest of my life.

I got my answer.

So retirement?

Not yet. Not for me.

Not when I can easily endure the raised eyebrows that hint at postponed endings and, perhaps, staying at the party too long.

Not when I can still turn ideas-into-words-into-print.

My husband is mildly disappointed that my deadlines keep us from carefree travel, the badge of honor of retirees. Happily, he is a patient man, and one who appreciates my slightly late start. Balanced with worthwhile and absorbing activities, he also is happy in solitude, a trait we both believe came from spending the first seventeen years of his life on a farm without neighbors close by.

So yes, I will go on jotting down ideas in supermarket checkout lines, using an eyebrow pencil because I never seem to have a pen and have not yet surrendered to the electronic toys that my children and grandchildren carry.

I try not to agonize over my clinging to work. Dr. Freud, after all, reminded us that love—and work—were probably the essential elements of a life well-lived.

I've been profoundly blessed. I've got the love—and I've got the work.

And for me, at least—and for now—one without the other just isn't enough.

~Sally Schwartz Friedman

Old Woman in the Mirror

The great secret that all old people share is that you really haven't changed in seventy or eighty years. Your body changes, but you don't change at all. And that, of course, causes great confusion.

~Doris Lessing

When I retired at sixty-four years of age, I had no idea how interesting growing old was going to be. I was just happy to wake up every morning, knowing I didn't have to go to work. Neither did I think of myself as elderly until a newspaper article regarding a sixty-year-old woman referred to her as "an elderly woman."

When I read those words, I remembered a dear friend who had once told me that when she accidentally caught sight of herself, she would wonder, "Who is that old woman in the mirror?" She had the spirit and the heart of a young woman until she died at eighty-nine years of age. Neither of us ever thought of her as elderly.

I was fortunate in my youth to have good friends who were thirty or forty years older than myself. I saw them grow old so gracefully, so beautifully, that I never thought of them as elderly. They were my mentors, my pole stars, my inspiration to live a long and fulfilling life.

So what is this aging business? Am I in denial because I feel no different than I did thirty years ago? When I look in the mirror, I don't exactly see an old woman, but neither do I see the woman I know myself to be. But then, does the mirror ever reflect our inner selves?

I have decided the mirror is not the culprit. It is modern society's perception of old age. There is a certain stigma to growing old in today's world. If we are retired, our value to society is questioned. Unfortunately, many buy into that theory. But not all of us!

I find myself excited for the first time in many years, because I am finally free to be as young as I feel. I have no job to define me, no boss to direct me, no career goals to achieve. I can call, e-mail and visit friends, spend time with beloved children and grandchildren, read for hours at a time, get involved in projects that help others or just do nothing. I can spend as much time in prayer, meditation and contemplation as I choose. I can dance around the house to my favorite music, but please don't spread that around. Senility is another of society's concerns.

I do acknowledge that my husband and I have an occasional "senior moment" which we joke about. A few months ago, I was writing a check at Walmart (having also shopped at Kmart and Target). It took me a moment to recall which store I was in, and I teasingly said to my husband, "Where am I?" Having a slight hearing problem in one ear, he looked at his watch and responded, "It's almost 5:00 o'clock." We laughed so hard that we had to lean against one another. The clerk looked a little nervous.

It is not my intention to play down the seriousness of those who do suffer with physical, mental or emotional problems. Having worked with hospice, I have great compassion for those who bravely face the end of their lives under difficult circumstances.

Neither do I deny that on a more superficial level, I now make different choices—shopping particularly. The woman who once wore uncomfortable shoes and control-top pantyhose has died. Please don't mourn that woman. She has found heaven right here on earth in comfortable, but hopefully still attractive, attire.

I can understand why the young ignore the rather obvious fact that they will one day grow old and die. I would like to reassure them, however, that the person who lives in the now young body will be the same person, if somewhat wiser and with less baggage, in an older body. An important bonus is thrown in for good measure. With age comes a marvelous freedom from caring what other people think of you and from trying to live up to their expectations.

I don't know if this last phase of my life will last a few months or many years. It is the not knowing that makes each day special. Of course, we didn't know how long we were going to live when we were younger either, but we didn't know that we didn't know. We were too busy living.

Since I am goal oriented, I chose a new goal when I retired. I decided to be too busy living to dwell on what the rest of the world is focused on—my age, my deteriorating body, my uselessness in a fast-moving modern society. I want to give of myself to life, to my family and friends. I want to learn new things, explore new possibilities. I want to be involved in helping others open their hearts.

So call me elderly if you like, but be careful how you refer to others. Words have power. Choose them carefully.

I once read that people may not remember exactly what you did, or what you said, but they will always remember how you made them feel.

~Libby Grandy

Eyes of Love

Anyone who keeps the ability to see beauty never grows old.
~Franz Kafka

"Doesn't he look old?" my dinner companion asked as she nodded at a man sitting across the restaurant.

I looked to see who she meant. It was a "girls' night out" for the two of us—husbands and kids, and in my case, grandkids, left behind for a couple of hours as we caught up on a little girl talk.

We had known one another since junior high school and had graduated in the same high school class. Time, careers, husbands and families had taken us on different paths in life, but recently she and her family had returned to our little hometown with its two stoplights. We were both in our mid-sixties now, and the outing tonight was our own private celebration of the renewal of our friendship.

I glanced again at the man sitting alone across the room, enjoying a solitary meal. We had all attended the same high school, although he was a year older than she and I.

"His hair has gotten so gray, that is what little he has left," my friend commented. "And look at all those wrinkles!"

I thought back to our high school years. He had been the "Fonzie" of the school—the "cool cat" with the black leather jacket and coal black hair combed into a "duck tail," the style of the day. He even rode a motorcycle, something almost unheard of for a high school kid back in the early 1960s—at least in our small town. In fact, back then very few teens had any kind of transportation they could call their own. Oh, the girls might beg to drive the family car for a Sunday afternoon spin with girlfriends, and if the boys did have a set of wheels, it was usually a "fixer upper" bought in a junkyard. That meant the guys would spend most Saturday afternoons under the hood trying to find why this hose leaked or that valve malfunctioned.

But not our friend across the room. He drove a Harley and was the envy of all the guys and the dreamboat for all the girls.

"His hands are even trembling," my companion exclaimed, and sure enough, when I glanced again, I saw a slight shaking as he lifted his coffee cup to his lips.

We had dated for a while when he was a senior and I was a junior. I remembered lazy summer afternoons on the back of the Harley, clinging to his leather jacket and laughing into the wind. Life had seemed so perfect and so innocent.

Then he had graduated from high school, and without any fanfare or notice, decided college wasn't his lot in life, so he joined the Army. Before long he was shipped overseas while I finished my high school years and went off to college. We lost touch then, as he never wrote, but one day he returned, bringing with him a girl he had met and married while stationed in Europe. She was pretty and outgoing, and I liked her. By then, I was married, too, and starting my own family. I would see the two of them occasionally at a community event or shopping in a local store. We would exchange pleasantries as people do while standing in the produce aisle. But when he and I looked at one another, there was something there—a smile, a remembrance, that passed between us quietly and innocently, and I could almost feel the wind in my hair once again.

"He just looks like a dried up little old man," my friend continued. "Doesn't he look old to you?"

I smiled.

"No," I said.

And I meant it. For when I looked at my friend across the table from me and the other sitting across the room, I still saw them as they once were. I saw my first love and my forever friend. I was looking at them with different eyes than perhaps most people saw them. I was seeing them through eyes of love. I knew neither would ever look old to me.

And as I glanced across the room once more, his piercing blue eyes met mine and he gave me that crooked smile. I thought—no, I am certain—that I felt the wind in my hair one more time. And it was a sweet memory indeed.

~Anna B. Ashby

Mushy Face Is No Disgrace

Inside every older person is a younger person wondering what happened.
~Jennifer Yane

In the mirror is a face,
Oh my goodness what a face!
Used to be so firm and full.
Hair as coarse as new clipped wool;
Now it's gone from black to gray,
Incremental, day by day.

Mushy face is no disgrace;
Loss of tone is commonplace.
Still, it's interesting to see
My youth vanish by degree.

In the mirror is a face
Of a man you can't replace;
Though it sags from ear to ear,
Not yet will it disappear.

Droopy cheeks and widow's peaks,
Older than valued antiques;

Strange that this image I see
Represents reality.
Really now, how can it be
That this old fossil face is me?

~Robert Tell

My Biological Clock
Is Quacking

No man is ever old enough to know better.
~Holbrook Jackson

My husband Bob and I have been talking about having
another duck. Since I've joined the ranks of the estro-
gen impaired, I think it's normal to think about these
things. And I'm sure our pet ducks, Spike and Grant, would like a
little pal.

"You know, Bob," I said, "if we wait much longer, we'll be too
old to play with them." He kept folding laundry. "Come on." I kissed
his neck softly. "Wouldn't you like to hear the pitter patter of little
webbed feet?"

He shook his head while we folded a sheet. "We're not so young
anymore. And we don't have the money."

"But we still have the incubator and the heat lamp. That is," I
nibbled at his ear, "if you want to try to hatch our own."

"I don't know," he said, scratching his irritated ear. "It would
be socially irresponsible to bring another duck into this world." He
folded our pillowcases. "And we'd have to adopt one."

"Would you care if it's a different kind of duck than ours?"

"Of course not," he said. "But you know my folks."

"Give them a chance. They had a problem, at first, with me being Jewish."

"I know. I'd hate to expose a duck to such prejudice."

He got a new bottle of fabric softener and headed downstairs. I followed him. "It's so damp down here and..." I looked around frantically, "there's no TV!"

"This is where the clean clothes fairy lives." He turned on the machine. "There are many down sides, so to speak, to a duck," he said. "Like less traveling."

"But we're empty nesters, Bob. Another duck would keep us young. And I'd give anything to hear a newborn's first quack again."

He looked up wistfully. "I remember when Spike took his first steps. He was only three minutes old."

We headed upstairs. "It's too late in our lives," he said. "We'll be decrepit when they have their own eggs."

"What if Golda Meir said, 'It's too late to be Israel's Prime Minister. After all, I'm seventy.' What if Alfred Hitchcock said, 'I'm too old to direct *The Birds*. I'm sixty-two'?"

"Maybe next year."

"You say that every year."

"People will think we're not acting our age."

"I can't think of a better way of being thought of."

I took his arm and led him to the backyard. "It's spring, sweetheart. Sap is flowing. Leaves are unfurling. Tulips are bursting. There's new life everywhere—at any age. Bob!" I grasped his hands in mine. "I want a baby duck!"

It wasn't until a few Sundays ago that he finally agreed to feather our nest.

"Come with me," I said and we drove to a small town near where we live on Cape Cod. And there, along with a few hundred people, we watched an extraordinary woman celebrate her eightieth birthday by tap dancing down Main Street.

I saw a well-known writer in the crowd. But I felt too shy to introduce myself. "Maybe next time," I said to Bob.

"You said that when you saw him at the July 4th parade. But

that's fine," he said playfully. "We'll postpone a duck until next time too."

And so, I forced myself to meet the author. He warmly responded to my overture. And together we watched the tap dancer show us that "acting your age" is probably never smart and is likely said only when someone's having fun.

Back home, we prepared the coop for our new little bundle of joy.

I often think of my mom, now gone, who decided early on that it was too late for her to enjoy most good things. Teeming with dreams that were never fulfilled, she inadvertently set an example for me of how not to live.

I owe to her my courage to change, though it terrifies me, my humor, and although she'd have a fit if she knew, my late-in-life duck.

~Saralee Perel

88

Who Moved My Marbles?

There was no respect for youth when I was young, and now that I am old,
there is no respect for age — I missed it coming and going.
~J.B. Priestley

few years ago, the book *Who Moved My Cheese?* was a best-seller. No one has moved my cheese, but marbles are a different story. It has become increasingly obvious to me that someone has made off with them.

I look back to just a few months ago when I managed a large government department. I had all my marbles then. I chaired committees, administered the budget and developed programs. I expected to be in the middle of the action and I got respect without even thinking about it.

Then came downsizing. I got a decent retirement package and happily quit the commute from hell. It was sad to lose the office and the secretary but it was, after all, an expected part of leaving. What I didn't expect to lose was my marbles.

I didn't know they were gone. I didn't see or hear them go. But somehow they left. My theory is that someone stole them because I'm careful with my stuff and I'm sure I didn't just mislay them.

My first hint came when I tried a new hairdresser. When she discovered I was retired, she called me "Dear" and showed me to the chair as if I might not be able to find it on my own.

Then I thought I should keep fit so I asked at the recreation centre about their swim schedule. The receptionist gave me a look that said someone my age should not be cavorting in their pool.

"Try the seniors' centre," she said, and gave me careful directions.

It's not two months since the director of that seniors' centre asked me for career advice. Three months ago I was keynote speaker at a conference of leaders of senior centres. Now I need directions to get there? What happened?

Something changed. Not me; I'm much the same as I was a few months ago—same salt-and-pepper hair, same clothes, same height. But before, everyone knew that I came with a full complement of marbles, and now they think I've lost them all. Well, they are not in my house or in my car and my office was thoroughly cleaned out. So I can only conclude that someone stole them.

Could I have been careless with them? All these years I never gave them a thought. Oh, I went to courses and conferences to add to my stock of marbles and the nature of my job meant that I used them often—every last marble had a good workout daily. But I didn't really pay attention to them. If I'd known someone was going to steal them I would have locked them away, insured them. I might even have put them in a safety deposit box.

Now that everyone knows they're gone I miss them. Who might want to steal my well-used marbles? Not my office staff—I selected them myself and each one has more than enough marbles to last a lifetime. My family? Not likely because they too are well supplied with marbles. The lad who helps the gardener? Well, he is rather short of marbles, but he doesn't have enough marbles to know how to go about purloining more.

So I'm left to wonder who might want my supply of slightly used but well polished marbles. Is there a not-so-dumb blonde who got tired of dumb blonde jokes? Is there a senior trying to eliminate senior moments? Perhaps I should check out friends who are both senior and blonde—the more I think about it the more suspect they seem.

But why would they want my marbles when they already have

plenty of their own? I know that because we have great discussions. They are bright and funny, just as they always were. They're sharp and perceptive and they know human nature inside out. They can find flaws in an argument, deflate inflated male egos, plan the itinerary for a trip to New York and analyze local politics.

If their marbles are all in working order they don't need mine. Who does need them? Could it be politicians, explaining the difference between what they promised and what they delivered? Could it be teens explaining how getting home "just after midnight" somehow encompasses 5 a.m.? Could it be drivers who need them to explain more brilliantly why the light wasn't exactly red when they sped through?

Whoever it was, that's okay. Enjoy them. Appreciate them. I've realized I don't need those old marbles anyway. I have a whole new life ahead of me, a second chance for fun and fulfillment. I'll find more marbles—shiny new, different marbles. I'll earn them, learn them, experience them.

So, to the unknown someone, make good use of the secondhand marbles you came across. I have a whole new life ahead.

~Valerie Fletcher Adolph

89

Life Is a Parade

If you're not in the parade, you watch the parade. That's life.
~Mike Ditka

A s a young girl I first saw the movie *Auntie Mame*. It is the story of an eccentric woman who, through lean times and flush, lives every day of her life to the fullest. To this day, that movie has had a profound impact on how I have lived my own life.

I have tried to teach my children and grandchildren that life is a parade, to be lived to the fullest with eyes wide open. Doors are made to be unlocked, and dreams are meant to be fulfilled.

I have had opposition! The first time I mentioned to my three young daughters that "life is a parade," they looked at me as though I was crazy. "You've never been in a parade, Mom," they said, "so how do you know?" It was the day before the 4th of July and there just happened to be a local parade in the small resort town of Mammoth Lakes. I knew I had to teach them by example, so I called the chamber of commerce and asked to enter the parade. They said we needed to have a float so I told them we had one! I looked at our group, thought of our Volkswagen and knew we had our float. Our theme? Looking at those young faces, I saw Becky Thatcher, Tom Sawyer, Indian Joe, and their friends. I knew right then and there that we would be Tom Sawyer and friends whitewashing Aunt Polly's fence. Of course we were accepted. My family was horrified!

We took white sheets, colored them with flowers and hung them from the windows inside the car. We tore more sheets into strips for the fencing around the car. We put an empty paper towel roll on the antenna with a Kleenex box on top saying "Aunt Polly's." That night we ate corn on the cob so we had our corncob pipes. We borrowed paintbrushes and paint cans from the complex we were staying in. And my husband had a beard... a little baby powder and a cowboy hat and he was Mark Twain on top of the car.

What fun they all had planning and working together to join that parade.

I continue to try new things. I'm afraid of small, enclosed areas, but when I was in Egypt, I took a deep breath and forced myself into the bowels of a pyramid. I'm afraid of roller coasters, but when given the opportunity to fly in an open cockpit, two-seat World War I plane over Santa Monica beach, I strapped on the harness, the Red Baron leather hat and goggles, and told myself "keep your eyes open" over and over as we flew loops in the sky!

At sixty-four years of age I now have grandchildren who tease, giggle and love to see life through the eyes of their sometimes-silly grandma. The older ones have traveled with me and relived the paths of history. For her high school graduation, I took my oldest grand-daughter, Nicole, to London and Paris. She is such a fashion hound. We spent hours in Harrods browsing the racks, smelling the perfumes, comparing prices with Nordstom at home. We walked the streets of Paris taking photos of the windows with contemporary furniture for her first apartment. We entered the wonderland of Louis Vuitton and marveled at the handbags she dreamed to one day own. As we wandered Versailles my granddaughter watched me imagine I was Marie Antoinette in flowing gowns of satin.

When her sister, Heather, graduated with a scholarship in soft-ball I thought what better place to take her than the home of the last summer Olympics—China! We visited the Olympic Stadium, the "Bird's Nest," wandered the Forbidden City, rode in rickshaws, had her tea leaves read, marveled at the Terra Cotta Warriors, and trekked the Great Wall of China. She watched as I danced with the seniors in the parks and tried to play their games. Through it all we played

"Imagine"—imagining we lived behind these walls, imagining the history unfolding before us.

The younger ones ask when it will be their turn. I'm looking forward to Italy four years from now with my soccer-loving grandson, Bailey.

I believe that, by example, my children have each lived every day of their lives to the fullest. I'm so proud that at an early age they learned, "You can either sit in the bleachers and watch the parade go by, be part of the crew that cleans up the mess when the parade is over, or stand right up, hold your head high and march in that parade of life."

~Kristine Byron

Sunday	Monday	Tuesday	Wednesday	Thursday	Friday	Saturday
		1 brunch at Smiths	2 Work 9-1	3 babysit Jessica	4 work 9-1	5 Pack
6 Pier 3 at 4 sharp	7 CRUISE!!	8	9	10	11	12
13	14 work 9-1	15 Jessica ☺	16 Work 9-1	17 Dog Shelter	18 work 9-1	19 Golf with Gene
20	21 Work 9-1	22 Dr.Miller - 10:30	23 work 9-1	24 dog shelter	25 Work 9-1	26 Dinner Party 7:00
27 DC trip 27th-29th	28	29	30 Work 9-1	31 Dog Shelter		

Chapter
9

Inspiration
for the
Young
at
Heart

Go For It

90

A New Window

It is possible at any age to discover a lifelong desire you never knew you had.
~Robert Brault, www.robertbrault.com

"Mom, don't feel bad if you don't get your story published," my son David said. "There are thousands of great young writers out there struggling. They're bright and talented, tough competition."

I smiled. "I know. But I have to try," I answered.

At sixty-three, with an introductory course in computer use newly under my belt, I launched my first project: writing family stories to preserve them for David and his cousins. I am the last of my generation, the last to remember our family history. I especially wanted to preserve all the humorous anecdotes and stories our family had shared with one another for generations. David so enjoyed one of the first stories I related that he had called to say, "Mom, this is so funny, you need to turn it into an essay and try to get it published!"

So I did. But now while months passed and I did not hear from the editor to whom I had sent it, David worried that I would be disappointed. As a published academic himself, he well understood literary competition. But I was not discouraged, and settled into a routine of writing every morning. I was happy for this new outlet for my energies. Arthritis in several of my aging joints was increasingly limiting me. I had injured my knees. Pain and stiffness were slowly closing the door to my favorite activities, hiking and gardening.

Then a few weeks after David expressed concern for my possible disappointment, along came an acceptance letter from a regional magazine for my story of an adventure in the Ozark Mountains when I was a teenager! A modest check followed, along with a copy of the magazine featuring my tale. What excitement! Suddenly, with the sale of that first article, a new window opened for me.

Within months I sold several more stories, anecdotes that had been shared around the dinner table at holiday gatherings. I am blessed to have been born into a family of amusing storytellers, and since early childhood had listened to them carefully. Now it was paying off in a surprising way.

I was so thrilled seeing family stories preserved in print that sometimes I had to remind myself to leave the computer and get a little exercise! Best of all was David's pride in my new accomplishment.

I expanded into fiction and poetry and, with careful marketing, sold those. As writing began to "take on a life of its own," it seemed, I found myself compelled to write every day. A subtle change occurred in all my relationships. After a lifetime as daughter, wife, mother and secretary—fine as that had been—now I was also a professional published writer. That overcame a lack of confidence I had felt since leaving college without graduating to marry when I was twenty-one. I joined the Writers' League of Texas and made new friends at a time in life when it is not always easy to make new friends. Old friends suddenly spoke to me with a new respect.

Nearly fifteen years have passed since that first story was published, and I have seen my work in print somewhere almost every month since. My oft-told family anecdotes and recollections and other works have appeared in national magazines, a number of anthologies including the *Chicken Soup for the Soul* series, and newspapers. Several of my stories have won awards. I have enjoyed my "five seconds of celebrity" in local bookstores promoting the anthologies that include my true tales. It is pure joy when someone tells me that they have been touched in some way by one of my stories or articles.

When I was inducted into the National League of American Pen Women, I was ecstatic and humbled to be counted among so many accomplished women. It was a poignant moment, as my mother had also achieved that honor in her seventies. Although long a published poet, she became a newspaper columnist in her late sixties.

"I should have known you could do it," my son said. "Grandmama did!"

What started as casual fun, a loving gift of remembrances for my family, has filled my so-called retirement years to the brim. As arthritis has claimed one physical joint after another, these might have been frustrating and isolating years. Instead, I have found myself in a totally unexpected late life career.

I do not plan to retire a second time. For old writers never retire: we just scribble away!

~Marcia E. Brown

The Pole Dancing Ladies of Marigold Drive

Those who bring sunshine to the lives of others cannot keep it from themselves.

~James Matthew Barrie

The moving vans were rumbling down Marigold Drive daily, each being led by a car with a license plate reading New York, New Jersey, Ohio, Vermont, Texas or Virginia. The aging baby boomers were settling in at our new active adult retirement community in South Carolina. Within two weeks, all the house closings had taken place and the new occupants were ready to meet and greet.

My neighbor Lynn shared an idea she had for a get-together. She planned to host a seniors' pole dancing party and wanted my opinion. My "GO FOR IT!" response bolstered her courage and she mailed the invitations. Twelve women were game to give it a try. With a surprise in mind, our hostess requested that each guest bring a costume and prop to represent the month of her birth.

Our young instructor arrived and was obviously shocked by the age of her students. She set up her professional dancer's pole and the lesson began. Following the instructor's example, each woman tried the demonstrated move. We had so many laughs as cameras flashed and videos whirled. Our final assignment was to put the newly learned steps together and create our own dance where we could each "strut our stuff!" The bonding that took place set the stage for our growing friendships and the beginning of quite a reputation for the ladies of Marigold Drive.

When our faces were hurting from too much laughter, our knees screaming, and our backs giving out, we started a photo shoot. Then the need for our costumes was revealed. We would create a Marigold Goes Wild Pole Dancing Calendar that would be sold for the benefit of the Alzheimer's Association. With help from a computer savvy son, the seniors put together a quality piece. The pole dancers changed hats and became saleswomen, promoting the calendar within the community, through newspaper articles and even through a local TV appearance! Copies were sold to friends and relatives across the United States.

Only Lynn, the organizer of the event, knew the amount of money raised and she kept it a secret until the Unveiling Party in January. We were thrilled to learn that our donation to the Alzheimer's Association exceeded $2,000.

We will forever be remembered in our retirement community as "The Pole Dancing Ladies of Marigold Drive" and our active street is the envy of the neighborhood. This experience gave us a wonderful opportunity to bond, have fun, and work together for a worthy goal. It was a win-win event. Are you inspired to give it a try? GO FOR IT!

~Mary Grant Dempsey

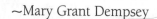

92

A Scholarship at Sixty?

Some day you will be old enough to start reading fairy tales again.
~C.S. Lewis

Positive thinking gurus declare, "It's never too late to start living your life. Believe in yourself and your special dreams."

So, after retiring from teaching kindergarten through third grade, I decided to pursue my dream of becoming a published children's book author.

I signed up for a university class, Writing Picture Books, taught by an award-winning author, and soon realized that writing for children isn't as easy as it looks. I had a lot to learn!

Next, I joined a critique group with several published children's book authors. They gently pointed out flaws galore in my writing and storytelling. One member told me how her writing improved after attending the weeklong Highlights Foundation Workshop for Children's Writers and Illustrators in Chautauqua, New York.

"Sounds wonderful," I said. "But I can't afford plane tickets from Arizona to New York, much less the tuition."

"They offer scholarships," she said. "It couldn't hurt to try for one."

"At my age?" I told myself the worst that could happen was that my application would be denied. So I applied. And miracle of miracles, at age sixty, I was awarded a scholarship that paid my airfare and most of the tuition!

My week in Chautauqua was hectic but heavenly. I gathered

valuable writing advice from editors, authors and fellow writers, some even older than me. Perhaps equally important, I learned that age isn't a barrier unless you let it be.

Spend your senior years doing what you've always wanted to do. Pursue your dreams. The years will fly by. You'll have fun, and you might even earn a little extra income. I've sold articles, stories and poems. And I realized my dream. I'm a published children's book author, earning royalties from my book. The gurus are right. It is never too late. At age sixty-five, I won a national writing contest!

~Charline Profiri

93

The Burning Boot

The road to success is dotted with many tempting parking places.
~Author Unknown

I've been a fitness enthusiast all my life. That is, for the first two weeks of every year. Each January 1st, I start out full of hope on a new regime, and every January 15th, I disgustedly realize once again I've given up without much of a fight.

I'm not sure what changed last year. Maybe it was the fact that I'd just turned sixty-four and was eyeing retirement with a mixture of elation and a "what am I going to do now" panic. Or maybe it was that for once I started, not on New Year's with all its pressure, but in November on my birthday. I started out small. I bought a Wii and then stood in line at minus thirty degrees Centigrade for a half hour at seven in the morning waiting for the store to open so I could claim one of the twelve precious Wii Fit games that were available. For some reason I began to take my fitness more seriously this time. Maybe it was that superior little voice on the Wii Fit prodding me and informing me I was unbalanced.

Then my daughter Heather breathed additional life into the program. More than twenty years ago we had lived on Vancouver Island. Every June, on the first Saturday of the month, they stage what is billed as North America's Toughest Pledge Walk—63.5 kilometers through the mountains, from the town of Gold River to the town of Tahsis in one day. While living there we had all had a go for our Burning Boot, the reward for completing the walkathon. My son

Gavin still holds the all-time record for the youngest walker to finish, at seven years old. Heather had gone back two years earlier with her sister-in-law and a friend. Now she was talking about a family get-together staged around the Walk. The next thing I knew I was registered and forced to start training.

I live on Brandon's North Hill, which as you would guess, provides the perfect training ground for mountain walking. I devised a five-mile circuit — over, down, across and up, which I repeated till I figured I should carry my cell with me so I could call Emergency Services when I went into cardiac arrest.

Two days before the event I arrived in Courtenay by bus, rented a car, and met my son at the airport. We drove the winding road to Gold River and then started the gravel logging road/goat trail that we would be walking shortly. It was longer than I'd remembered. And steeper. There we met Heather and her family and arranged our schedule.

All my insecurities about the state of my fitness had come rushing to the forefront after driving that road. What did a sixty-four-year-old couch potato think she was trying to prove? I peered at the emergency vehicles that would patrol the Walk and wondered if I would find out what they looked like inside.

We left Tahsis on a school bus around 1 a.m. to make the drive to the Gold River bridge, starting point for the day of torture. 4:30 was lift off, and everyone had to finish by sundown. They pulled any stragglers off the road then, as bears were common and cougars not unknown. Everyone milled around as we waited, sharing previous experiences with total strangers, having that last sip of coffee or the last trip to the Porta-Potty.

At the starting gun we all surged forward in a herd like the start of a buffalo stampede. The serious walkers and runners soon left the rest of us straggling in small groups as we realized the enormity of what we were doing. Twelve checkpoints marked the way. Each one had water, Gatorade, fruit and snacks. Selected ones had sign-in sheets. The first checkpoint was the farthest away, at the 7.8 kilometer mark. When I got there and thought of eleven more, I couldn't imagine finishing, so I set my sights on Checkpoint 6, the halfway point where they gave out the T-shirts.

By Checkpoint 6, I was sore, exhausted and no longer planning to settle for just a T-shirt. I knew 6 to 9 were the toughest, all uphill, and that once at 9 the elevation reversed. I struggled on the longer hills, stopping repeatedly to check my heart rate, looking around nervously for the emergency vehicles. Some walkers say the downhill is the hardest, your knees go on you and you push harder into your runners, worsening your blisters. I was lucky—no blisters—but my back and shoulder muscles were killing me and I began to look for bridges, logs or large rocks so I could sit for a minute and let my back muscles unlock. By now, I was zoning out, almost in a zombie state. As checkpoint volunteers cheered the walkers on with words of encouragement, I hardly heard them. I remembered what Heather's sister-in-law Megan had said at around Checkpoint 10 when they went two years ago. "Never, ever again. I would rather give birth to twins in a wilderness tent, breech, with only a rawhide to chew on than to ever do this again." I understood how she felt.

All I could think of was the next stop. By Checkpoint 12, I knew I was going to finish, because it was only 3.6 more kilometers. I knew it was going to kill me, but I was going to finish. Now, it wasn't mountains anymore, just little rolling hills, and I counted them down. At last I glimpsed the water as I rounded the bend where the cedar mill used to stand. Now came that last little shot of adrenaline as I passed the Tahsis welcome sign with the note on the reverse that says, "last to leave, please turn out the lights." I could hear the horns and honks of the police car and fire engine as they welcomed each walker to the finish line. Dehydrated, my eyes still found enough moisture to brim over as I knew I'd made it, in just thirteen hours and forty-nine minutes. Just a few more yards and I was ringing the bell by the big wooden cut-outs of hiking boots and getting my reward—the medal with the Burning Boot and the words "I Did It." Checking the list later I found out I was 165th of 194 to finish, but I felt like a winner.

I knew tomorrow I'd be hurting even more than I was now, but it didn't matter anymore. Those three words on the medal said it all. I did it!

~Sharon McGregor

Five Years

Difficult things take a long time, impossible things a little longer.
~André A. Jackson

hree days after my forced retirement, I was sitting at the kitchen table feeling sorry for myself. Two severely arthritic hips had made it impossible to continue in my pediatric practice. What meaningful activity would hold my interest and enhance the rest of my life? I had wracked my brain, but as yet had not devised a plan.

When the phone rang, I hoped my wife Dotty would answer it. After several rings, I reached for the phone, realizing she wasn't home. It was my good friend Allan.

After the usual pleasantries, he asked, "How'd you like to take a course with me at the Lifelong Learning Institute at Florida International University?"

"What course?"

"It's a creative writing course."

"You're kidding?"

"No, I always wanted to write, and I'd love company."

"I got brung up in Brooklyn and ain't even loined to talk a gooda English," I chided. "No way do I want to write."

"Come on," he said. "It'll be fun."

"Nah!"

"Please, you'll love it. We'll spend some time together."

"Nah!"

"Keep me company."

Just to get him off my back, I finally agreed. I thought he'd forget about it when the time came to take the course.

"Great," he said. "I'll pick you up in ten minutes."

Damn, what had I gotten myself into?

One of the first assignments the teacher gave us was to write an opening sentence about a trip we had taken. We were to make it interesting so the reader would want to learn more. I wrote, "As our ship entered the fjord, the sight of rugged cliffs undulating to the sea, and the sweet smells of multicolored flowers at their bases, presaged the wonders of Norway we were about to see."

"Very good," the teacher said. "Maybe a little overuse of big words, but it grabs our interest."

I could do this, I thought. By the time the class was over, I was hooked.

Several months later, I decided to take a writing course at the university itself. I learned that before I could take more advanced courses, I needed to complete Creative Writing 101. I tried to enlist my friend Allan.

"We'll have fun," I said. "It won't cost you anything. When you're over fifty-five, they let you take any course free with the permission of the instructor."

"Sounds too elementary," he said. "Besides, I'm still working and can't make a class in the middle of the day."

I took the course anyway, and found myself thrown in with a group of eighteen- to twenty-one-year-olds. It was interesting to hear about their dreams and passions. They were not too dissimilar to the ones I had at their age. One of the assignments was to write a twenty-six sentence story, each sentence starting with a different letter of the alphabet from A to Z. I told the story of Abraham Zenobia, an elderly gentleman who was trying to regain his youth. When I came to the end I concluded, "Youth couldn't be revisited. Zenobia sadly became resolved to his fate." Then I realized that although youth couldn't be revisited, hopes and dreams needn't die. I had found a new passion, creative writing.

The next term, I enrolled in the more advanced class of Narrative Technique. I enlisted Allan to come with me, as the course was given in the evening. On the first night of the class, the professor, who was head of the department, wanted to know who had taken Creative Writing 101. I raised my hand. He asked all those who didn't have this prerequisite to leave. I felt sorry for my friend Allan as he walked out the door. He was the one who always wanted to write and he had started me on this path. Yet, I was the one pursuing it.

The accolades I had received in the first two courses for my writing skills were now few and far between. I seemed to have no concept of what constituted a good story. Each exercise I handed in was ripped to shreds by the professor. At first I thought he was doing that because in his mind I was dallying with writing and was taking the place of someone who wanted to write professionally. Then I realized what I was writing was generally awful.

I made an appointment to see the professor. "Will I ever be able to write a good story?" I asked.

"How long have you been writing?" he said.

"A long time. At least seven or eight months."

He smiled. "You can't expect to write anything decent for at least five years."

"Really?"

He nodded.

I continued taking classes with different professors, trying to hone my skills. I even published my first story, in *Chicken Soup for the Sports Fan's Soul*. I thought this was just luck since I still wasn't really sure what made a good story.

The focus of the classes I had been taking was on fiction. Someone suggested that I might enjoy taking a course in creative nonfiction that was being offered that term. The first assignment was to describe a culinary delight we had experienced. I described my grandmother's savory chopped liver. The professor's comment on my story was "B+, good." The second assignment had to do with writing a story about one of the rooms we lived in growing up. I wrote about sneaking into the dining room Friday nights when the male members of my extended family played pinochle. When the professor returned the story, the comment and the grade were the same: B+, good. The third assignment was to go home and write a story about an object in your house. I chose my mother's soup tureen that adorned our dining room table. I told the story of how, at the age of fifteen, I traveled by train to Chicago, to meet my mother, father, uncle and aunt to attend my brother's graduation from a Master's degree program at the University of Illinois. I couldn't drive out with them because I needed to take several New York State Regents Exams.

After the graduation, we traveled in a packed car through Canada, stopping at every antique barn along the way. At the first barn my mother found a silver coffee and tea server that I thought was ugly. My father said we couldn't buy it because there was no room in the car. My brother, who loved it, suggested that it be shipped, and my father acquiesced.

At the next barn my mother sniffed out a large tureen hidden between an ornate candelabra and a set of old English fire irons. Although my brother said it was ugly, my mother and I loved it. My father said it was too big to fit into our stuffed car, and too fragile to ship. I saw the sad look on my mother's face. "If we buy it, Pop, I'd be willing to hold it on my lap till we arrive home. Mom really loves the tureen."

My father nodded.

"I clutched the boxed tureen the entire trip, as if by releasing my grip I would lose my hold on my mother."

When the professor handed this story back, she wrote "A+, excellent." I spoke to her and said I didn't like this story as much as the other two. I thought I spent too much time on the description of the tureen.

She smiled. "That's easy to correct. Do you see how the story highlights the differences between you and your brother in a subtle way, and shows your feelings toward your mother?"

I nodded, and really did see it. I finally realized what constituted a story.

I entered the story into the all-University contest and when I won, the head of the department presented the award to me. He said, "Paul once asked me if he would ever write a good story. I guess this is his answer. I told him it takes at least five years to write something good. If I'm not mistaken, that's how long it has been since he started writing."

~Paul Winick, M.D.

95

Our Great Expectations

*Nobody succeeds beyond his or her wildest expectations unless he or she
begins with some wild expectations.*

~Ralph Charell

On my seventieth birthday, my husband of just seven years
photographed me amidst our scarlet Asian lilies. Then he
donned an elegant taupe striped shirt, splashed on his
woodsy signature Devin cologne and escorted me to an Early Bird
Supper at Stephani's Oak Street Grill in Colville.

We toasted with huckleberry iced tea, and then Ken patted my
hand. "Enjoy your dinner, baby. I'm glad I still can take you out for
special occasions. But I want to ask you something. Now that you've
reached seventy, is there anything you've always wanted to do that
you haven't gotten around to?"

His question surprised me. Ken wasn't one for introspection,
though he'd become more reflective since his recent cardiac bypass
surgery. I took a bite of my lemon garlic salmon and considered.

"Well, there's that government education award from my VISTA
service. I'd like to study literature and history at the University of
Cambridge International Summer School."

Ken smiled. "It sure would be something to brag about. Is there
a deadline on that award?"

I calculated. I had to use it within seven years of the conclusion
of my service. "I have until 2013," I said.

"Then I expect Cambridge can wait a while. You'll go someday. I don't have enough energy for any more trips."

I understood his concern. After his kidneys had taken such a hard hit from his surgery, Ken believed that his time was running short. He'd decided against dialysis. I doubted we'd be going anywhere far away ever again. And there was little at Cambridge to hold his interest.

Then one evening several months later, Ken surprised me.

"Remember your birthday when I asked if there was anything you still wanted to do? I've been thinking it over. I want to see the Rosetta Stone and Loch Ness. Think you could book us one last trip? Let's do it all… England, Wales, Scotland, maybe even Ireland."

I went to our computer and tapped away. "What luck," I announced. "There's a sale on flights to Heathrow right now. We have enough frequent flyer miles for one fare, and we can buy a second for half price if we go in March."

"Let's do it," Ken said. "We can get a BritRail pass, and take the trains everywhere."

"Except we'll need a ferry to get to Ireland," I replied, laughing.

So we went, expecting to do it all. A cryptographer while in the Air Force, Ken frequently mentioned his fascination with that ancient Egyptian stele, the Rosetta Stone. He managed the walk from our London hotel to the bus stop, but he sighed when we stepped off the double-decker in front of the British Museum.

"I can't take another step, baby. I'll just sit in the lobby."

I pointed to the collapsible wheelchairs by the entrance. "We've come all this way. You're going to see that Stone!"

He relented. "I guess you could push me here. Nobody we know is going to see me."

That was so like Ken. He placed great stock in keeping up appearances. Didn't want to look sick… didn't want to look frail… even when he was.

He made some last valiant efforts. When we toured the Guinness brewery in Dublin, Ken plodded up the ramp to the top floor. When we got to our B&B in Inverness, though, he dispatched me to fetch a takeaway curry, and acknowledged we'd need a taxi to meet the tour going to Loch Ness the next morning. He couldn't navigate the few blocks to their office on foot. But he grinned the entire time we boated across the lake, alert to glimpse the fabled Nessie. By the time we met up with old friends in Bristol a few days later, Ken claimed to be plain tuckered out. I could see the weariness in his eyes.

Once we returned home, we rarely went out, even to the movies. The last one we saw together was *The Bucket List*, where a pair of terminally-ill men travel the world with their final "to do" wish list.

"I guess seeing Loch Ness and the Rosetta Stone completed my bucket list," Ken said as we exited the Alpine Theatre. "You make certain you get to Cambridge University one day."

That autumn we learned Ken's eldest son would remarry. The wedding would be in Colorado Springs. Ken's other boys and all the grandkids planned to be there.

"I'd like to see my three sons together once again. Final bucket list request," he said.

"Would you agree to let me order wheelchairs for the Spokane and Denver airports?"

He hesitated for just one second. "Yes."

That was our final trip together. By Valentine's Day we learned that Ken now had cancer, as well as kidney failure. Tough to the last, he stayed at home, dogs flanking his recliner, until the end.

After he died I moped for months. Then I remembered what Ken had said. Despite reservations that at seventy-three I'd be too old to fit in with a college crowd, I applied for the 2010 Cambridge summer school. I selected three courses, all in Victorian literature and history. I especially looked forward to taking "Criminals and Gentlemen: the Victorian Underworld in Charles Dickens' *Oliver Twist* and *Great Expectations*."

The moment I set foot on the grounds of Cambridge's Selwyn College, where I'd live for two weeks, I felt at home. I loved studying in my Ann's Court dorm, and savoring supper in the dining hall. I wandered through this storied town that dates back to medieval days, sipped cider at the Anchor Pub on the banks of the River Cam and debated Dickens and Victorians with new friends of all ages, from dozens of countries. Most of all, I pondered the layered nuances of *Great Expectations*.

The novel's title alludes to inheritance, the expectation of a legacy. That's the literal meaning, from the moment a lawyer tells Pip, the hero, that he'll have money coming from an anonymous benefactor. The title's ironic, as well; it references Pip's other expectations, beyond that said fortune. Then there are the expectations that Pip believes others have of him, those great things he believes God or fate or his own conscience expect. The title even hints at what readers might expect when they read a Dickens novel.

I considered our own expectations. When Ken and I married in 2000 we didn't expect to come into a fortune. But we did well enough when I retired, selling a townhouse near Washington, D.C., and buying a country home in Northeast Washington State. Ken hadn't expected to travel, but we did, watching glaciers shard in Alaska's Inner Passage, photographing the Leaning Tower of Pisa, hefting steins at Munich's Oktoberfest.

I didn't expect to lose my husband so soon. But Ken left me a legacy, an appreciation for that "bucket list." I've fulfilled most of my personal expectations, writing my narrative essays and continuing with community service. And there's still some money left in that education award, so I'm not quite through with Cambridge.

I expect I'll return there this coming summer. I've even picked my course. It's "Napoleon and His Enemies." Now there was a man with great expectations!

~Terri Elders

96

Scooter Chicks Rule

Middle age is when we can do just as much as ever — but would rather not.
~Author Unknown

I t happened almost twenty years ago, but I remember it like it was yesterday. Turning my minivan absentmindedly into the driveway on the day before my fortieth birthday, I almost hit the motorcycle parked there. Not just any motorcycle, mind you, but a shiny black Honda Rebel cruiser with a black leather seat, black leather saddlebags, and chrome fenders so dazzling they almost blinded me. A fire-engine-red helmet, complete with American flag decal, rested atop the sissy bar.

My husband George was straddling the bike and grinning from ear to ear.

I got out of the van and slammed the door. Hard. "Don't tell me you've bought another one!" I was as tight-lipped and hands-on-hips exasperated as I'd been six months earlier when he told me he was thinking about buying a motorcycle. Which he did, despite my protests that such a toy was not only impractical and dangerous but a sure sign of a mid-life crisis. "Why in heaven's name do you need two motorcycles?"

"I don't," he said, still grinning. "This one's for you."

"You've got to be kidding." I shook my head in disbelief. I'd never even been a passenger on the back of George's bike, let alone considered piloting one of my own. "I can't ride that thing!"

"Sure you can. Anybody who can balance a bicycle and drive a straight shift car can ride a motorcycle." He eased the helmet onto my head and showed me how to lace its strap through the D-rings. "Get on."

I did. And my schooling as a motorcyclist began.

Lesson One was mastering the terminology. The first — and most traumatic — phrase I learned was "dropping the bike," commonly known as "falling over" by those unfamiliar with biker lingo. In Lesson Two, I learned that the best place to work on my clutch-and-throttle skills was a deserted country road, not at our town's busiest intersection. Over time, I learned how to avoid dead possums in the road, how to stay in my own lane while negotiating sharp curves, and how not to lock up the brakes when I hit a patch of loose gravel. I became a fan of padded jeans and bright yellow rain suits and thick leather gloves. I learned the difference between full-face helmets and open-face helmets and barely-legal bean pot helmets, and between a water-cooled engine and an air-cooled one.

And along the way, I discovered that there really is nothing like the open road experienced from a motorcycle. The sights, the sounds, the smells were like nothing I'd ever encountered in a car. Every time I rode the motorcycle, I felt awake, alert, and alive. And happy. Ecstatically, deliriously happy.

My favorite T-shirt bore a message I fervently believed: BIKER CHICKS RULE.

So why, as the years passed, did I find myself riding my motorcycle less and less often? Lots of reasons. I accepted a library job that required hauling boxes of books from one branch to another. (You can't haul books on a motorcycle.) I adopted a dog who loved to run errands with me. (Dogs make lousy motorcycle passengers.) On the days I'd set aside an hour or two to ride, the weather never seemed to cooperate. (Motorcycling in a thunderstorm is no fun, even in a bright yellow rain suit.)

Or the bike's battery would be dead. Or my leather jacket would be covered in mildew. Or birds would have built a nest in my helmet.

My shiny black motorcycle was eventually rolled into the back corner of the garage where it sat, dusty and forlorn, for almost five years. I had to admit to myself, though I never said it aloud, that even if I charged the battery and scrubbed the mildew off the jacket and cleaned the bird nest out of the helmet, I probably wouldn't be eager to ride it.

I'd lost my edge and wasn't sure I could get it back, even if I wanted to.

So imagine my surprise when, not long before my fifty-sixth birthday, I absentmindedly turned my car into the driveway and almost hit the motor scooter parked there. It was a Honda Reflex—fire-engine red with a black leather seat and a molded fiberglass trunk on the back.

George was standing next to it and grinning from ear to ear.

"Thought you might want to give one of these a try," he said. "Step-through mounting, automatic transmission, even a radio!"

"What makes you think I want another motorcycle?" I stammered. "I don't even ride the one I have."

"Not a motorcycle," he said. "A motor scooter. No more clutching and shifting. No need to straddle a gas tank. No burning your bare legs on the exhaust pipe." He pointed to the wide footrests. "And you put your feet on those instead of pegs." He eased the old red helmet—now cleared of any hint of a bird nest—onto my head. "Get on. Take it for a spin and see how you like it."

I laced the helmet strap through the D-rings as he explained how the scooter worked. I adjusted the mirrors, cranked the engine, and gently rolled the throttle toward me. Easing the scooter onto the street, I was amazed at how smooth and uncomplicated it was to ride. No clutch. No gears. No tank. No exhaust pipe.

Wow, I muttered to myself. A little old lady could ride this thing.

Such a thought was enough to make me slam on the brakes. Was that what I'd become? A little old lady not tough enough to ride a real motorcycle? Maybe I should just skip the scooter and trade my motorcycle in for a rocking chair. Perhaps even go ahead and reserve a spot in the nursing home.

I was feeling pretty down as I circled the block and headed for home. Until three guys on tricked-out Harleys appeared. The first two flashed me the peace sign, as is the custom when one motorcyclist meets another. The third rider? He winked and mouthed the words "cool bike" as he whizzed past.

That's when I knew I wasn't ready to give up the pleasures of the open road experienced from my very own set of wheels. And I sure wasn't ready for a rocking chair. So without regret—not too much, anyway—I traded my shiny black cruiser for the fire-engine-red scooter. I learned once again how to avoid dead possums in the road and how to stay in my own lane when negotiating sharp curves and how not to lock up the brakes when I hit a patch of loose gravel.

I bought a new favorite T-shirt, too. One with a slightly different message printed on it: SCOOTER CHICKS RULE.

Yeah baby.

~Jennie Ivey

97

Holding Babies

*A child needs a grandparent, anybody's grandparent, to grow a little more
securely into an unfamiliar world.*
~Charles and Ann Morse

The seat belt sign had just come on during our flight to New
Orleans. My long-term companion Carol Lee was reading
her book. "Carol Lee, what do you want to do in life?" I
asked. I expected her to say she wanted to travel to Europe again.

Carol Lee turned to me and said, "I would like to hold babies."

"Hold babies?" I was stunned. "You've got grandchildren!"

"I would like to work in a hospital nursery and just hold the
newborns."

Newborns? Her desire was one to ponder, which I did with each
salty peanut I crunched. I looked out my little round window at New
Orleans in the distance.

Hold babies? Was she serious?

We relaxed in the Big Easy, even though there was so much to
do. A beignet at Café du Monde, the French Quarter, a walk and a
tour of the Garden District. St. Charles Avenue and the streetcar ride;
moonlight dancing aboard a Mississippi riverboat; a final dinner at
Emile's. Then, our time was gone.

We returned the rental car, took off our shoes, got our bags
through security and walked to our departure gate. We then had a
two-hour wait for our flight home. Carol Lee sat and read her book,
but I'm not good at waiting. Electric carts with irritating beepers, a

crowd of noisy people in plastic chairs near Carol Lee, and a crying baby by the windows bothered me. I got up and explored the terminal. I knew how to entertain myself. One of my pastimes is to look for celebrities. Wouldn't it be cool to be able to say, "You know who I saw in New Orleans?" And then deal with someone's awe? But, in Louis Armstrong International, as in other airports, all the celebrities had shown poor judgment by eluding me.

Six postcards later, I came back. Carol Lee was blissfully reading her book. I tried sitting still, but the crying child and the loud voices annoyed me, so I got up and paced the floor. When I sat down again, Carol Lee motioned towards the windows and said, "I'm going to see if I can help that baby." I knew the only thing to do was to watch.

Carol approached the baby slowly with a smile on her face, love in her heart and peace on her mind.

Understandably, the parents looked up. What did this little white-haired lady want? Carol Lee said something to the parents. They looked at one another and then at Carol Lee. They couldn't speak English. Carol Lee couldn't speak their language, but that didn't matter. Hand motions spoke volumes. Behind me, the noisy people were aggressively discussing something. Carol Lee remained resolute and focused on the crying child.

She opened her arms, the universal expression of acceptance. She forgot herself and her needs. She concentrated on the troubled and innocent child's needs. Sunlight shone through the windows behind her as, miracle of miracles, the parents handed over the crying baby to a peaceful stranger. Carol stood holding the baby and talking in the ubiquitous language of grandmothers. She cooed. She shushed. She hummed. She swayed rhythmically and held the infant close. She instantly became the Universal Grandmother loved by babies, welcomed by tired parents, treasured worldwide. Her calmness was like a pebble thrown into a pond. The first ripple caused the child's anxieties to disappear. The next ripple caused the child's parents to relax. Another ripple caused me to relax.

Carol Lee motioned to the parents that she was going to walk around the seating area with the child. The parents nodded their approval. Carol Lee nodded. I nodded, but I don't know why. The noisy people were touched by the next ripple and watched in awe as Carol Lee performed the ancient ritual of ignoring all commotion and moving around a room full of people while being alone with an infant. When she returned to the smiling, grateful, tearful mother, the child was asleep. The noisy people began to whisper and I, well, I was spellbound. On the flight home, I stopped crunching peanuts when I realized I had walked all over that airport terminal looking for famous people and had seen someone more important than any celebrity. She was not an athlete, not a movie star, and not Donald Trump. But she was someone who had the gift of demonstrating unconditional love.

When she first told me she wanted to hold babies, I confess that I did not see the magnanimity of her calling, but then, simple mission statements are often the most profound. Today, I translate her creed to look like this: If all babies get held and loved, they grow up to be happy children, ergo happy adults. If everyone is loved and loving, and holding newborns, who could take up arms and go to war?

It's a lesson grandparents can teach and learn while waiting in an airport.

~John J. Lesjack

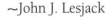

98

Oh My Word!

It is never too late to be what you might have been.
~George Eliot

During high school and college I had a friend who responded to most anything I said with, "Oh my word!" Soon all of us in our close-knit group picked up her habit. "Oh my word," punctuated our conversations. We conveyed the intended message—concern, excitement, disbelief—by the inflection in our voices, the words we emphasized, and the expressions on our faces. After our group scattered, my use of the phrase diminished. It popped up again years later when my longtime employer offered retirement three years earlier than I expected. I burst into tears at the surprise. As the shock wore off and my mind embraced the possibilities, I exclaimed, "Oh my word!"

I had enjoyed my job as a school social worker and early intervention specialist, but it was time for me to answer another calling, to be a writer. Others may take scenic trips or volunteer for worthy projects. "Oh my word" described my desire. I could journey with my words and honor my creative spirit. I could write what I wanted, explore styles, and improve my writing craft.

In its own way, writing has always held a prominent place in my life. In high school, when I wrestled with decisions about my future, my dad wondered about a career that would employ my love of writing.

"Maybe you could be a writer or a journalist."

I didn't pursue his idea wholeheartedly. Not then. Today I can imagine why he concluded that a writing career might suit me, but I'll never know for sure since he died more than thirty years ago and I had never asked. I bet his thought was based on his observation of my childhood and teen years.

I loved stories and books. Both my parents read to me when I was young, instilling in me a passion for reading. I was enchanted with the books I owned or checked out from the library.

Though he was always on the go with his sand and gravel business, Dad appreciated the written word. He read *National Geographic*, *The Saturday Evening Post*, *Reader's Digest*, and *Popular Mechanics*. Every night he read our newspaper, *The Emporia Gazette*, with my mother and me. Emporia was the home of the famous journalists William Allen White and William Lindsay White, a likely reason for my father suggesting a writing career.

Growing up, I wrote long letters to my grandmother, aunts, and pen pals while perched at the edge of the mammoth desk in the dining room. Or, I stretched out on the living room floor with our ginger cat lounging on my back. After I moved to the upstairs bedroom, I sat at my desk penning poems and meditations along with letters and journal entries.

During my teen years I had a few items published in church and camp newsletters and church-related periodicals. As a social worker I authored articles in professional journals, edited a school social work journal, wrote countless evaluation reports, and gave workshops to motivate practitioners to share their wisdom by writing. I journaled through most years, chronicling my challenges with health issues and describing the joys and laments of life.

Over the years, I viewed writing as an option I could fall back on if my congenital hearing loss worsened or my weak voice declined to the point of encumbering my day-to-day job interactions. That time never materialized. For more than three decades I worked with children who had special needs and with their families. So when agency reorganization resulted in that early retirement offer in 2007,

I accepted. My husband had already retired, plus I wanted a pace of life that matched my energy level.

A precursor to writing in retirement had occurred several years before when I participated in a writing workshop. After our facilitator moved out of state, I joined others from the workshop to form our own writing group. This group made me accountable for my goals and gave me courage to devote time each day to creative writing.

I wondered if I could stick with my plan. Soon I recognized that my optimism and persistence—evident from my social work practice and from my approach to personal health issues—also applied to successful writing. My ability to communicate effectively by observing, listening, reflecting, and reframing situations transferred to penning evocative pieces. I wrote what came to mind: wisdom gleaned from my family and growing up, and lessons learned about empowering myself and others.

I believe that words inspire, inform, and heal. All people long for connection, the kind that springs from kindness, compassion, and cooperation. Now, in retirement, I craft stories to inspire and connect others.

Writing fits my retired life. It opens me up and gives voice to my life. I unearth a richer understanding of my experiences. I bridge my insights with those of others. Through writing I take fascinating journeys. I travel unseen roads. I dive into oceans of information.

Sometimes parents don't know the seeds they've sown. Like my dad, a parent may not live to see those seeds grow and flower. Yet, the confidence my dad gave me boosts me up. I want to say, "Dad! See, I did it. I followed your guidance and you were right. I can write!"

My husband Bill acts as my number one writing cheerleader now. He shares with others his enthusiasm for my writing. When we're asked about what I'm doing in retirement, he says, "She's writing! I'm so proud of her. She's doing exactly what she said she'd do."

That's true. In retirement I do what I vowed I'd do and more. I didn't begin creative writing with the goal of publishing my work. I wrote because of my passion for words. Slowly, bit by bit, my work found a home in print.

These successes affirm what my dad recognized all those years ago—I have an inspiring message and I can use my writing skills to share it. My writing transforms into a gift I give to make the world a better place.

Every now and then my path astounds me and my heart fills with joy. I think, "Oh my word—I'm a writer!"

It's never too late to follow a dream. Unexpected early retirement rendered the right time for me. When I write, my words frolic on the page, spinning stories that stood still until a cherished dream got up to dance.

~Ronda Armstrong

99

Stretching from Within

I tried yoga once but took off for the mall halfway through class,
as I had a sudden craving for a soft pretzel and world peace.
~Terri Guillemets

I walked in and unfolded my yoga mat like a matador unfurling her cape. I looked in the mirror and dared myself to stay in this room for the whole ninety minutes. Already, the heat coaxed out sweat on my arms and behind my knees. I was thirsty and I was wondering why I had thought I was capable of doing Bikram (or "hot") yoga.

Every year, I like to try a different physical activity, something I'm not good at. When I first heard about "hot yoga," I couldn't imagine why anyone would want to spend ninety minutes in a room heated to 108 degrees, rapidly going through a routine of yoga poses. The yoga classes I had taken long ago were slow and contemplative; the teachers were intuitive and experimental in choosing the next poses. There was a gentle flow, punctuated by breaks and conversation.

The Bikram method featured the same twenty-six poses every session with no time for anything but focus and concentration.

"You'll love it," my friend Liza had promised me. I loved the introductory price — $10 for as many classes as I wanted to take in ten days.

The teacher entered the room and everyone rose. Feet together, arms by our sides, we stood like well-behaved schoolchildren ready to walk to lunch. Listening to her instructions, we interlaced our fingers, folded our hands under our chins, pressed our arms together, and began with breathing. Then we moved into stretching, knee bending, and balancing postures. I wobbled; I shook; I fumbled. The heat, which was supposed to help deepen stretching as well as cleanse organs, was wiping me out. I felt woozy, dizzy and dumb. Halfway through the class, I fled the room.

"How did you like it?" Liza called to ask later that evening.

"It was terrible. I was terrible," I told her.

"You're just not used to it. You need the point system. You get fifty points just for showing up. You get another forty points if you stay in the room for the whole session. Even if you're lying down half the time, you still get those forty points. Then you get another ten points for trying the poses."

She knew me too well. I liked the idea of amassing points. I liked the idea of measuring myself. I wanted to achieve at least ninety points before I quit.

I went a second time, determined to stay in the room. Only two poses in, I already felt dizzy. I lay on my mat, embarrassed by my weakness.

"Look in the mirror. Keep focused on yourself," the teacher advised. "Breathe. Breathing is the most important component of this practice."

I stood up to rejoin the group. I looked at myself and sent an affirmation: "You are very brave." I realized just how brave I was when my attention wandered and I saw I was the least supple person in the class.

To touch the floor, I had to bend my knees. My backward bend was a slight lean. When everyone else was gracefully curling her spine upward from the floor, I was barely raising my head. I had never been so inept in such plain view of so many people. "Don't judge yourself," the teacher said. "Just try your best."

My best at that point was sitting down again while the class went into another stretching pose. I dabbed at the sweat, then stood up to do the Tree, a balancing posture I'd done at home, a posture I was usually good at. But instead of posing as a graceful willow, I stumbled across my mat like a piece of tumbleweed.

Each pose seemed harder than the next. I felt like an awkward crow among lovely, lithe finches. Then I reminded myself that this was a spiritual practice as well as a physical workout. I was an acolyte seeking knowledge.

Somehow I stayed in the room the whole ninety minutes, although I was flat on the mat during a third of the poses. Still, at the end, when we all lay on our backs, relaxing and letting the benefits of the exercise come deeper into our bodies, I felt a small sense of calm and accomplishment.

The next class, I managed to try every exercise.

I called Liza to report my progress.

"You have 100 points," she said. "You should be so proud."

I was. Too proud, perhaps. Three classes later, during the one-legged tree pose, I peeked over at the strapping strong man next to me and noticed I was better at balancing then he was. I smiled inwardly and instantly fell out of the posture. My friend hadn't mentioned deducting points for competitiveness and comparisons: the yoga practice took care of that.

"What's the rest of the point system?" I asked Liza, two months into my practice. "Do I get points when I learn to do the Camel? What about the Crow? That arm balance looks really difficult."

Liza smiled at me and shook her head.

"What's really difficult is now to let go of achievement and just enjoy where you are in the practice."

I stared at her. "I'm terrible. I still can't touch my toes. My chair posture looks like a bar stool."

"Are you showing up? Are you breathing?" she asked.

I nodded.

"Then enjoy the process."

That Saturday, walking into the warm studio, I felt a sense of humility, joy and ease. Though my body was slow to show improvement, something inside me was blossoming. I liked being in a roomful of people of all ages and all different types of bodies and abilities, each of us pursuing the same spiritual and physical practice. I liked leaving more emotionally flexible and more relaxed, knowing that no matter how deeply I stretched or how aptly I balanced, I still had so far to go and so much to learn.

~Deborah Shouse

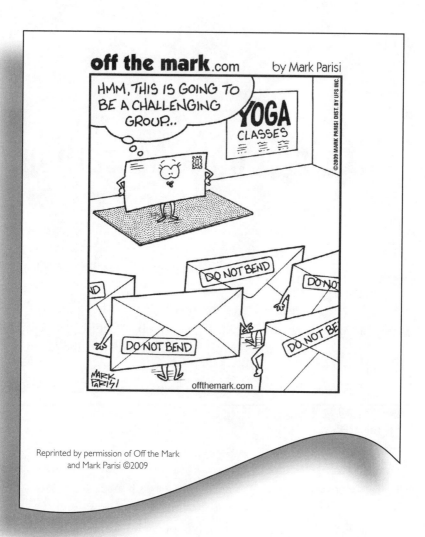

Reprinted by permission of Off the Mark
and Mark Parisi ©2009

Musings on a Marathon

Arriving at one goal is the starting point to another.
~John Dewey

I could hardly believe I was there, amidst a hoard of people waiting for the starting shot that would begin the 1995 Portland Marathon. Although I'd been telling myself for months as I trained that I could do this, I still had doubts. Could I really finish the twenty-six point two mile race and make it across the finish line standing up?

What was I doing there anyway, sixty-five years old, the granny in our group, and never having competed in anything longer than a 5K race before?

Until my late fifties, I was a confirmed couch potato. Give me a good book and somewhere to sit and I was content. Then I remarried. My new husband, Leonard, turned out to be a geriatric jock with a sweet steamroller way of talking me into anything. First we took walks together. Gradually the strolls grew longer and moved at a brisker pace.

Before I knew it, I was entered in my first race. I walked most of the way while Leonard ran. The next race seemed easier and so did the one after that. As my walk rate increased, a competitive streak I never knew I had kicked in. I would set my sights on a slow moving runner ahead of me and pump up my pace until I overtook him. I would feel energized by my little victory and search out the next target, a jogger or power walker who looked vulnerable. After a couple of years, I owned the 5K and had first place ribbons to prove it.

Leonard considered my conversion to walking one of his greatest achievements in our marriage. He didn't care that I wasn't running. Fast walking was good enough to prove he'd gotten me off the couch and into a more healthful activity. When we moved to Bainbridge Island, he discovered the Saturday Striders, a newly formed runners and walkers group, and signed us up. When he became terminally ill and bedridden, members of the group would often visit and talk running with him. After one such visit, our friend Judy asked as she was leaving if there was anything she could do for him.

"Yes," he said. "Keep Marcia walking."

She promised and took it as a sacred pledge not to let his proud achievement die with him. She showed up daily and we walked. Walked and talked. Our outings became more than exercise. They were my therapy, a time when I could strip away the cheery mask, vocalize my despair and not care if it made me cry. We walked regularly, all through Leonard's illness and after he was gone. It became a habit, a stabilizing part of my life that eased my grief.

A year later, during a Striders meeting, I listened with admiration as Judy, Sarah and Druse talked about going down to Portland, Oregon to do the Walkers' Marathon. Kay, the Striders' leader, was enthusiastic about their plan. She worked out training schedules for them and continued to motivate and encourage.

My walks with Judy began to follow her training schedule, gradually increasing in distance and speed. I was glad to be able to support Judy in this, as she had supported me through Leonard's illness. We marked down the days to the marathon. The closer that loomed, the more excited the Portland threesome became in reporting their progress to the group. I began to feel left out. I'd joined Judy through all the training, but I wasn't going to the big event, the grand finale, the race itself.

A thought began to nag at me: Why not? I knew the answer. I was way older than Sarah and Judy and even a bit older than Druse, who was a guy with big strong legs. But the thought wouldn't go away. The question rattled around in my head every time I laced on my running shoes.

I went to Kay for advice. I knew, with her nursing background and trainer expertise, she'd be honest with me, remind me I'd turned sixty-five that year and finally turn off the question in my head. What she said wasn't what I expected.

"Oh Marcia, what a wonderful tribute to Leonard. Do you realize the race is almost exactly a year since he passed away? Of course you should do it."

She was right about the date of the race. I hadn't realized it before. The Portland trio became a foursome.

Marathon day arrived all too soon. Was I ready? Could I maintain the minimum speed required to complete twenty-six point two miles before they re-opened the streets to traffic? Would I have any energy left to run for my life if cars and trucks came roaring down the street at me? I was filled with doubt, but as I started to pack and tucked my race number into my bag, I felt confident again. That piece of paper with those big black digits and Portland Marathon printed on it gave me a thrill. I was an official entrant.

We were up early the next morning for the start of the race. I stashed a PowerBar in my fanny pack to nibble for energy along the way. I added a bottle of water and a photo of Leonard for encouragement.

The chatter and anticipation all around me at the starting line had everyone in a party mood and I was raring to go. Judy, Sarah and Druse were soon ahead of me and out of sight. It didn't matter. I was having a grand walk, feeling fit and moving at a good speed.

But the walk was a long haul. I hit every Porta-Potty because I didn't know how far it would be to the next one. I was losing time, becoming one of the back of the pack stragglers.

The miles dragged on. My feet felt like lead. It was getting harder and harder to lift them. I didn't stop at Porta-Potties anymore. I was afraid that if I sat down I wouldn't be able to get up. Better to just keep the feet moving, one after the other, on automatic pilot.

I pulled out my PowerBar. It tasted like chocolate-flavored

cardboard. I took a long drink from my water bottle and returned it to my fanny pack. My hand touched Leonard's photo as I did. I imagined him inhabiting the picture and giving me a good kick in the rear to get me moving. I laughed and quickened my pace.

I resorted to mind games. Five miles left. That's about the distance from my house to town. I can do that. Two miles left. That's the distance from the highway to the Wilkes School. I can do that. One mile left. That's the distance from town to the ferry. I can do that.

Soon I was moving over the finish line, still on automatic pilot and surprised when someone hung a medal attached to a white and blue ribbon around my neck. I looked down at it. Finisher-Portland Marathon, 1995. Finisher—is there a more beautiful word in the whole wide world?

~Marcia Rudoff

All in Good Time

We don't grow older, we grow riper.
~Pablo Picasso

ince I was an eight-year-old child, propped up on my elbows using a flashlight in a rain-soaked tent in Stokes State Forest, New Jersey, reading comics for hours on end about mythical beasts and beautiful princesses, I've wanted to write for publication. Being published means someone else recognizes the merit of your words and will invest time, effort, and money in you. I never considered self-publishing or vanity press. That always seemed to me like giving oneself a card on Valentine's Day.

As with many far-off dreams, I had multiple starts. I'd keep a diary for a while. Sometimes, I'd record meticulous details of some trip to a far-flung corner of the world, only to lose track of where I put the journal a month later. In my mid-twenties, I honed the fictional beginnings of the greatest American novel since *Gone with the Wind* on some loose leaf paper in a three-ring notebook. After a few weeks, I lost steam and my muse. The writing habit never took root.

Life always got in the way of chronic writing. I went to college. I got a job. I married. I bore four children. I raised them. I joined clubs. I gardened. I played tennis. I did everything but what I felt driven to do. I avoided writing. I was too busy. I told myself that someday I'd give it a go!

Whether one of my myriad excuses for not "doing it" was genuine or whether I harbored the fear of failure or whether I was too lazy to work at my craft, no matter. The simple truth was I never wrote, never joined a group of writers, never attended a conference for writers, never submitted a thing anywhere, decade after decade. I was a talker with entertaining anecdotes, nothing more.

Then, my life changed radically, quickly and unexpectedly.

Six years ago, my failing father moved in. As he lost his independence, so did I. During this new phase of life, with my 24/7 duties caring for Dad, a penitentiary silence day after boring day enveloped me. I decided that although a door closed on my former life, I'd force open a window and shout out a new life! I had no reason to defer my childhood goal—to become a published writer. The confinement thrust on me as caregiver could be my opportunity to realize my longtime dream.

While Dad napped, I scribbled. Within nine months, I birthed a 103,000-word novel. Next, I bought books on literary agents. I studied the recommendations and shot off a ream of splendid queries via cyber-mail and traditional post. Those sad SASE's boomeranged back with standard rejection slips. "Just one editor's opinion, that's all," they'd say.

Undaunted, I attended a writing conference—The Harriette Austin Writers Conference in Athens, Georgia, in July 2007. I met a columnist, Sheila Hudson, who told me that a publisher is rarely interested in a novel without agent representation and no agent takes on a writer without credentials. To procure those, I needed to shelve my novel and write articles or short stories for magazines and anthologies.

Sheila and I chatted during meals. When she learned my circumstances, she told me she received a call-out for stories about Alzheimer's from an anthology. She suggested I write my story for them. I wrote it fast and furious and from the heart, with tears streaming down my face. The deadline was a couple of days away. By December 2007, I learned my tale was a finalist: one of 55 for 50 slots. By January, I had made the cut. My non-fiction narrative would appear in an anthology in October 2008. I signed the contract; I'd become a bona fide author.

Since then, I have blazed with writing passion and scrawled thousands of words that spring into my head at the most unlikely moments. I have attended more conferences, and my pieces have been accepted by Chicken Soup for the Soul and other publishers, travel magazines, newspapers, secular magazines, regional magazines, religious, and inspirational ones. I've even been published in Australia, where I've never set foot! I've been assigned articles and am on the staff of a magazine dealing with health issues. I've been a finalist in ten contests, and I've placed and won prizes in others. I've been paid for more than forty of my articles! My 103,000-word novel was published November 1, 2010.

I'm achieving the goal I set as a kid. I'm accomplishing my dream. Some days, I wish I had started this process years ago. Had I begun writing right after college, I would have produced more by now. Nevertheless, I enjoyed my years as a wife, stay-at-home mom, PTA president, Girl Scout leader, and garden club enthusiast as well as the decade I spent teaching teens. Some folks say one hasn't experienced enough of the world to write about it until age forty anyway. A silver lining hitches to every cloud, and one finds those thin threads—those life altering moments—when not searching for them.

"All in good time," I say. The moment's right now for me to reflect on the human condition and my life experience and separate the wheat from the chaff for penning purposes. Those more talented than I may view this as a cautionary tale and begin their adventure to become the next Margaret Mitchell at a younger age. Yet, the fruit of my labor tastes sweeter because it stayed on the vine longer and plumped up ripe before I harvested it. I count my blessings every day. I am fortunate I can take care of my aged dad at my home with my understanding spouse and helpful children and that when finding "a door shutting," I've been inspired to "open a window" and hurl my words from it!

Becoming a caregiver isn't easy; nothing worthwhile in life is. I never foresaw that my dad's dementia would open my eyes to the joy gained from giving of oneself. Additionally, I've achieved the satisfaction of pursuing long-pondered aspirations. Life's fulfilling when a soul recognizes her passion and then circumstances put that body in the right place to pursue it. Lucky am I. I can say to myself about my dream: "Mission Accomplished."

~Erika Hoffman

Meet Our Contributors

Valerie Fletcher Adolph was born and educated in England and now lives near Vancouver, Canada. A published author of both fiction and non-fiction, her latest book is *The Story Solver*. An accomplished public speaker, she mentors young writers and speakers. She enjoys walking her dog, reading and gardening.

Nancy Allan retired after thirty years as a news editor for the former *Greenfield Observer* newspaper. She is a freelance writer and also enjoys writing a column for her condo newspaper, *Colonial Columns*. She has also had her poetry selected a number of times for the *Wisconsin Poets' Calendar*.

Ronda Armstrong's stories appear in two Midwest anthologies, *Amber Waves of Grain* and *Knee High by the Fourth of July*; several *Chicken Soup for the Soul* books, and *The Des Moines Register*. Beyond writing, she and her husband dance, chase their two cats, and keep in touch with others. E-mail her at ronda.armstrong@gmail.com.

Anna B. Ashby has written since junior high for both her junior high and high school newspapers, and as an adult for more professional venues, including a daily newspaper and several magazines. She currently writes feature/human interest stories and a monthly column for a small town newspaper. She has won numerous awards over the years.

Lil Blosfield is the Chief Financial Officer for Child & Adolescent Behavioral Health in Canton, OH. In addition to writing she enjoys hot sunny days and backyard barbecues with her husband, Ted, daughters, Amanda and Elizabeth, and other family and friends who come to play. E-mail her at LBlosfield40@msn.com.

Jan Bono's latest book, *Just Joshin', A Year in the Life of a Not-so-ordinary 4th Grade Kid*, is available through Sandridge Publications. She also writes one-act plays, dinner theater plays, and an every-other-day blog. Much of Jan's writing can be found at www.JanBonoBooks.com.

Barbara Brady, a retired RN, lives in Topeka, KS, with Merris, her husband of fifty-five years. She is an active member of Kansas Authors Club and submits prose and poetry to the annual convention competition. She enjoys family and friends, reading, writing and the opportunity to learn new things.

Jean Brody has a B.S. degree in Journalism and Education plus graduate work in Animal Behavior. This is her eighteenth story in the *Chicken Soup for the Soul* series. She writes a weekly newspaper column and a monthly magazine column. She and her husband Gene live on their horse farm.

Marcia E. Brown lives in Austin, TX, and is a widow and freelancer. She loves sharing family stories in magazines, newspapers and anthologies, including several in the *Chicken Soup for the Soul* series. She is now trying her hand at children's stories, especially to please her grandson.

Penelope Burbank received her B.S. from Utah State University in 1994. She teaches students with disabilities at a middle school in Utah. Penelope enjoys gardening and spending time with her grandchildren. She believes everyone has a story to tell. E-mail her at pburbank@dsdmail.net.

Beverly Burmeier, a retired public school teacher, has been writing professionally for more than ten years. She loves trying new adventures like zip lining in Belize, rafting the Colorado River at the Grand Canyon, dogsledding in Alaska, desert surfing at Dubai, and biking through Amsterdam. Contact her at www.beverlyburmeier.com or beburmeier@austin.rr.com.

Kristine Byron worked as a trainer for Tupperware and in later years as an interior designer. She loves to cook and entertain. Kristine also loves to travel with her husband and spend quality time with her five grandchildren.

After seventy-plus years of misbehaving, **Robert Campbell** settled into humorous reminiscences of his youth in Boston, sailing adventures in the Caribbean and elder age in Florida trying to amuse his wife with such stories. As a cancer patient, writing keeps his pulse on the value of humor.

Annis Cassells, a freelance writer whose articles have appeared in local and hobbyist magazines and professional journals, also teaches memoir writing. A life coach and speaker, Annis coaches individual clients and presents workshops. She enjoys travel abroad and in the U.S., often by motorcycle. E-mail her at HeyAnnis@aol.com.

Emily Parke Chase continues to enjoy subbing in the schools. She is a popular speaker and the author of six non-fiction books including *Why Say No When My Hormones Say Go?* and also *Help! My Family's Messed Up.* She is currently working on her first novel. Visit her at emilychase.com.

After years of caring for her family, **Jane McBride Choate** reached for her dream of writing. Being published in the *Chicken Soup for the Soul* series is truly a dream come true.

Linda S. Clare is the author of several books, including *The Fence My Father Built,* (Abingdon Press 2009). She teaches and coaches writing for George Fox University and Lane Community College. She lives with her family in Eugene, OR. She blogs at GodSongGrace.blogspot.com, or e-mail her at Lindas352@comcast.net.

Linda J. Cooper writes creative songs, poems and tributes to be delivered at special events. She puts the words together with the presenter's feelings so that he/she offers a meaningful tribute. She is currently writing a novel about senior living in south Florida. E-mail her at ljcooper@ix.netcom.com.

Tracy Crump has more than 100 writing credits. She is a CLASS graduate, moderates an online critique group, and enjoys teaching other writers through Write Life Workshops. She was recently promoted to the exalted status of grandmother and will talk about Nellie to anyone who listens. Visit her at www.TracyCrump.com.

Margaret P. Cunningham lives on Alabama's Gulf coast where she writes about humor and romance in middle age. She is a frequent Chicken Soup for the Soul contributor and the author of two quirky, southern romance novels: *Lily in Bloom* (Golden Rose Award winner—Best Contemporary Romance, 2008) and *One True Place*. Contact her at www.margaretpcunningham.com.

Barbara Curtis, professional author and mother of twelve—including four sons with Down syndrome (three adopted)—presides over a steadily-emptying nest and dreams of traveling someday with her husband Tripp. Visit her at BarbaraCurtis.com or MommyLife.net.

Pat Davis writes from her home in Philadelphia. Her articles, essays and short stories have appeared in other *Chicken Soup for the Soul* books, *Guideposts*, *GRIT* magazine, *The Lookout*, *Woman Alive* and other publications in the U.S. and U.K. She has completed an inspirational romance set in the WWII era. Visit her at patjeannedavis.com.

Mary Grant Dempsey is a former New Jersey early childhood teacher.

Following her teaching career, she was co-owner of an independent book shop in Clinton, NJ. She has had short stories published in local newspapers, newsletters and in American and Canadian magazines. Mary is now retired and resides with her husband in Bluffton, SC.

Frieda Dixon received her religious education degree from New Orleans Baptist Theological Seminary. She and her husband own an Atlanta-area aerospace engineering company. Frieda likes to swim and volunteer at her church. She is writing her memoir, of which this story is a part. E-mail her at friedas@bellsouth.net.

Terri Elders, LCSW, lives near Colville, WA. Her stories have appeared in many anthologies, including a dozen *Chicken Soup for the Soul* books. She is a public member of the Washington State Medical Quality Assurance Commission. In 2006, she received the UCLA Alumni Association Community Service Award. She blogs at atouchoftarragon.blogspot.com.

Joy Feldman, a retired executive secretary, vigorously works out, studies and practices organic gardening, studies the violin and writes poetry and articles. Her biographies and poetry have been published in the local newspapers. She enjoys her garden's bounty, writing, museums, live theater and her family. E-mail her at Joyfeldman@ verizon.net.

Christiana Flanigan lives in Orangeville, Ontario, Canada and is a retired administrative assistant. She holds two diplomas from the Institute of Children's Literature. Christiana enjoys reading, gardening, hiking, cycling, cross-country skiing and skating. Since childhood, writing has held a special place in her heart.

A graduate of the University of Pennsylvania, **Sally Schwartz Friedman** has been writing about family and feelings for over three decades. She has contributed to *The New York Times*, *The Philadelphia Inquirer*, *Ladies' Home Journal*, *Family Circle*, *Brides* and other national and regional publications. Her most important work is as wife/mother/grandmother! E-mail her at pinegander@aol.com.

Pamela Goldstein has followed her passion for writing for twenty years. She has completed three manuscripts, four plays and has several short stories published, many in the *Chicken Soup for the Soul* series. Her play, *The Interview*, opened April 1, 2011. Pamela is honoured to be part of the Chicken Soup for the Soul family. E-mail her at boker_tov2002@yahoo.ca.

Jane Goodwin is dedicated to making the most of her daily life through volunteering. No longer a youngster, she searches for exciting activities that help others, and has learned to savor what comes her way. Reading her true-to-life stories to family and friends is one way of encouraging others.

Libby Grandy lives in Claremont, CA, with her husband Fred. She has published numerous magazine articles and is currently marketing a mystery (*Desert Soliloquy*) and a women's fiction trilogy (*Promises to Keep*, *Lydia* and *True Abundance*). Learn more at www.libbygrandy.com or e-mail her at quillvision@aol.com.

Jonny Hawkins draws cartoons full-time from his home in Sherwood, MI. Since 1986, over 600 publications have used his work. He also has several books out including *The Hilarious Book of Heavenly Humor* along with his five Cartoon-a-Day calendars. E-mail him at jonnyhawkins2nz@yahoo.com.

Even as a small child, **Margery M. Henderson** felt the need to meet the needs of others. That need and ability grew as she grew and attained knowledge. Margery spent six years in Liberia as a teacher. She is now educating two Liberian college students.

Miriam Hill is a frequent contributor to *Chicken Soup for the Soul* books and has been published in *Writer's Digest*, *The Christian Science*

Monitor, Grit, St. Petersburg Times, The Sacramento Bee and Poynter Online. Miriam's manuscript received Honorable Mention for Inspirational Writing in a Writer's Digest Writing Competition.

Erika Hoffman used her childhood name, Riki Vogel, as her nom de plume when she penned her novel, *Secrets, Lies and Grace* under the ISBN # 978-1-935361-43-5. Its subject is teen bullying. The novel's website is www.secretsliesandgrace.vpweb.com.

Gary Ingraham is a documentary producer, a freelance writer, and bass player in a 60s cover band. He has previously been published in *Chicken Soup for the Dog Lover's Soul* and he writes a column on classic movies for Examiner.com. Contact him at gril@cornell.edu.

Jennie Ivey lives in Tennessee. She is the author of numerous fiction and non-fiction works, including stories in several *Chicken Soup for the Soul* anthologies. Her latest book is *Soldiers, Spies, and Spartans: Civil War Stories from Tennessee.* E-mail her at jivey@frontiernet.net.

Yvonne Kays recently retired from careers as a teacher and a Prevention Specialist. She lives in Central Oregon with her husband and two dogs; she loves spending time with her grandchildren, hiking, fishing, camping and being in nature. She writes personal stories and poetry.

April Knight is a frequent contibutor to *Chicken Soup for the Soul* books. She is also the author of several books about Native Americans, including *Crying Wind* and *My Searching Heart* and others written under her tribal name, Crying Wind.

Kathleen Kohler is a writer and speaker from the Pacific Northwest. Her articles, rooted in personal experience, appear in books and internationally in magazines. She and her husband have three children and seven grandchildren. She enjoys bird watching, gardening, traveling, painting, and of course dancing. Learn more at www.kathleenkohler.com.

Mitchell Kyd spent her first career as a communications professional for Fortune 500 companies. She now speaks and writes frequently on the topic of "Who's Writing Your Story?" Her stories and journaling workshops reflect the joy and poignant moments of small town life in rural Pennsylvania. E-mail her at mitchellkyd@gmail.com.

Jeannie Lancaster is a freelance writer living in Colorado. As she ages, she finds that the greatest joys come from the simplest of things. She is grateful to her family and friends, who laugh with her, cry with her and help her see each day as an exciting new adventure.

Annette Langer grew up in Chicago and spent a rewarding career with the Federal Government before retiring. Then she trained for her "life after" and became a travel agent, work she enjoyed for many years. Now retired, she immerses herself in volunteer work and creative writing. Contact her ar www.AnnetteLanger.com.

Ruth Lehrer, a New York City elementary school teacher, published her first personal essay at age sixty-two, after she retired. Now, twenty years later, she's written over one hundred stories, and published her first book, *My Book of Ruth: Reflections of a Jewish Girl*. E-mail her at ruthartl@gmail.com or visit her website at www.reflectionsofajewishgirl.com.

John J. Lesjack and Carol Lee are septugenarians and retired school teachers. They have traveled most of the United States and live in Sonoma, CA. John, an avid collector of *Chicken Soup for the Soul* books, has been published in four of them. Carol is a licensed practitioner at the Center for Spiritual Living in Santa Rosa, CA. E-mail them at Jlesjack@gmail.com.

Dawn Lilly is a former TV news anchor who swapped the spotlight for diaper duty over thirty years ago. She hasn't looked back since.

A freelance writer, Dawn has written for DaySpring Cards, *The Secret Place*, *Evangel* and *Chicken Soup for the Soul: Thanks Dad*. E-mail her at 22dlilly@gmail.com.

A frequent contributor to the *Chicken Soup for the Soul* series, **Linda Lohman** thanks her parole officer, Lucy, the four-footed Yorkie that encourages use of the exercise yard daily. Living in Sacramento, CA, she is retired and loving life as a Red Hat Society Ambassador. E-mail her at laborelations@yahoo.com.

Gloria Hander Lyons has channeled thirty years of training and hands-on experience in the areas of art, interior decorating, crafting and event planning into writing creative how-to books, fun cookbooks and humorous slice-of-life stories. Learn more at www.BlueSagePress.com.

David Martin's humor and political satire have appeared in many publications including *The New York Times*, the *Chicago Tribune* and *Smithsonian Magazine*. His latest humor collection entitled *Dare to be Average* was published by Lulu.com. David lives in Ottawa, Canada with his wife Cheryl and their daughter Sarah.

Tim Martin is the author of five books, including *The Legend of Boomer Jack*. His novel *Scout's Oaf* is due out in 2011 published by Cedar Grove Books. Tim has completed nine screenplays and is a contributing author to seven *Chicken Soup for the Soul* books. E-mail him at tmartin@northcoast.com.

Hank Mattimore is both a former elementary grade teacher and the Director of the Fairfield, California Senior Center. He is currently a surrogate grandpa at the Children's Village, an intergenerational home for twenty-four abused or neglected children in Santa Rosa, CA. E-mail him at hmattimore@yahoo.com.

Maryann McCullough spent most of her professional life in the company of sophomore boys, all eager to understand the mysteries of geometry. Retirement provided her the opportunity to become a sharer of stories. You can read more of her work at www.maryannmccullough. wordpress.com or e-mail her at msm100@cox.net.

Sharon McGregor is a semi-retired grandmother of five who enjoys reading, writing short mystery stories, and walking, although not always 63.5 kilometers in one day. She is looking forward to moving back to the country next year and spending more time with her pets and gardening. E-mail her at sharonmcgr@hotmail.com.

Caroline S. McKinney recently retired from the School of Education at the University of Colorado where she was an adjunct for over twenty years. Now she spends time with her seven grandchildren, hiking Colorado's mountains... and trying to play her flute! She enjoys writing poetry for religious publications.

Marc Tyler Nobleman is the author of more than seventy books including *Boys of Steel: The Creators of Superman* and one due out in 2012 about the "secret" co-creator of Batman. His cartoons have appeared in more than 100 international publications. At noblemania. blogspot.com, he reveals the behind-the-scenes stories of his work.

Caroline Overlund-Reid grew up in Oregon. She attended St. Olaf College in Northfield, MN, and was employed as an executive assistant prior to retirement. She enjoys her family and friends. Working, writing, painting and gym workouts keep her busy. She resides in Bakersfield, CA. E-mail her at creid@bak.rr.com.

Mark Parisi's "off the mark" comic, syndicated since 1987, is distributed by United Media. His cartoon feature won the National Cartoonists Society's award for Best Newspaper Panel in 2009. Mark's humor also graces greeting cards, T-shirts, calendars, magazines, newsletters and books. Lynn is his wife/business partner. Their daughter,

Jen, contributes with inspiration, (as do two cats, one dog and an unknown number of koi). Learn more at www.offthemark.com.

Ava Pennington is an author, speaker, and Bible teacher. She has published numerous magazine articles and contributed to twenty-one anthologies, including fifteen *Chicken Soup for the Soul* books. She has also authored *One Year Alone with God: 366 Devotions on the Names of God* (Revell, 2010). Learn more at www.AvaWrites.com.

Saralee Perel is a national award-winning columnist and multiple contributor to Chicken Soup for the Soul. Her book, *The Dog Who Walked Me*, is about her dog who became her caregiver after Saralee's spinal cord injury, the initial devastation of her marriage, and her cat who kept her sane. E-mail her at sperel@saraleeperel.com or www.saraleeperel.com.

Lori Phillips has a B.A. in communications and Master's of Education. She is an editor for BellaOnline.com and writes about living simply, Japanese food, marriage, self-help and spirituality. E-mail her at hope037@hotmail.com.

Kay Conner Pliszka and her husband, both former teachers, live in The Villages, FL—a retirement community that boasts more than thirty golf courses, two town squares with free, live entertainment every night, dozens of pools, tennis courts and much more. Kay says the residents all agree that in retirement "Life is Good!"

Charline Profiri's publication credits include *Highlights for Children*, *Highlights High Five* and *Pockets*. She loves sharing her books and tips on writing during school, library and conference presentations. When not writing, Charline enjoys reading, laughter, yoga and water aerobics. Learn more at www.cprofiri.com.

CR Rae has been a published writer since 1999. Making people laugh through her column, "Out of My Mature Mind" and humorous speaking programs is her passion. Rae writes for *Suburbanite* newspapers, various publications, websites and began a magazine insert, "The Next Fifty." She also loves travel writing. Contact Rae at www.carolynnrae.com.

Virginia Redman received her B.A. in English from Loyola Marymount University in 1970. She received her Master of Arts in English from San Diego State University in 1990. Virginia is a retired English teacher and lives in Southern California. She is writing her first young adult novel.

Carol McAdoo Rehme spends hours dreaming, reading, and writing in the spacious, window-banked office of her towering Victorian. She is discovering anew the joy of making a home out of a house and memories out of adventures. She is also the co-author of *Chicken Soup for the Soul: Empty Nesters*. Contact her at www.rehme.com.

Bruce Robinson is an award-winning internationally published cartoonist whose work has appeared in many consumer and trade magazines including the *National Enquirer, The Saturday Evening Post, Women's World,* etc. He is also the author of the cartoon books, *Good Medicine* and *Bow Wows & Meows*. E-mail him at CartoonsByBruceRobinson@hotmail.com.

S. Ann Robinson received her BBA from The University of Texas at Austin. She enjoys working with preschool literacy programs and events for deaf adolescents. Ann currently teaches Workforce Development for community colleges in Virginia and Maryland. She writes for anthologies, as well as a history project entitled "Swing County." E-mail her at sarwood@aol.com.

Sallie A. Rodman is an award-winning author whose work has appeared in numerous *Chicken Soup for the Soul* anthologies, magazines, and *The Orange County Register*. She mentors other writers, is working on a book and does mixed media art. She never knew she could be so busily retired. E-mail her at sa.rodman@verizon.net.

Marcia Rudoff is a newspaper columnist, memoir writing instructor and freelance writer in Bainbridge Island, WA. She is the author of *We Have Stories—A Handbook for Writing Your Memoirs.*

Jacqueline Seewald taught high school English, also creative, expository and technical writing at the university. She's worked as an academic librarian and an educational media specialist. Ten of her books of fiction have been published. Her short stories, poems, essays, reviews and articles have appeared in hundreds of magazines, newspapers and anthologies.

Alison Shelton received her B.A. in English and history and her Masters degree in education. She taught high school for thirty years and, since retiring, has enjoyed traveling, art classes, writing workshops and especially her five grandchildren. Alison is a columnist for a senior magazine and also has published several articles in other magazines.

Deborah Shouse is a speaker, writer and editor. She loves helping people write books and facilitating creativity and storytelling workshops. Deborah donates all proceeds from her book *Love in the Land of Dementia: Finding Hope in the Caregiver's Journey* to Alzheimer's programs and research. Visit www.thecreativityconnection.com or deborahshousewrites.wordpress.com to learn more.

Barbara L. Smith writes a humor column for the *Norwalk Citizen* (CT). Her work appears in regional magazines and on numerous websites. An award-winning playwright, she has been published by Samuel French, and produced round the country. At work on a book of humor, Barbara welcomes comments at blsith283@aol.com.

Sheila Sowder has been living the workamping lifestyle for the last several years, traveling throughout the country, from Death Valley to Maine, working seasonal jobs at resorts and RV parks and writing about her experiences. For more information about workamping, e-mail her at sksowder@aol.com.

Brian Staff was born in England, has travelled throughout much of the world, and now lives in California. He has published a novel and a collection of stories/essays. His works in both fiction and non-fiction have also appeared in magazines and anthologies. Find more of his work on www.wordisworth.com.

Kent O. Stever is a long-term educational leader and lifetime resident of Minnesota. He earned his Ph. D at Texas A&M University in 1973. He has served as a high school principal and a university lecturer. He enjoys gardening, fitness, reading, carving, writing, fishing and family at his lakeside home in Lakeville. E-mail him at kojl@frontiernet.net.

Joyce Sudbeck is enjoying the abundant free time retirement is providing. While she has a number of hobbies, writing short stories and poetry remains her most favorite. She has been published numerous times in *Chicken Soup for the Soul* books, magazines, and anthologies. Life is good.

Robert Tell nurtured his writing skills while working as a healthcare executive. His published work includes poetry, fiction and creative non-fiction. Bob was educated in Public Health and English at Columbia and Long Island universities. He lives in Michigan and winters in Florida. Contact him through his website at www.bobtell.com.

Susan Tornga lives and writes in southern Arizona. She enjoys hiking in the beautiful Sonoran Desert and traveling throughout this fascinating world of ours. She writes mysteries, both historical and current day, that celebrate the courage of women in the West. E-mail her at susantornga.writer@comcast.net.

Samantha Ducloux Waltz is an award-winning freelance writer in Portland, OR. Her personal stories appear in the *Chicken Soup for the Soul* series, *A Cup of Comfort* series, and numerous other anthologies. She has also written fiction and non-fiction under the name Samellyn Wood. Learn more at www.pathsofthought.com.

Mary Ellen Warner is an award-winning speaker and a freelance writer who works with people to overcome communication barriers created by the onset of adult hearing loss. Please visit Mary Ellen at www.marbilwarner.com to learn more about living with hearing loss.

Donna Weaver's greatest inspiration comes from her children and four grandchildren. When she's not studying at Colorado Christian University or working as office manager for a medical practice, she enjoys art, journaling, reading and church activities. Donna writes a weekly devotional blog and hopes to have her Christian children's books published soon. E-mail her at donna_a_weaver@hotmail.com.

Raymond P. Weaver is in his seventies, retired and lives in Clearwater, FL. He has had numerous short stories and articles published in newspapers and magazines. His first novel, *Tightrope to Justice*, was published in May, 2010. He is currently working on his second novel, *Miami Justice*. E-mail him at raymondellie@aol.com.

Judy A. Weist is a writer who uses her experiences of everyday life to fill the pages of her short stories and memoirs. She delights in teaching dance to young children, and loves to write. Judy has written several children's books which she plans to publish in the future. E-mail her at weistjudy@yahoo.com.

Paul Winick lives with his wife Dorothy in Hollywood, FL, where he practiced pediatrics for thirty years. He would like to dedicate this story to his good freind Allan, an ophthalmologist, who was an integral part of the story. Before his sudden demise, Allan encouraged Paul to publish the story. E-mail Dr. Winick at paulwinick@pol.net.

Ann Michener Winter lives in Santa Barbara, CA, and is a published poet and freelance author of creative non-fiction. She is an avid photographer, enjoys reading, yoga, scrapbooking, tap dancing, singing Doo Wop and loves to travel. E-mail her at amwinter@cox.net.

Ernie Witham writes the humor column "Ernie's World" for the *Montecito Journal* in Montecito, CA. He is the author of two humor books including *A Year in the Life of a "Working" Writer*. His stories have appeared in more than a dozen *Chicken Soup for the Soul* books. He is also a humor workshop leader at several writers conferences.

Linda C. Wright is a member of Romance Writers of America and the local chapter, SpacecoasT Authors of Romance. She has been published in *Chicken Soup for the Soul: My Dog's Life*. Linda enjoys traveling, reading, walking her four-legged friend, Ginger and bike riding with her husband, Richard. She is currently writing a novel. E-mail her at lindacwright@ymail.com.

Phyllis W. Zeno has had stories in seven *Chicken Soup for the Soul* books. She was the founding editor of *AAA Going Places* for twenty years and editor/publisher of *Beach Talk Magazine* until that fateful day when she met Harvey Meltzer on Match.com. Both eighty-three years old, they were married August 22, 2009. They are still madly in love.

Meet Our Authors

Jack Canfield is the co-creator of the *Chicken Soup for the Soul* series, which *Time* magazine has called "the publishing phenomenon of the decade." Jack is also the co-author of many other bestselling books.

Jack is the CEO of the Canfield Training Group in Santa Barbara, California, and founder of the Foundation for Self-Esteem in Culver City, California. He has conducted intensive personal and professional development seminars on the principles of success for more than a million people in twenty-three countries, has spoken to hundreds of thousands of people at more than 1,000 corporations, universities, professional conferences and conventions, and has been seen by millions more on national television shows.

Jack has received many awards and honors, including three honorary doctorates and a Guinness World Records Certificate for having seven books from the *Chicken Soup for the Soul* series appearing on the New York Times bestseller list on May 24, 1998.

You can reach Jack at www.jackcanfield.com.

Mark Victor Hansen is the co-founder of Chicken Soup for the Soul, along with Jack Canfield. He is a sought-after keynote speaker, bestselling author, and marketing maven. Mark's powerful messages of possibility, opportunity, and action have created powerful change in thousands of organizations and millions of individuals worldwide.

Mark is a prolific writer with many bestselling books in addition to the *Chicken Soup for the Soul* series. Mark has had a profound influence in the field of human potential through his library of audios, videos, and articles in the areas of big thinking, sales achievement, wealth building, publishing success, and personal and professional development. He is also the founder of the MEGA Seminar Series.

Mark has received numerous awards that honor his entrepreneurial spirit, philanthropic heart, and business acumen. He is a lifetime member of the Horatio Alger Association of Distinguished Americans.

You can reach Mark at www.markvictorhansen.com.

Amy Newmark is Chicken Soup for the Soul's publisher and editor-in-chief, after a thirty-year career as a writer, speaker, financial analyst, and business executive in the worlds of finance and telecommunications. Amy is a *magna cum laude* graduate of Harvard College, where she majored in Portuguese, minored in French, and traveled extensively. She and her husband have four grown children.

After a long career writing books on telecommunications, voluminous financial reports, business plans, and corporate press releases, Chicken Soup for the Soul is a breath of fresh air for Amy. She has fallen in love with Chicken Soup for the Soul and its life-changing books, and really enjoys putting these books together for Chicken Soup's wonderful readers. She has co-authored more than three dozen *Chicken Soup for the Soul* books and has edited another two dozen.

You can reach Amy through the webmaster@chickensoupforthesoul.com.

Thank You

We owe huge thanks to all of our contributors. We know that you poured your hearts and souls into the thousands of stories and poems that you shared with us, and ultimately with each other. We appreciate your willingness to open up your lives to other Chicken Soup for the Soul readers and share your own experiences as dynamic, busy seniors. We loved your stories and all of us here at Chicken Soup for the Soul, especially those of us within spitting distance of those retirement years, were very encouraged by how much fun you are all having!

We could only publish a small percentage of the stories that were submitted, but we read every single one and even the ones that do not appear in the book had an influence on us and on the final manuscript. We owe special thanks to our editor Barbara LoMonaco, who read every submission to this book and narrowed the list down to a few hundred finalists, and then proofread the final manuscript. Our assistant publisher, D'ette Corona, worked with all the contributors as kindly and competently as always, obtaining their approvals for our edits and the quotations we carefully chose to begin each story. And editor Kristiana Glavin performed her normal masterful proofreading and made sure the book went to the printer on time.

We also owe a very special thanks to our creative director and book producer, Brian Taylor at Pneuma Books, for his brilliant vision for our covers and interiors. Finally, none of this would be possible without the business and creative leadership of our CEO, Bill Rouhana, and our president, Bob Jacobs.

Improving Your Life
Every Day

Real people sharing real stories—for seventeen years. Now, Chicken Soup for the Soul has gone beyond the bookstore to become a world leader in life improvement. Through books, movies, DVDs, online resources and other partnerships, we bring hope, courage, inspiration and love to hundreds of millions of people around the world. Chicken Soup for the Soul's writers and readers belong to a one-of-a-kind global community, sharing advice, support, guidance, comfort, and knowledge.

Chicken Soup for the Soul stories have been translated into more than forty languages and can be found in more than one hundred countries. Every day, millions of people experience a Chicken Soup for the Soul story in a book, magazine, newspaper or online. As we share our life experiences through these stories, we offer hope, comfort and inspiration to one another. The stories travel from person to person, and from country to country, helping to improve lives everywhere.

Share with Us

We all have had Chicken Soup for the Soul moments in our lives. If you would like to share your story or poem with millions of people around the world, go to chickensoup.com and click on "Submit Your Story." You may be able to help another reader, and become a published author at the same time. Some of our past contributors have launched writing and speaking careers from the publication of their stories in our books!

Our submission volume has been increasing steadily—the quality and quantity of your submissions has been fabulous. We only accept story submissions via our website. They are no longer accepted via mail or fax.

To contact us regarding other matters, please send us an e-mail through webmaster@chickensoupforthesoul.com, or fax or write us at:

Chicken Soup for the Soul
P.O. Box 700
Cos Cob, CT 06807-0700
Fax: 203-861-7194

One more note from your friends at Chicken Soup for the Soul: Occasionally, we receive an unsolicited book manuscript from one of our readers, and we would like to respectfully inform you that we do not accept unsolicited manuscripts and we must discard the ones that appear.

Chicken Soup for the Soul.

Grandmothers

101 Stories of Love, Laughs, and Lessons from Grandmothers and Grandchildren

Jack Canfield, Mark Victor Hansen & Amy Newmark

The moment a grandchild is born, a grandmother is born too. This collection of stories by grandmothers about being a grandmother, and by grandchildren about their grandmothers, celebrates these special relationships. Personal stories about legacies and traditions, grandma's wisdom and lessons from grandchildren as well as the joys and challenges of grandparenting, will touch the heart of all grandmothers.

978-1-935096-64-1

Classics for Grandmothers

Chicken Soup for the Soul

Empty Nesters

101 Stories about Surviving and Thriving When the Kids Leave Home

Jack Canfield,
Mark Victor Hansen,
Carol McAdoo Rehme,
Patricia Cena Evans

This book provides support during an emotional but exciting time for parents—sending their children off to college, new homes, or careers. These heartfelt stories about gazing at surprisingly clean bedrooms, starting new careers, rediscovering spouses, and handling the continuing, and often humorous, needs of children will inspire, support, and amuse parents. They'll nod their heads, cry a little, and laugh a lot, as they read these oh-so-true stories.

978-1-935096-22-1

Classics for Parents

Nearly everyone thinks their own family is "nutty" or has at least one or two nuts. With 101 stories of wacky yet lovable relatives, funny foibles, and holiday meltdowns, this book is usually hilarious and occasionally poignant. This book shows readers that we all have the same family matters and what really matters is families. It is a quirky and fun holiday book, and a great bridal shower or wedding gift!

978-1-935096-55-9

Classics for Families

Chicken Soup for the Soul.

Shaping the New You

101 Encouraging Stories
about Dieting
and Fitness...
and Finding
What Works for You

Jack Canfield,
Mark Victor Hansen & Amy Newmark
Foreword by Richard Simmons

No one likes to diet, but this book will encourage and inspire readers with its positive, practical, and purposeful stories of dieting and fitness. Readers will find hope, help, and hints on getting fit and staying healthy in these 101 stories from those who have been there, done that, and maintained it. Stories about wake-up calls and realizations, moving more and eating better, self-esteem and support, make this a great book for anyone starting fresh or needing a boost.

978-1-935096-57-3

Classics for Healthy Living